SHELLEY AND GREECE

Shelley and Greece

Rethinking Romantic Hellenism

Jennifer Wallace
College Lecturer and Director of Studies in English
Peterhouse, Cambridge

First published in Great Britain 1997 by
MACMILLAN PRESS LTD
Houndmills, Basingstoke, Hampshire RG21 6XS and London
Companies and representatives throughout the world

A catalogue record for this book is available from the British Library.

ISBN 0–333–65569–9

First published in the United States of America 1997 by
ST. MARTIN'S PRESS, INC.,
Scholarly and Reference Division,
175 Fifth Avenue, New York, N.Y. 10010

ISBN 0–312–16548–X

Library of Congress Cataloging-in-Publication Data
Wallace, Jennifer.
Shelley and Greece : rethinking romantic Hellenism / Jennifer
Wallace.
p. cm.
Includes bibliographical references and index.
ISBN 0–312–16548–X (cloth)
1. Shelley, Percy Bysshe, 1792–1822—Knowledge—Greece.
2. English poetry—Greek influences. 3. Greece—In literature.
4. Romanticism—England. 5. Classicism—England. 6. Hellenism.
I. Title.
PR5442.G65W35 1997
821'.7—dc21   96–49850
                                                                                 CIP

This book is printed on paper suitable for recycling and made from fully managed and
sustained forest sources.

10   9   8   7   6   5   4   3   2   1
06   05   04   03   02   01   00   99   98   97

Printed and bound in Great Britain by
Antony Rowe Ltd, Chippenham, Wiltshire

In memory of
VALERIE MARY WALLACE
1938–86

Contents

Acknowledgements

This book has been written in two Cambridge colleges which have provided me with just the right balance of authority and freedom required to write about the classics. The fellows of Newnham College first encouraged my interest and allowed me the time to study both classical and English literature. Later, the fellows of Clare College welcomed me as a research fellow and offered me the chance, through many informal conversations, to learn 'things foreign' and enlightening for my research. Earlier versions of Chapters 5 and 6 appeared in *Romanticism* and the *Byron Journal*, and I should like to thank the editors of these journals for the opportunity to test my ideas in the public domain.

Numerous individuals have contributed to the writing of this book. In particular, Adrian Poole, originally my doctoral supervisor, has lent his own acute eye for subtlety and ambiguity in language to guide my research. Among those who have read earlier drafts of this work and who have offered sharp and helpful comment, I should like to thank: John Beer, Marilyn Butler, Paul Cartledge, Pat Easterling, Jean Gooder, Edith Hall, Susan Manning, Gregory Nagy, Ralph Pite, Nicholas Roe, Dominic Scott, Chris Stray, Timothy Webb, Penny Wilson. Finally I must thank my family: my father, Fleming Wallace, for his legalistic scrutiny of my work; Gillian, Linda, Val and Pete for their lively interest; and especially my husband, Simon Targett, a most unelusive 'second self', who has shared in this enterprise from its beginning and without whose enthusiastic encouragement it could not have been written.

List of Plates

List of Abbreviations

BLJ	*Byron's Letters and Journals*, ed. L.A. Marchand, 12 vols (1973–82)
ELH	*English Literary History*
KSJ	*Keats–Shelley Journal*
Letters	*The Letters of Percy Bysshe Shelley*, ed. F.L. Jones, 2 vols (Oxford, 1964)
Loeb	Loeb Classical Library
Matthews/Everest	*The Poems of Shelley*, ed. G. Matthews and K. Everest (London, 1989)
MSJ	*The Journals of Mary Shelley*, ed. P.R. Feldman and D. Scott-Kilvert, 2 vols (Oxford, 1987)
MSL	*The Letters of Mary Wollstonecraft Shelley*, ed. B.B. Bennett, 2 vols (Baltimore, 1980–83)
PMLA	*Publications of the Modern Language Association of America*
Prose	*Shelley's Prose: or Trumpet of a Prophecy*, ed. D.L. Clark (Albuquerque, 1954; 3rd edn, 1988)
PV	Aeschylus, *Prometheus Bound*, ed. M. Griffiths (Cambridge, 1983).
Reiman and Powers	*Shelley's Poetry and Prose*, ed. D.H. Reiman and S.B. Powers (New York, 1977)
SIR	*Studies in Romanticism*
SPW	*Shelley's Poetical Works*, ed. T. Hutchinson, corr. by G. Matthews (2nd edn, Oxford, 1970)

Explorations

For too long, writing about hellenism has been associated with the study of a perfect civilisation. Again and again, the ancient Greeks are portrayed as an exemplary race, living at the dawn of the world and supposedly sharing its dewy freshness. They surpass later ages both in simplicity and in sophistication. Generations of critics have compared them to an innocent child, 'younger, with fewer lines and wrinkles on its features and with more definite and deliberate purpose in its eyes'.[1] Schiller contrasted the childlike contentment of the ancient Greeks with the adolescent unfulfilled yearning of his contemporaries: 'They are what we were; they are what we should become again . . . a representation of our lost childhood, which remains eternally most precious to us.'[2] Escaping the degeneration and corruption of later ages, the ancient Greeks for centuries have led admirably uncomplicated lives, seeing the world with direct clarity and without the furrowed brow of adulthood. Generations of critics have also called them the epitome of genius. Because they lived before the Romans, the Normans, the Venetians, they thought of everything first, they invented all the hallmarks of cultivated society, they practised all the arts of western culture to a prodigious level.

Since the Greeks have been perceived to be so perfect, they have become a model for subsequent generations. It is thought enough for later disciples to imbibe as much of Greek civilisation as possible and then to incorporate its values in their lives and their work. A clearcut choice seems to lie before the critics. Without Greece, 'our civilisation' becomes 'much thinner, more fragmentary, less thoughtful, more materialistic'.[3] With Greece, civilisation is 'renewed', made more 'valuable'.[4] The notion of the influence of the Greeks on subsequent peoples is simple and one-dimensional. It is unequivocally beneficial, and it is devoted to the task of making us ever more like them. In order to do this, Greece needs only to 'touch' us with 'its living flame', offer a 'Hellenic current', provide 'flashes of insight', and we will respond with grateful imitation.[5] This is a remarkably unsophisticated view of influence, but because it has been the predominant one, students of hellenism

1

have tended to concentrate on the laborious process of source-hunting and cataloguing areas of obvious similarity like latter-day Casaubons retreating behind the defences of their massive libraries.[6]

The notion of Greece as an ideal example touching with flames is especially prevalent in the study of the hellenism of previous centuries. In this century, the ideas of Freud and Nietzsche and the anthropological approaches to the ancient world practised by Jean-Pierre Vernant and Pierre Vidal-Naquet have unsettled unthinking identification with the ancient world. Since these writers depicted Greece as a violent and primitive world, some critics have begun to wonder whether twentieth-century writers have lost belief in the imaginative benefits of Hellas.[7] Louis MacNeice's famous lines about Greece – 'It was all so unimaginably different / And all so long ago' – are commonly seen as the turning-point in the growth of doubt.[8] Oliver Taplin describes the 'new return to ancient Greece' in the last quarter of the twentieth century. 'Instead of trying to reconstruct or imitate Greece as a whole', he observes, 'the new return recognises the vast differences between now and then, in tension with the similarities, and the fragmentariness of the evidence and of our knowledge; and recognises how any picture of ancient Greece must be selective, prejudiced, not innocent'.[9]

But the assumption is still that the interest in Greece during the Romantic and Victorian periods was far less questioning and far more adulatory than it is today. 'The Victorians appropriated the ancient Greeks', Bernard Knox mocks, 'inspired them as contemporaries, and used their writing as weapons in their own ideological wars. If they had been attuned to modern advertising techniques, they might have reversed Shelley's claim and launched the slogan GREEKS 'R' US'.[10] Looking back at the past, most critics tend to see the study of Greek art and literature by artists and writers in previous centuries as enforcing notions of conformity, defining the moral standards of the nation and encouraging people to accept orthodox taste. Some critics argue that Greece offered ideal possibilities of escape into a Platonic transcendent world.[11] But all are agreed that in previous centuries classical Greece provided an unproblematic endorsement of the nation's concerns and values.

The picture changes, however, if one considers the work of individual writers, thinkers and artists in the period. The varied response to Greece by different writers reveals the heterogeneity of classical influence. The interest in ancient Greece becomes less a case of simple conformity when, with different ideas of the ancient world emerging, it becomes unclear exactly to what model of Greece all writers can and do conform. Moreover, individual writers reveal the complications of responding to the Greek world, complications which become simplified and ignored when a general picture is painted. By focusing on the work of the individual writer, one sees the detailed process of selection and appropriation of Greek culture; and the integration or juxtaposition of hellenism with the rest of the writer's interests and concerns modifies an otherwise monolithic account.

This is particularly the case if the focus is upon Shelley. Romantic hellenism has tended to be associated either with Keats or with Byron.[12] Keatsian hellenism is predominantly aesthetic. It is interested in sculpture and urns, mythical landscapes and beauty. Since Keats could not read Greek, he encountered Greek culture by viewing physical objects, such as statues and vases, and by reading books of mythology. These, potentially, reduced him to the position of passive spectator. He also relied heavily upon his imagination, welcoming Psyche into the temple of his mind as an alternative to the public temples frequented in the researches of Greek scholars:

> Yes, I will be thy priest, and build a fane
>   In some untrodden region of my mind,
> Where branched thoughts, new grown with pleasant pain
>   Instead of pines shall murmur in the wind . . .
> And there shall be for thee all soft delight
>   That shadowy thought can win,
> A bright torch, and a casement ope at night
>   To let the warm Love in![13]

Imagining Greece in Keats's highly personal and secretive way renders it intensely sensual, 'all soft delight'. Hellenism, if associated with Keats, thus becomes a sensual and illogical escape from mundane cares into the beautiful world of the imagination, evoked by beautiful art and landscapes.[14]

Byron's hellenism is similarly passionate. Unlike Keats, Byron could read Greek, but he chose not to do so. When travelling round Greece he preferred to go swimming while his companion John Cam Hobhouse studied the ruined columns of ancient temples.[15] 'He often said', according to Trelawny, 'if he had ever written a line worth preserving, it was Greece that inspired it.'[16] For him, Greece was a mood as well as a physical landscape described in his poetry. It evoked the spirit of adventure, turning him into the hero which dominated his literary work.[17] And it provoked melancholy and nostalgia, because of the discrepancy between its past greatness and present disintegration. For Byron, Greece became an easily appropriated metaphor, almost a cliché, for the gloomy sense of self which he portrayed, and later interrogated, in his work. Byronic hellenism thus becomes the creation and subtle questioning of stereotypes, pictures drawn from the instinctive emotions rather than from cool reason.

Yet if attention is turned to Shelley, the impression of Romantic hellenism is very different. Instead of the passive and emotional response to Greece, the response is rather intellectual. Shelley spent his life reading Greek, ranging widely through the corpus of ancient literature, philosophy and history. As a result, his idea of Greece was not only based upon the imagination and descriptions of statues and landscapes, but crucially upon a series of texts. Rather than passively imbibing the translations and mediations of other scholars and dilettanti travel writers, he actively struggled to read the texts in the original, and hence Greece appealed directly to his mind as well as to his emotions. It is partly to stress this departure from a typical Keatsian aesthetic or Byronic emotional hellenism that my book is subtitled 'Re*thinking* Romantic Hellenism'. Shelley's reliance upon a wide number of texts means that his impressions of Greece are far more varied. Of course Shelley was an extremely diverse writer, experimenting with genre far more than either Keats or Byron, and so his need to draw upon Greece would alter according to the particular circumstance of each literary work. But reading Greek literature allowed him to realise the heterogeneity of Greek culture – after all, ancient writers themselves differed and disputed – and to reflect that variation in his own writing.

Besides its textual and protean qualities, Shelley's hellenism is overtly political. He wrote to Thomas Love Peacock in 1819: 'I consider Poetry very subordinate to moral and political science, and if I were well, certainly I should aspire to the latter.'[18] His commitment to radical politics meant that, for Shelley, poetry was primarily important for its potential to change opinions, to bring about a revolutionary improvement in society. 'Poetry', he insisted, 'awakens and enlarges the mind itself by rendering it the receptacle

of a thousand unapprehended combinations of thought. Poetry lifts
the veil from the hidden beauty of the world and makes familiar
objects be as if they were not familiar.'[19] The interest in Greece
served a similar purpose, to unsettle fixed opinions and to offer
visions of other ways of organising society. It was for this reason
that an intellectual Greece, one that required an active thinking
mind, was so important because it was needed to engage more
cutting-edge ideas and broader thoughts than the emotional closed
world of a sensual Greece could achieve. By focusing upon Shelley's particular response to Greece, this book overturns the conventional picture of Romantic and Victorian idealistic and conforming
hellenism.

The book also rethinks Romantic hellenism by considering the
whole question of classical influence and classical tradition. Increasingly, within other academic fields, notions of influence and
the relationship with other cultures are being explored. Once the
heterogeneity of ancient Greece is appreciated, the way in which
modern writers respond to it should also be perceived as far more
ambiguous. Hellenism raises issues of the relationship with the
past, with foreign cultures, with other peoples. Harold Bloom's
Anxiety of Influence developed a terminology for describing the
complicated and subtle way in which writers respond to their
predecessors. To avoid what W.J. Bate described as the psychological 'burden' of being found inferior to the past, writers deliberately
'misread' or create their own version of their predecessor's work.[20]
Responding to the literary heritage thus becomes a process of
subtle self-conscious reinvention and alteration, rather than a
straightforward one of imitation and passive acceptance. While
critics since Bloom prefer to look at the problem of influence in less
psychological terms and, rediscovering the work of Mikhail Bakhtin and Julia Kristeva, are beginning to replace the image of two
competing male poets with that of the plural text endlessly offering
possibilities for selection or omission, nevertheless the same distrust of the notion of a simple influence informs their work.[21] The
past becomes something actively recreated or imagined, rather
than passively inherited.

The past, as L.P. Hartley famously mused, is a foreign country,
and Bloom's ideas about our complicated relationship with our
predecessors can be compared with studies of our relationship with
other countries and with other cultures.[22] Although Edward Said
writes about a world further east in *Orientalism*, and significantly

ranges Greece and classical literature with the western world, yet in his analysis of the west's domination and control of the Orient, he opens up the whole issue of the relationship between cultures. He links the ability to gain knowledge of and write about another culture with political imperialism, so that knowledge becomes politically problematic, not only controlling its subject but cultivating it and even, he argues, 'producing' it. 'Orientalism', he explains, 'is a western style for dominating, restructuring, and having authority over the Orient.'[23] The west defines itself in contrast to the east, with the result that the two concepts are dependent upon a series of opposing values. Each culture gains its sense of identity from its contemplation of the other. The east is not known at all except as the mirror image of the west; orientalism, indeed, 'involved a narrowing of the imagination and intensified feelings of the innate and categorical superiority of European civilisation'.[24] It has 'less to do with the Orient than it does with 'our' world'.[25]

Said's argument, that cultures virtually invent and then control alien cultures, is given material support by Martin Bernal in *Black Athena*. Bernal posits the theory that the ancient Greeks were originally descended from the ancient Egyptians and Phoenicians, and that this fact was universally accepted until a later explanation for their origins was fabricated in the nineteenth century. While it is still highly debatable whether Bernal's African Greeks ever existed or possess any historical validity,[26] what emerges from his book is a telling account of the conscious efforts made by the west to discredit the suggestion of Greek difference and to create what Bernal terms an 'Aryan model', a Greece which belongs to the west, is endowed with western qualities and is treated as the revered ancestor of the west, the origin of western civilisation. 'The establishment of the Aryan model', he argues, 'can best be seen as attempts to impose the Romantic ideals of remoteness, coldness and purity on this most unsuitable candidate.'[27] Crucially, the relationship with Greece is consciously created, not natural or given. While Said has articulated the process of controlling and defining the foreign, Bernal describes what it is to appropriate and define one's own identity and to resist other relationships and explanations.

Though ostensibly about the geographical gulf between countries, Said's and Bernal's works speak predominantly about identity and self-perception, about how they are defined and how they are maintained. They draw upon the work of French feminists

– notably Simone de Beauvoir, Luce Irigaray and Hélène Cixous –
in their use of the term the 'other', to describe other cultures.
Feminist theory, which describes the relationship between the
sexes, offers useful metaphors and images for the articulation of
other types of relationship. The relationship between the sexes
is informed by an interest in personal identity and sources of
knowledge. Feminist critics dramatise the implications of obvious
biological difference, the fear and attraction of the other, and
the covert desire for sameness and sympathy. Since, as Cixous
demonstrates, 'thought has always worked by opposition',
masculine and feminine qualities are interdependent, defined as
polar opposites.[28] As a consequence, personal identity and self-
perception are externally determined and become relative concepts. Indeed, Irigaray unsettles everything by suggesting that
woman is unknowable, since she is always a reflection of male
desire and speculation and cannot be known outside that sphere of
knowledge.[29] Knowledge of the other and the self, under feminist
theories, becomes something invented or created in order to evade
the abyss posed by the prospect of the impossibility of knowledge
or of communication.

The effect of new ideas from cultural and gender studies and
from the study of literary influence is to destabilise the assumption that the relationship with other cultures and other writers
is natural and unproblematic. Knowledge of other peoples,
whether in the past or in different circumstances, becomes a process of invention, construction and imagination rather than an
objective immediate identification. An awareness of how we
respond to otherness, the degree of imaginative construction
involved rather than simply passive inheritance, should inform the
study of hellenism. In recent years, Said's ideas have prompted
a flurry of academic interest in colonialism and the traces it has
left on nineteenth-century literature. Scholars are eager to expose
various Victorian novelists and poets as closet imperialists
who were influenced, in their representation of other countries,
by the current distorting stereotypes and depictions of these
places and by their own subconscious feelings of superiority.[30]
Behind apparently innocent descriptions of life abroad and life
at home, it is argued, lurk the dynamics of power and manipulation
which ensure that no literary representation is objective or simple.
Even the Romantic period, a time when the British empire was still
at an early developmental stage, has been shaken by the new

interest, not least by Said's own controversial views of Jane Austen.[31]

But the understanding of Greece is more complicated than that of the Orient or of the Empire since it is unclear whether the ancient Greek world is to be understood as entirely different from the western world or unquestionably the same. The treatment of the Greeks, both ancient and modern, shares correspondences with the treatment of colonised peoples. But ancient Greece, and the classics in general, were also bound up with the strategy for colonising others. The glory that was Greece – and was now Britain – was an integral part of the imperial mentality. The Indian civil service examination, for example, not to mention the examinations for the Foreign Office and the domestic civil service, was heavily dependent upon a knowledge of Latin and Greek. As a result, the ways of approaching Greece call for both an orientalist treatment and an occidentalist one. Paul Cartledge deals with the problem of how like or unlike the ancient Greeks were to western eyes by exploring the fissures within Greek culture.[32] The Greeks themselves were empire-builders and strenuously sought to define their own identity by distinguishing their superior character from others – women, slaves or foreigners. Indeed they invented the xenophobia essential for imperial aspirations when they coined the onomatopoeic word, *barbaros*, or barbarian, for anyone who spoke a non-Greek language which sounded to their untuned ears like gibberish.[33] Those tensions within Greece between self and other are echoed and developed in the relationship between Greece and Britain.

The question of how different or similar Greece should be considered was particularly relevant during the Romantic period, during the last few decades of the eighteenth century and the first few of the nineteenth. It is possible to identify an increasing public acceptance of Greece as a national icon during the eighteenth and early nineteenth centuries. In the first half of the eighteenth century, Latin was in the cultural ascendency. Political writers used Roman historical parallels to support their case and Virgil and Horace were quoted for moral guidance.[34] Meanwhile Greek literature and history were hardly studied in universities and Greek art little known or admired. While Alexander Pope translated the *Iliad*, he attempted to render it as Latinate as possible, feeling uncertain about the unruliness of the gods and the primitive passions of Achilles which could not easily be contained within his neoclassical couplets. Edward Gibbon articulated the general consensus when he argued that Greece constituted only a developmental stage before the sophisticated peak of Roman civilisation.[35] But gradually Greece was rediscovered and appreciated. In 1748, excavation was begun at Pompeii, the city in southern Italy which was founded as a Greek colony, so stimulating interest in the factual details of the Greek way of life.[36] Three years later, James Stuart and Nicholas Revett were dispatched by the Dilettanti Club to make the daring trip to the distant Greek mainland where they sketched the buildings and ruins they discovered. The descriptions and drawings which they brought back gave many people in Britain their first idea of Greek architecture.[37] In 1767, Robert Wood published his study of the historical identity of Homer, and as a result initiated renewed interest in the poet and in the historical reality of Greek civilisation.[38] Meanwhile, on the continent, Johann Joachim Winckelmann, inspired by the excavations at Pompeii, chose to study Greek rather than Roman sculpture, albeit in Roman copies, and drew up what were exciting and challenging theories about Greek art and standards of beauty.[39] And Jean Jacques Barthélèmy brought the ancient streets of Athens to life with an imagined depiction of Greek life in his novel *Le Voyage du Jeune Anacharsis en Grèce*.[40] The novel sparked off a debate across Europe about the nature of ancient Greek life and provoked rival attempts to produce the authentic account. Christoph Wieland's fictional *The History of Agathon*, written a few years earlier, had stressed the historical accuracy of his descriptions;[41] while August Wilhelm Schlegel dismissed these earlier accounts and claimed that his own work was closest to the truth. 'To feel the ancients as we ought,' he wrote, 'we must have become in some degree one of themselves, and breathed as it were the Grecian air.'[42] Even Shelley entered the debate, criticising Wieland and Barthélèmy and attempting to offer a more historically objective picture in his translation of Plato's *Symposium*. What is most important is that the official account of Greece did not yet exist, with the result that these writers were still able to dispute and reshape their ideas. These new ideas of Greece were seen as pioneering and radical, emanating from outside the standard cultural expectations and institutional values.

But, in time, the ideas of Greece became more organised and were given official sanction. The discoveries in archaeology, literature and art encouraged further explorations. More and more people travelled to Greece and wrote about their experiences, which encouraged further travel.[43] The accounts followed an increasingly accepted route through Greece and described the appropriate emotions for particular sites, until the distinction between travelling and touring the country became hard to make.[44] Following Wood's book, Homer became a topic for scholarly debate, provoking a number of publications disputing his historical identity and the geographical site of Troy.[45] This also prompted tourism to Troy. In 1801, Lord Elgin's party visited the supposed site of Troy, where they met the Rev. Edward Daniel Clarke and almost came to blows in the passionate argument over the exact location of the most famous city of their education.[46] Years later, Byron, who also visited the Troad, recalled the devastating impact of Jacob Bryant's sceptical book: 'We *do* care about the authenticity of the Tale of Troy. I have stood upon that plain daily, for more than a month, in 1810; and, if anything diminished my pleasure, it was that the blackguard Bryant had impugned its veracity.'[47] The passion of these memories testifies to the concern about how the official account of Greece and its literature would finally be settled. The question over whether Homer had existed or not affected the earliest notions of heroism, adventure and nobility imbibed since childhood and supposedly investing the British character. Byron went on to explain the implications of Bryant: 'Who will persuade me, when I reclined upon a mighty tomb, that it did not contain a hero? – its very magnitude proved this. Men do not labour over the ignoble and petty dead – and why should not the dead be Homer's dead?'

Meanwhile in Britain, Greek was becoming integrated into academic institutions. Publication of Greek texts rapidly outnumbered those of Latin ones during the early nineteenth century, while the turn of the century witnessed a blossoming of translations from Greek.[48] Most dramatic was the change in educational practices. Even by the end of the eighteenth century, Eton concentrated mostly on Virgil and Horace along with Latin grammar and composition. Greek was learnt only in the last three years of school and pupils read just the Greek New Testament and Homer's *Iliad*.[49] Other leading endowed grammar schools followed the Eton curriculum, concentrating upon Latin exclusively and introducing the brightest pupils to Greek in their last years at school in haphazard fashion.[50] But by the early nineteenth century, education was becoming more organised and defined. Classical degree examinations were introduced in Oxford in 1807 and in Cambridge in

1824. Feeling the threat of the rapidly improving and increasingly popular grammar schools, Eton introduced exams in 1829 when it instituted the Newcastle Scholarship. One of the results of the formalising of school curricula was the greater concentration on the study of Greek. Chief pioneers of this reform were Samuel Butler at Shrewsbury and Thomas Arnold at Rugby.[51] They demanded that the range of authors which the pupils read should be considerably widened to include Herodotus and Demosthenes, as well as more dramatists.[52] They also, more significantly, encouraged a completely different pedagogical approach. Pupils now devoted their time not only to the niceties of grammar and the process of construing but to the appreciation of the spirit of Greece and Greek culture. The study of Greek was no longer just an academic exercise of the brain, additional to Latin, but, according to Arnold, it was essential for the development of the character and moral education of the young. In an article which significantly picked up Schlegel's rhetoric of authenticity stemming from breathing Grecian air, Arnold argued that 'the mind of the Greek is in all the essential parts of its constitution our own', and maintained that consequently education should concentrate upon making young boys more and more like 'moral' replicas of the Greeks: 'they are virtually our own countrymen; and . . . having thus seen in a manner in our eyes what we cannot see for ourselves, their conclusions are such as bear upon our own circumstances, while their information has all the charms of novelty, and all the value of a mass of new and pertinent facts, illustrative of the great science of the nature of civilised man'.[53]

An illustration of the change of attitude towards Greece over the turn of the century is provided by the Elgin Marbles controversy. Between 1801 and 1806, Lord Elgin removed all the statues from the Parthenon and shipped them to England. He wanted to improve the British 'National Taste' and provoke a semi- revolution in the arts.[54] At first, however, the government was suspicious. It was unwilling to take responsibility for the statues and Elgin was compelled to house them in a shed in the garden of a rented house in Piccadilly. The government was also reluctant to purchase the statues. A committee was set up to investigate their value before any decision to buy them could be guaranteed. It was anxious to discover whether the close imitation of nature shown by the statues detracted from their excellence, and whether they were of less value because they had not been restored like most of the statues in the Vatican, then much admired. The committee was almost persuaded by the vigorous arguments of the art connoisseur Richard Payne Knight who thought that the Elgin Marbles were probably not genuinely classical and, in any case, that they were second-rate.[55] However, the government was finally convinced of their worth by Benjamin Robert Haydon and a few other contemporary artists, and in 1816 the Parthenon statues were purchased and moved from the shed to the British Museum. Within a few years men were appointed to engrave and catalogue the statues and international statesmen brought to view them. Casts of the statues were sent to museums and art schools around Europe. Greek sculpture was now no longer on the periphery of British interest, but literally in the centre of the art world, in the most important museum in the country, leading, as Elgin had wished, a revolution in taste.

By the nineteenth century, Greece had moved from the margins of culture to a central position attracting national attention. It had replaced Rome as the cultural and political model, strengthening the moral fibre of the nation from childhood. There was always room for dispute over the implications of Greek history. Athenian democracy was appropriated by both sides contesting parliamentary reform during the Victorian period and presented either as liberal or chaotic. George Grote's highly flattering depiction of Athenian democracy, which obviously alluded to the contemporary British constitution, provoked a direct response from the future Prime Minister William Gladstone, whose *Studies on Homer and the Homeric Age* suggested that the early Bronze Age assemblies of Homer's epics were more like the ideal British constitution than the unruly Athenian gatherings.[56] Behind this dispute lies the basic question which dogged political appropriation of Greece: namely, which Greece? Usually when Greece was cited for political argument, it was Athenian Greece that was intended. But the Spartan regime could also be used as a model and so could the primitive world of the Homeric epic. It was to Greece in some form, however, that writers now turned in their discussion of the contemporary political system.[57] Rome was alluded to only as a counterpoint, a model to be avoided and resisted – even if, at times, it seemed worryingly closer than Athens.[58]

The Romantic period thus marked a crucial turning point, a 'transitional period', in the reassessment of Greece and its integration within national culture.[59] Neither completely novel and marginal, as in the eighteenth century, nor institutionalised and central as in the later nineteenth century, Greece at the turn of the century challenged readers and writers to determine the degree of its closeness to their culture. This was hard, not least because the centre of culture itself seemed to be fragmenting. The popularity of writers such as Robert Burns was spurring a fashion for literature from the provinces. Wordsworth and Coleridge's *Lyrical Ballads*, and their espousal of 'the language of men', were part of the new exciting interest in dialects and in other ways of communicating beyond the metropolitan use of language defined by Samuel Johnson's dictionary. Resistance to the centralised way of writing carried political significance. Some investigated local dialects and resurrected old regional poets in order to encourage national instincts and to counter the power of London.[60] Others celebrated a 'plain' way of speaking which derived from ordinary people and which therefore offered an alternative voice to that used by those perceived to be the ruling classes.[61] The proliferation of publications, of newspapers and journals, during the period emphasised the general sense of the fragmentation and dispersal of society. Writers became 'radically uncertain of their readers'.[62] But nothing better illustrated the way society could tear itself apart than the reports of the massacres and mob violence in the streets of Paris during the revolutionary early 1790s. Shelley epitomised the tensions which were dividing and isolating parts of the country. He was an aristocrat who sympathised with the needs of the ordinary people and who shunned all the expectations of his class – a seat in parliament as a Whig, a hereditary baronetcy. He had enjoyed a privileged education and practised a highly sophisticated literary style, and yet he expressed revolutionary sentiments that would have been more popular with the mass illiterate audience than with his natural readers. As a result, much of his energy was devoted to worrying about his connection with or distance from an indeterminate and often scanty reading audience.[63]

It is because the last years of the eighteenth century and the first decades of the nineteenth were so tumultuous and destabilising that, according to Jerome McGann, writers, and particularly poets, were driven to finding a way of thinking which appeared to transcend the messiness of their lives.[64] McGann's notion of a 'Romantic ideology', which stabilised the nation's sense of itself and repressed the historical conditions of writers' lives, has now become an orthodoxy in Romantic criticism. The ideology, which included the celebration of the imagination, the belief in a transcendent world, the emphasis upon the individual and an isolated landscape denuded of fearsome crowds, was the result of a calculated effort to resist acknowledging the real changes which were happening to the country. Many of the passions which we associate with Romanticism – the Lake District, the mythological world, the seductive beautiful woman – become, under McGann's New Historicist eyes, covert displacement activities for the political anxieties which really concerned the writers. One of the purposes of this book is to consider how far Greece constituted another displacement activity. On the one hand, the distance of Greece and the imaginative possibilities of its mythology, offered a similar retreat into a simple homogeneous society which the Lake District offered Wordsworth. Both locations operated like a typical pastoral landscape, displacing political concerns within a stylised topos while leaving the *status quo* unaltered.[65] On the other hand, the difference and indeed alien world, which ancient Greece also tokened, could have a fragmenting effect similar to that of the revolutionary interest in native heroes or primitive local dialects. In contrast to McGann's ideas, the work of L.J. Swingle suggests a very different Romanticism, one that is concerned with Wordsworth's 'obstinate questionings' and a sceptical attitude to belief rather than one which represses difficulties and the external world.[66] If Swingle's ideas are accepted, Greece can become another troubling question, disrupting certainties and positively dis-integrating fixed belief.

The dilemma between a McGann-influenced view of Romantic Greece and a Swingle one is well illustrated by attitudes to Ossian's poetry. James Macpherson's controversial forgery of an ancient Scottish bard's poems polarised opinion at the end of the eighteenth century, and still tantalises today.[67] One of the points of controversy is Ossian's relation to Homer. Some see Ossian as the antithesis of Homer, representing the culmination of a growing dissatisfaction with the classics and a movement towards the primitive, domestic origins of Britain.[68] Under this interpretation, Greece becomes part of the centralising ideology which McGann identifies, and one which is resisted by local writers from the grassroots in touch with their history. But others prefer to find analogies between Ossian and Homer.[69] Homer seems to have provided a literary model when Macpherson composed his epic of *Fingal*.[70]

And indeed the writing of Ossian in turn influenced receptions of Homer, so that he was seen as more primitive and simpler, like Ossian, and attractively different from the sophisticated Virgil.[71] Under this interpretation, the primitive and localised Greeks become icons of resistance against the prevailing ideology.

A further way of countering the fragmentation and instability of the Romantic period, besides the ideology which McGann has described, was through the development of education and discipline. Discipline involved organisation and definition, distinguishing branches of knowledge into different disciplines, as well as the injection of rigour and order into the minds of pupils. The classics had long been associated with the drawing of distinctions between different qualities, different disciplines. Charles Sainte-Beuve explained the exclusivity of the term 'classic' from its origins in Roman culture: 'The *classici*, properly so called, were not all the citizens of different classes, but only those of the highest class, who possessed, at least, an income of a certain fixed figure.'[72] Later, the term was appropriated to apply specifically to writers: 'a writer of worth and mark is a *classicus assiduusque scriptor*'. The distinguishing of writers 'of worth' necessitated collating lists of writers to perpetuate the distinction. Effectively, classics depended upon canons drawn up by those who wanted to perpetuate their view of distinctiveness, and implied as much about the selectors as the selection.[73] As was noted recently, 'a classic work of literature is a work that for political reasons those in power have decided to call a classic'.[74] University degree courses were divided into different disciplines with the institution of subject examinations. Indeed, it is even argued that one of the motives for establishing the examination in Classics at Oxford University was to control what men read and prevent unlicensed forays into literature not on approved lists.[75]

Besides the capability of organised classics to control and define, there was the added benefit that classics was perceived to be hard to learn. Learning Latin and Greek disciplined the mind, making it tougher and punishing it with grammar so that it would eventually become sharper and outshine other, feebler minds. The study of classics was believed to be difficult because of the abstract nature of language work and because of the requirement to subject oneself to a tradition, to an age-old method of learning, without asserting any form of independence. The difficulty of classical discipline was marked more sharply by the exclusion of women from classical

education. Mary Shelley was denied Greek education while
Elizabeth Barrett Browning was unusually able to learn Greek with
her brother and later to read it with a local scholar – a training
which Barrett Browning felt qualified her to become the first serious woman poet.[76] Her classical upbringing had disciplined her
mind sufficiently to rival male poets in rigour and earnestness. As
a result of the punishing reputation of classics, critics of English
literature have tended to associate the subject with the demands
of school and authority, while avoiding it, for them, constitutes
a glorious truancy. Olivia Smith's polarisation of society in the
Romantic period into the 'classically-educated' elite who repress
any other social groups and the sympathetic 'vulgar language'
users, who resist the political hegemony, implicitly carries this
belief.[77] Consequently, the study of the Romantic interest in
classical Greece can erroneously be seen as an attempt to focus
back regressively upon the canon, to discipline new writers and
writing.

But this is a consciously *inter*-disciplinary book. I mean this of
course partly in the obvious sense that it is intended both for
literary scholars interested in Shelley and the Romantic period and
also for classical scholars studying the reception of texts and
notions of the classical tradition. But I also mean that the book is
concerned with the question of what it is to be interdisciplinary, to
attempt to link or compare discrete areas of knowledge and to
break the rigidity of isolating disciplines and their effects. Shelley's
writing repeatedly confronts what he sees as the enervating sta-
bility of tradition and conformity and contemplates the terrifying,
awe-inspiring alternative. Thinking and writing – marking 'the
before unapprehended relations of things' – unsettle the fixed distinctions of thought and language and allow glimpses of what lies
beyond or between. 'We are on that verge', he admits in *Essay on
Life*, after much thinking, 'where words abandon us, and what
wonder if we grow dizzy to look down the dark abyss of how little
we know.'

The two critics whom I have found most helpful in my reading of
Shelley both describe Shelley's writing 'on that verge'. Richard
Cronin's *Shelley's Poetic Thoughts* examines Shelley's exploration and subversion of poetic genres.[78] Cronin spells out the
consciousness and sophistication behind the poet's invocation
and manipulation of poetic tradition and language. Jerrold E.
Hogle has analysed in admirable detail the continual 'transference'

in Shelley's writing from a state of stasis to one of process, a Derridean celebration of deferral.[79] While Hogle's discussion remains remarkably abstract, it is possible to detect a mental movement between stasis and process in Shelley's relationship with Greece. The intellectual leap required in moving over to Greece as a subject matter allows for fluidity in thought and language. But there is always the danger that Greece is a stabilising, displacing and authoritative force, as already discussed. Stasis thus threatens. But the uncertainty over the significance of Greece itself keeps the mind working, thinking, and not content to rest. The western poet's ambiguous relationship with Greece, like the male poet's elusive relationship with a beautiful female muse figure – which features so often in Shelley's writing – replicates the general problem of the poet's mastery over his subject. Shelley's mastery over his subject, a sense of authority which Cronin touches upon in his discussion of poetic tradition, is highly desirable for him and indeed necessary for any communicable form of expression. Yet mastery is at the same time problematic, fraught with literary and political uneasiness. It is to test the limits and possibilities of his poetic mastery that Shelley moves to other fields of knowledge and inspiration. My concentration upon Shelley's hellenism, therefore, sheds new light upon the tension between discipline and freedom within his writing.

The chapters which follow explore the wide range of responses to, and ideas of, Greece which permeated the Romantic period. Each chapter focuses discussion of an aspect of Greece through a reading of one or more of Shelley's poems, thus examining how Shelley reacted to and interrogated contemporary concepts of Greece. The first chapter looks at classical education in schools, which provided the first experience of Greek culture for most educated men. It uncovers a vigorous debate about the benefit of classics, a debate which prompted Shelley's poems *Queen Mab* and *Alastor* and which they in turn illuminate. The next two chapters confront the question of the political significance of Greece: the first explores the possibilities of democratic Greece for Shelley's subversive writing while the second pushes New Historicist ideas about pastoral displacement further to consider the pastoral genre and the process of translation as metaphors for the difficulty of radical writing in the period. Chapters 4 and 5 contrast notions of Greece as seductively different, with the image of Greece as an awesome example, close and comparable. The difference of Greece was conveyed by its links with the Orient, and the confusion which followed, between an orientalist and occidentalist representation, is articulated in Shelley's *Epipsychidion*. Meanwhile the growing acceptance of Greek culture and art as the supreme example of western civilisation provoked anxious feelings of inferiority among artists and writers, feelings which prompted Shelley's battle with Aeschylus for authority over Prometheus. The final chapter describes the consequences of the various ideas of Greece explored earlier in the book. The Greek War of Independence was the result of the enthusiastic but colonising ideas of Greece which had developed during the Romantic period, constructions of Greece as western, free, beautiful and the generous source of contemporary culture. Shelley's *Hellas* dramatises the tensions behind the philhellenic rhetoric which determined the course of the war.

1

'Things Foreign'?: Classical Education and Knowledge

> It gives men liberal views; it accustoms the mind to take an interest in things foreign to itself.
>
> Hazlitt: 'On Classical Education'

When Charles Lamb came to look back upon his days at Christ's Hospital, his clearest memory was of his consciousness of distinction:

> For the Christ's Hospital boy feels that he is no charity boy; he feels it in the antiquity and regality of the foundation to which he belongs; in the usage which he meets with at school, and the treatment he is accustomed to out of its bounds; in the respect, and even the kindness, which his well-known garb never fails to procure him in the streets of the metropolis; and he feels it in his education, in that measure of classical attainments which every individual at that school, though not destined to a learned profession, has it in his power to procure – attainments which it would be worse than folly to put in the reach of the labouring classes to acquire.[1]

Although Christ's Hospital was founded for poor sons of respectable families and a third of its pupils were 'on foundation' or financially supported by the school, Lamb is anxious to point out that he was 'no charity boy' and that he was distanced dramatically from the poor. Unlike the poor at conventional 'common charity schools', he is distinguished by the 'well-known garb' and the 'classical attainments'. The 'well-known garb', a long blue tunic and yellow stockings, a 'venerable fashion' which Leigh Hunt believed was 'the ordinary dress of children in humble life during the

19

reign of the Tudors', was as physically distinctive as 'classical attainments' were socially distinctive.[2] Although the wearing of uniform at Christ's Hospital was unique among schools, one can find in it an analogy for the perception of classical education at the time. Tidy and correct, ancient with no attempt to reform or update, uniforming and anachronistic – the blue coats provided an external manifestation of the educational practices carried out within the school walls. They bestowed the same distinctiveness as the possession of a solid classical education.

In fact when Lamb remembered his sense of distinction based upon his outfits and his classical education, he confirmed all that critics now feel about classical education in the early nineteenth century. There is a common perception among critics that classical education was crucial in determining hierarchies of class and political groupings.[3] Education served to polarise the refined and vulgar, the rulers and the ruled. By extension classical education also determined, it is thought, political power and political opinions. Since there was a direct connection between classical education at school, entrance to university, and subsequent career in the government, church or courts, it is assumed that classical education ensured a role within the establishment and a desire to maintain the *status quo*, both within the realm of education and in the government of the country as a whole. The authority of the classics derived from its position at the bedrock of the British establishment, and was drawn upon to maintain and justify that establishment.

In this chapter, I examine the validity of this opinion by considering the range of educational experiences during the Romantic period. While there was a strong element of elitism and power linked to classical education, there were also a number of literary writers and educationalists who were eager to create other ways of teaching the classical world and other ways of reading and drawing upon the classics without being caught up in the cultural establishment. There was indeed a debate being conducted into the merits and advantages of reading classical literature, and one that drew in a range of people from different backgrounds and political opinions. Could reading the classics, and particularly Greek, give one 'liberal views' if conducted the right way? Could education return to its original meaning and 'lead out' young minds to other worlds, rather than imprisoning them with the continual bombardment of grammar and rules? To continue the analogy, Coleridge and Leigh Hunt dreamed of other things, discovering Pindar and Greek mythology while shut in their school-rooms, wearing their blue coats. Could those dreams adequately transcend the blue-coated uniformity?

These questions were particularly pressing for Shelley, who, as the son of a baronet, had been educated at Eton and, briefly, Oxford, with a solid and uninterrupted grounding in classics. After Oxford, he was eager to question the whole political system in the country, from a perspective contrary to the expectations of his background and education. His participation in the debate is therefore exemplary and highly important for a whole class of writers. It is also highly problematic. For while arguments were mooted for the possible liberating effects of reading classical literature, it was evident that the reading of classics was to a certain extent based upon the opportunities afforded by class, wealth and gender, so that any amount of arguing could not ensure that reading and writing about the classics would be divorced from prejudices about classical education. While a man might dream about Pindar and Greek mythology, the metaphorical blue-coat rather spoilt the disguise.

Two of the major works in which Shelley explored the possibilities and ambiguities of knowledge of the classics as it was perceived by its liberal advocates are *Queen Mab* and *Alastor*. These early poems, sometimes relegated to the juvenilia section in collections of Shelley's works, represent Shelley's efforts to educate himself in the writing of poetry as well as tackling the subject of education as their theme. Criticised and misunderstood at the time, the poems could be seen to make problematic the notion of the acceptability and power or powerlessness of the classics and classical education. These works are therefore discussed in this chapter as poems of forbidden knowledge, after consideration has been given to the political implications of classical education.

THE EDUCATION DEBATE

One of the chief criticisms lodged against classical education by radical campaigners in the late eighteenth century was that it was socially divisive and served to enforce and maintain the differences between classes. William Cobbett, the son of a farm-worker and smalltime farmer, received comparatively little education, possibly

attending a village school but mainly learning reading and arithmetic from his father between ploughing, according to his own
later (self-mythologising) autobiography.[4] He felt the inverted
snobbery of resentment against the social classes who enjoyed the
benefits of classical education. As he saw it, since knowledge of the
classics appeared to be the main shibboleth by which one judged
the social background of anyone, men therefore set out to acquire a
classical education only as a fashionable badge or accessory, and
should be condemned for doing so: 'All such attempts to apply this
schoolboy sort of learning, which, in fact, arise from the vanity of
appearing to know more than the people at large; all such attempts
are ridiculous.' Vicesimus Knox, headmaster of Tonbridge School
and author of a treatise which would have confirmed all of Cobbett's worst prejudices, conceded that classics should be learnt in
part because, as a mark of good breeding, it allowed entry to the
hallowed circle of gentlemanly discourse:

> Supposing for a moment, that a truly classical education were not
> the best preparation for every liberal pursuit, as well as the most
> efficacious means of exalting or refining the mind; yet as the
> greater number are still trained in it, who would chuse to be a
> stranger to that, in which almost every gentleman has been in
> some degree initiated.[5]

Knox recommends the learning of classical texts by heart for,
besides sharpening the memory and elevating the mind with the
finest language, it is extremely impressive or, as he puts it, 'common and agreeable', to be able to drop the occasional quotation into
conversation.[6] But such abilities are required only by a certain
class, and he endorses Cobbett's feelings about the social divisions
highlighted and maintained by classical education in even more
forthright fashion:

> There are cases in which classical learning may be properly dis-
> pensed with; such is that of a very dull intellect, or a total want of
> parts; and such is that of the boy who is to be trained to a
> subordinate trade, or to some low and mechanical employment,
> in which a refined taste and a comprehensive knowledge would
> divert his attention from his daily occupation. It is certain that
> money can be acquired, though not enjoyed with liberality, with-
> out either taste or literary knowledge. And indeed the good of the

community requires, that there should be grosser understandings to fill the illiberal and servile stations in society. Some of us must be hewers of wood and drawers of water, whose minds Nature has rendered less capable of ornament.[7]

Radicals also attacked classical education because it was deemed not useful. In *The Age of Reason*, Tom Paine criticises the study of classics for its concentration upon words rather than things, and for its sinister ability to distract from the politically important subjects of enquiry. 'Learning', he writes, 'does not consist, as the schools now make it consist, in the knowledge of languages, but in the knowledge of things to which language gives names.'[8] The knowledge of things leads the scholar to learn about science and cosmology, and to question religious doctrine and the *status quo*. As a consequence, he argues, it has been repressed by the nervous authorities: 'therefore it became necessary to their purpose to cut learning down to a size less dangerous to their project, and this they effected by restricting the idea of learning to the dead study of dead languages'.[9] Cobbett likewise considered that classical languages were not useful. Workers should be learning skills relevant to their future labour on the land; the classics were not relevant. He told the story of the British aristocracy's contempt for Napoleon's lack of classical knowledge which only briefly abated when the 'attention of the learned and the witty had been called off by the news of the battle of Austerlitz, which served, too, as a sort of practical illustration of the inutility of Latin and Greek in the performance of the great actions of the world'.

There was some justification for the radical attack on the classics. Classical studies did dominate the curricula of leading public schools. At Eton, even by 1830, a typical week's lessons in the fifth form consisted of reading seventy lines of the *Iliad*, seventy lines of the *Aeneid*, a few pages of *Scriptores Graeci* and *Romani* (classical anthologies), twenty verses from the New Testament, learning a few pages from the grammar book and completing some Latin translation exercises.[10] Most schools apparently modelled themselves on Eton, and followed similar timetables. Nicholas Carlisle's survey of schools records that the Eton grammar books were used at numerous endowed grammar schools, including Thetford (Paine's school), Hawkshead (Wordsworth's school), Shrewsbury and Merchant Taylors'.[11] Since classics formed the daily routine of the schoolroom, it was solely in knowledge of Greek and Latin that a pupil was tested and his intelligence assessed. Thomas De Quincey's entrance examination to Manchester Grammar School, for example, consisted of the translation of a couple of pages of *The Spectator* into Latin. The strict diet of classics continued at the only two universities in England, Cambridge and Oxford. While there was no official curriculum or degree at the universities until 1807 at Oxford and 1824 at Cambridge, the only medium of instruction at university consisted of translating or construing classical texts to a tutor, who might interject the occasional correction.[12] Cambridge also offered mathematics, but this was based upon Euclid and was linked to classical study, even after the introduction of the tripos in 1824.[13] From Oxford and Cambridge, students passed to careers in government, at the Bar or in the church, the three principal arms of the Establishment given the task of ruling, adjudicating over and guiding the country. Thus there seemed to be a natural link between the study of classics and the wielding of power and authority.

Admittedly, the path to this dubious bliss was more open than some critics have implied. Byron and Shelley were born into aristocratic families and so were educated at the premier educational institutions in the country, Harrow and Eton. However, if one believes De Quincey's description of what he had heard of Eton from his friend – 'you may judge of the discipline of the school when I tell you that a week ago they beat an old porter (in defiance of the masters, some of whom were standing by, and hardly trying to prevent them) with such brutality that his life, I hear, is despaired of' – the desirability of an education at either Eton or Harrow becomes doubtful.[14] Other good schools, the endowed grammar schools, appear to have been comparatively affordable and accessible and yet also often had sufficient reputation to select a couple of the best pupils for places at Oxford or Cambridge. Tom Paine's school at Thetford cost, besides the expense of books and quills, only a two shilling and sixpence fee, which Paine's father, a staymaker, managed to afford until his business began to fail and Paine had to leave.[15] Though a little more expensive and so offering more, Wordsworth's grammar school at Hawkshead cost only two guineas to enter and two guineas yearly fee payable at Shrovetide, yet it regularly sent pupils to Cambridge. One of the principal reasons for sending the orphaned De Quincey to Manchester Grammar School was the fact that the school awarded a few grants of £40 a year for pupils to attend Brasenose College, Oxford. The money set aside for De Quincey's education from his father's legacy, earned from his successful linen business, appeared not sufficient to send him to Oxford without an award; but later, after De Quincey had run away from Manchester Grammar School, he was able to attend Worcester College, Oxford – without a scholarship– on £100 a year. Coleridge also reached Cambridge, though an orphan, through Christ's Hospital and its university scholarship for the senior 'Grecian' – the final-year pupil – of £40. One of the most dramatic examples of the access to higher education offered to some people of humble background is provided by the experience of the classical scholar Richard Porson. Porson was the son of a weaver, and attended a village school, with the expectation that he would follow his father to the loom. But a clergyman spotted his talents and offered to educate him until the age of 13. At that point Porson was sent, on foundation, to Eton and from there progressed to Cambridge, where his subsistence was provided by a fund sponsored by wealthy old Etonians. After winning the Craven University scholarship and being elected fellow of Trinity, he was later, at the age of 32, appointed Regius Professor of Greek.

Porson's case is unusual. For most, access to university was dependent upon wealth and social background. Charles Lamb and Leigh Hunt, who also attended Christ's Hospital, did not go on to university. Both apparently 'stuttered too much to be a clergyman', the only purpose for which the school trustees would provide for pupils in the final 'Grecian' year of school, and both, as a result, expressed feelings of inadequacy and lifelong awe of the senior Grecians of their acquaintance. Keats's access to classical education was most pointedly linked to fluctuations in his parents' financial affairs. While both his stable-keeping but socially aspiring parents were alive, he was sent to a small academy in Enfield with the prospect of subsequent progression to Harrow. But after both his parents had died and nothing of their small legacy had reached him or his siblings, at the age of 15 he was removed from the school and apprenticed to a local apothecary, so that he could earn his living and do something useful, as his guardian perceived it.[16] So grammar schools opened up possibilities for some poor pupils from respectable backgrounds to reach university, but social backgrounds and wealth were of enormous importance in determining what a child was taught and thus his subsequent career. As William Godwin wrote in *Political Justice*, 'How long has the genius of education been disheartened and

unnerved by the pretence that man is born all that it is possible for
him to become?'[17]

However, the experience for all these men, whether or not they
were able to attend university, was very different from that of the
majority of working people in the country, the people for whom
Paine, Cobbett and others were speaking. The most common provi-
sion was the Sunday school, run by the parish, at which a little
reading tuition was provided. Not only could parents not afford
the fees of grammar schools, but they also could not afford for their
children not to work. William Pitt's Factory Act of 1802, which
stipulated – ineffectually as it turned out – that children should be
given four years of tuition in reading and writing during their
seven years of apprenticeship at the factory, indicates the low level
of education for the majority of the country. The experience of
Cobbett's father was typical. When he was 'a little boy', Cobbett
recalled, he 'drove the plough for two pence a day; and these
his earnings were appropriated to the expenses of an evening
school'.[18]

The radicals were justified, too, in feeling that classics, as it was
taught in schools, did not seem very useful. School lessons were
very regimented and unimaginative. In his autobiography, Leigh
Hunt describes the narrow classical curriculum of the 'Grammar
School' of Christ's Hospital and his consequent dislike of Greek
literature in his youth. 'Homer', he remembers, 'I regarded with
horror, as a series of letters which I had to learn by heart before I
understood him.'[19] Classical literature was allegedly spoilt also for
Byron by its mistreatment at the hands of school-teachers:

> I abhorred
> Too much, to conquer for the poet's sake,
> The drilled, dull lesson, forced down word by word
> In my repugnant youth.[20]

In essence the teaching of classics involved the rote learning of
particular texts and details of grammar, and the construing of
ancient languages into their grammatical forms and structures.
This was accompanied by the translation of ancient languages into
English and the translation of English into Latin and Greek. There
was no attempt to consider the historical or literary background to
the classical works; they merely provided ammunition for the serious technical study of language and grammar. The number of texts

studied was also circumscribed. At Eton, the only classical works read in their entirety were Virgil, Horace and Homer. There was also an anthology of extracts from Greek and Latin prose writers. But most of the time was spent on the Eton grammar, and parse book. It is small wonder that when Thomas De Quincey arrived finally at Oxford, after several 'years out', he found that most of his fellow students knew nothing of English literature or indeed any book beyond the few classical works stipulated on the school curriculum and the few pages of the *Spectator* which they had translated into Latin.[21]

It was the experience of these 'drilled, dull lessons' which motivated some liberals to question the authority of the classics. Byron, ever the rebel, turned against classical scholarship completely as a result of his experience and boasted an indifference to Greek architectural remains. But others sought alternative, more attractive ways of teaching classical languages. Thomas Love Peacock recognised the fault in British classical education when preparing the prospectus for his proposed small school for boys in the Lake District. 'The instructors of youth', he wrote, 'aim only at communicating the knowledge of the words and rules of a language, without exciting the taste of the student to penetrate into the beauties of the authors who have written it.'[22] His school would aim to rectify all that, by conveying what he perceived to be the spirit of Greece, rather than just the letter. William Godwin shared similar ideas about the need to replace facts with enthusiasm:

> The imagination, the faculty . . . [which I] aim at cultivating . . . if cultivated at all, must be begun within youth. Without imagination there can be no genuine ardour in any pursuit, or for any acquisition, and without imagination there can be no genuine morality, no profound feeling of another's sorrow, no ardent or persevering anxiety for their interests. This is the faculty which makes the man, and not the miserable minutenesses of detail about which the present age is so uneasy.[23]

To cultivate children's imagination, Godwin set about publishing books conveying the classical world to children which would circumvent the classroom.[24] Both Peacock and Godwin were influenced by the example of the Dissenting Academies, where lecturers such as Joseph Priestley, who taught William Hazlitt at Hackney Academy, were exploring alternative teaching methods

and other subjects of study. '[Children] should be able to read
and understand the classics, but their compositions should be in
English', Priestley urged.[25]

A second way of resisting the authoritarian influence of school
classics was to read books which were not taught at school. Byron
notably talked of the coercion behind the choice of reading matter,
and how different things could be:

> My mind could relish what it might have sought,
> If free to choose . . .[26]

Peacock, in particular, relished the task of seeking out the unusual
and the previously forbidden. Indeed at the turn of the century,
most of Greek literature was not studied at school and so had the
cachet of novelty. Greek tragedy and comedy by Aeschylus and
Aristophanes, poetry by Pindar or Theocritus or the obscure
Nonnus, and the dialogues of Plato constituted exciting discoveries
and were not tinged with memories of the school-room. Even Latin
texts could be found which had not been included in the ten-year
diet of Latin. Peacock and Shelley particularly enjoyed Lucretius
and Lucan. Precisely because these texts had not been taught in the
schoolroom, they assumed the aura of forbidden knowledge, the
world beyond authority.

But besides these practical methods of reading the classics in a
different way, the liberal writers set out to consider the theoretical
issue of the utility of learning ancient Greek and Latin. Paine's
radical attack on classical learning was answered by other liberal
writers, spearheaded by William Godwin. In his essay 'On the
Study of the Classics', written a year after *The Age of Reason*, Godwin argued that prejudice and despotism were not assisted by
classical education. Instead they were actually avoided through its
enlightening power and ability to open the mind:

> From the Greek and Roman authors the moderns learned to
> think. While they investigated with unconquerable perseverance
> the ideas and sentiments of antiquity, the feculence of their
> own understandings subsided. The shackles of superstition were
> loosened. Men were no longer shut up in so narrow boundaries
> nor benumbed in their faculties by the sound of eternal monot-
> ony. They saw; they examined; they compared . . . the love of
> truth displayed itself, and the love of liberty.[27]

The classical world opened the minds of scholars through its contrast with their own world and expectations, so that they were compelled to re-examine their assumptions. William Hazlitt adopted a similar argument in his essay 'On Classical Education', which appeared in *The Round Table*:

> The peculiar advantage of this mode of education consists not so much in strengthening the understanding, as in softening and refining the taste. It gives men liberal views; it accustoms the mind to take an interest in things foreign to itself.[28]

The 'softening and refining' of the taste involves the exercise of the mind, which is more important, Hazlitt argues, than the 'knowledge of things'. Godwin reiterates this belief in his pamphlet of 1818, *Letter of Advice to a Young American*: 'Language is as necessary an instrument for conducting the operations of the mind, as the hands are for conducting the operations of the body; and the most obvious way of acquiring the power of weighing and judging words aright is by enabling ourselves to compare the words and forms of different languages.'[29] And he goes on to tackle Paine's arguments directly:

> It has often been said by the wise men of the world, what a miserable waste of time it is, that boys should be occupied for successive year after year, in acquiring the Greek and Latin tongues! How much more usefully would these years be employed in learning the knowledge of things, and making a substantial acquaintance with the studies of men! I totally dissent from this.

Godwin countered Paine's call for the knowledge of things with the argument that education was not about knowledge, but about the training of the mind, the exercise of the mind through contrast and difference, the 'process of knowledge', as Hazlitt termed it, for its own sake. In this both writers were influenced by the theories put forward by Rousseau in *Emile*. In this treatise, Rousseau had significantly put more weight upon the capacity of the mind to confront any intellectual problem which might arise than upon the cumulative retention of facts: 'Emile has a mind that is universal not by its learning but by its faculty to acquire learning; a mind that is open, intelligent, ready for everything, and, as Montaigne says, if not instructed, at least able to be instructed.'[30]

However, despite their enthusiasm, the liberal advocates of classical education did reveal ambiguities and uncertainties in their arguments. For example, Godwin's defence against Paine's call for a knowledge of things went on to argue:

> As to the knowledge of things, young men will soon enough be plunged in the mire of cold and sordid realities, such things as it is the calamity of man that he should be condemned to consume so much of his mature life upon; and I could wish that those who can afford the leisure of education, should begin with acquiring something a little generous and elevated.[31]

The classics here seem close to being considered diversionary, shielding young men from 'sordid realities', just as Paine thought. Moreover, according to Godwin, the classics are the preserve of those who can afford such an education, the preserve of a leisured and 'elevated' elite. It is 'young men' who are expected to enjoy the privilege of a classical education. Hazlitt emphasises this when he writes that 'we do not think a classical education proper for women', a view with which even Vicesimus Knox would moderately disagree.[32]

Along with the liberal sentiments of these writers is a whiff of intellectual snobbery and elitism. They reveal a wish to distance themselves from the popular, radical leaders – notably William Cobbett and Thomas Paine – who speak without the privilege of education, and this influences their reception of Greece. The danger was that, by retreating to the 'generous and elevated' world of classics, the writer could be associated with those who advocated classics with similar arguments but who came from very different political positions. For example, a Lincolnshire clergyman, the Rev. David Henry Urquhart, wrote of the improvement of taste and the 'temporary asylum from the ills of life' offered by Greek and Latin.[33] But his main political purpose – to provide a nation of patriots who would defend the *status quo* and privilege their country over all other personal and family ties – was far from the liberal politics of Godwin and Hazlitt.

As well as the suggestions of elitism and the dangers of appearing an advocate for the wrong political parties, there is a further element of ambiguity in the liberal support for classical education. This is evident in the debate over whether Greece should be represented as different or ultimately the same, as a liberating contrast or an inspiring model. Liberals, as has been discussed, alluded to Greece in order to reveal how society could operate differently; while conservative thinkers appropriated Greece in order to confirm the *status quo* and to keep things the same. Godwin and Hazlitt used the concept of the difference of Greece to liberate the mind. They claimed to believe that Greece could free the mind from its narrow bounds by the contrast and difference it provided. However, there are hints in their writing that they also considered Greece as the highest example of western – or even British – culture to which all should aspire. If Greece was represented as a confirmation of western values, its radical potential, derived specifically from its difference, could be diluted. In his *Letter of Advice*, Godwin talks of 'studying the best models', and being 'imbued' with the classics. Hazlitt also represents classical Greece not as being a distant and distinct culture, but as a model which reveals the best aspects of national culture. The study of the ancient world 'teaches us to believe that there is something really great and excellent in the world, surviving all the shocks of accident and fluctuations of opinion', he announced in his essay, 'On Classical Education'. The active, evaluating power which Godwin and Hazlitt apparently valued is not evident when approaching Greece. Hazlitt writes: 'By conversing with the mighty dead, we imbibe sentiment with knowledge; we become strongly attached to those who can no longer either hurt or serve us, except through the influence which they exert over the mind.' Greece is obediently and passively 'imbibed', and the exercising, comparing power is forgotten.[34]

SHELLEY'S EDUCATION

Shelley negotiated his way through the different arguments of this liberal debate about the classics. He had himself undergone a vigorous classical education at Eton where he was noted for his ability in classical composition.[35] Later even Hogg admitted that Shelley possessed a wide classical knowledge: 'in his short life, and without ostentation, he had, in truth, read more Greek than an aged pedant'.[36] But when Hogg first met Shelley at Oxford, he wrote that Shelley showed more enthusiasm about science and metaphysics than about Greek literature. Hogg recounts Shelley's first meeting with his tutor, who impressed upon him the need to assimilate various prescribed Greek texts, and in particular Euclid and

Aristotle.[37] According to Hogg, Shelley was downcast by this discipline, and preferred pottering round his chemical experiments, burning holes in his carpet in the process. Hogg's account is some-what biased, designed to render the poet more comically eccentric than in reality. Even so, in his time at Oxford and for a few years afterwards, Shelley seemed deliberately to shun Greek reading. He immersed himself in English philosophy and contemporary novels, and remonstrated in 1812 against William Godwin's advice that he study Greek and Roman writers:

> I am not sufficiently vain and dogmatical to say that now I have no doubts on the deleteriousness of classical education, but it certainly is my opinion, nor has your last letter sufficed to refute it, that the evils of acquiring Greek and Latin considerably over-balance the benefits.[38]

Shelley's attitude, like Byron's, might partly be explained by the typical student's hatred for his school-enforced intellectual diet. Godwin was a father-figure for Shelley, one who inspired rebellion as well as veneration, and perhaps his reading-list reminded the poet of school. But Shelley's resistance and unease go further than that, consciously echoing the sentiments of his radical heroes, and Thomas Paine in particular. He criticised classical education for concentrating upon the knowledge of words rather than things, for distracting radical thinkers from the important issues with false knowledge. He explained to Godwin in a letter:

> You say that words will neither debauch our understandings, nor distort our moral feelings – you say that the time of youth could not be better employed than in the acquisition of classical learning. But words are the very things that so eminently contribute to the growth and establishment of prejudice.[39]

The acquisition of language only leaves the scholar vulnerable to the delusions of prejudice, and also, he goes on to argue, denies him access to the more politically empowering realms of knowledge:

> Nor can I help considering the vindicators of ancient learning . . . as the vindicators of a literary despotism, as the tracers of a circle which is intended to shut out from real knowledge, to which this fictitious knowledge is attached, all who do not breathe the air of

prejudice, and who will not support the established systems of politics, Religion, and morals.

Greece was used to displace radical, political attention from pressing current issues. As a result, in his early days, Shelley associated it with the establishment and with the manipulations of despotism.

But gradually Shelley adopted more of the arguments put forward by writers like Godwin and Hazlitt as he began reading and drawing upon a greater number of classical authors. Episodes from Greek history appear in his correspondence and literary work, to contrast with contemporary events in order to support his arguments. He cited the paganism of the ancient world in order to confront contemporary orthodox Christianity. There was not 'ever a period of greater tranquility in which the name of religion was not even mentioned', he wrote of the classical world to his father, when engaging in the bitter row over his rejection of Christianity.[40] And to Godwin he wrote that 'the first doubts which arose in my mind concerning the genuineness of the Christian religion as a revelation from the divinity were excited by a contemplation of the virtues and genius of Greece and Rome'.[41] The difference of Greece, and its lack of what he considered oppressive religion and prejudice, loosened 'the shackles of superstition'.

Yet the easy distinction of Greece from contemporary society becomes blurred. In his letter to Godwin, he goes on to ask, 'Shall Socrates and Cicero perish whilst the meanest hind of modern England inherits eternal life?'[42] The contorted thinking behind this sentence reveals the difficulties involved in the attempt to force a distinction between the two cultures. There were elements in contemporary society which were equally present in ancient culture. Even within Shelley's examples of the liberated nature of Greek civilisation, there were signs of the oppressive and corrupting aspects of the society. 'What do you think of Eaton's trial and sentence?', he wrote to Godwin, 'I mean not to insinuate that this poor bookseller has any characteristics in common with Socrates and Jesus Christ, still the spirit which pillories or imprisons him, is the same which brought them to an untimely end.'[43] If there were aspects of Greece which were distinct and enlightening for Shelley's society, there was paradoxically very little change in government or public attitudes. The same spirit of unthinking prejudice informed both ancient and modern societies. Shelley had realised this in his Paineite letter to Godwin: 'Was not the government of republican Rome, and most of those of Greece, as oppressive and arbitrary, as liberal of encouragement to monopoly as that of Great Britain is at present?'[44]

The difficulty of distinguishing whether Greece was to be understood as different from or the same as contemporary Britain led to these ambiguous feelings about drawing upon the classical world. Shelley's arguments, at one time appropriating Greece to contrast with Christian Britain and at another time admitting a long line of descent between the cultures, highlight the similar but unacknowledged confusion in Godwin's and Hazlitt's line of reasoning. But there was also a further dimension to Shelley's attitude to classical education. Women and their illicit reading of classical texts lent the subject an extra frisson, and it is noticeable that Shelley's relationships with women tended to be pedagogic. Certainly one of the main attractions of his second wife was her radical but untrained mind. Despite being the daughter of Mary Wollstonecraft, Mary Shelley did not receive the same education as her brothers. While they were sent to Charterhouse, she was educated at home, by a tutor and by her father when he had time. She learnt a little Latin, but no Greek, despite Godwin's emphasis upon the importance of Greek for the development of a child's mind.[45] As a result she held Greek, and men who could read it, in great awe, because it represented forbidden knowledge. Significantly, it was when she had met and declared her love for Shelley, over her mother's grave, that she began to learn the language. Her promise to Shelley that she 'will learn Greek', written in a letter planning their elopement in 1814, suggests that she considered Greek a *rite de passage* to the illicit world of free love.[46] And Shelley seemed to share her views. His letters to her at this time were sprinkled with Greek, more than any other of his letters. Sometimes the Greek references are quotations from classical texts – at one point, he quotes from *Prometheus Bound* to express his feelings about the bailiffs whose vigilance was compelling the lovers to stay apart.[47] Sometimes they are simply Greek words coined as a special lovers' code. 'I did not forget', Shelley writes to Mary 'to kiss your εἴδωλον κενον before I slept.'[48] The uncertainty and the intensity of love seem to be matched in Shelley's thinking by the mysteriousness of Greek, its appropriate medium. He wrote to Mary: 'I shall clasp you again – forever. Shall it be so? shall it be so? This is the ancient language that love alone can translate.'[49] The obscurity and renowned difficulty of the Greek language, which requires translation, mirrors the ineffability of love. Some parallel to Shelley's adoption of Greek in his love letters could perhaps be seen in Byron's use of Italian to recount his amorous affairs and, obviously, later to communicate with Teresa Guiccioli. The exotic associations of a foreign language perhaps seemed appropriate to describe the exciting strangeness of love. Perhaps also the freedom of pagan Greece suggested the life of free love upon which Shelley and Mary were embarking.

Through his explorations of the different representations of Greece, Shelley was coming in these early years to appreciate its ambiguous nature. Greece, it seemed, had the potential to be liberating and radical. It could be used to contrast with present society, so that 'men were no longer shut up in so narrow boundaries'. It could represent a radical alternative world, where the restrictive taboos surrounding free love and class equality were abolished. But at the same time, there was no ensuring the inviolability of these radical political implications. Writers supporting the establishment were able to appropriate the learning of Greek to bolster the hegemonic culture by maintaining traditional methods and approaches to the subject. Classical Greek learning could therefore constitute a retreat from politics, the repression of dissent, the abrogation of responsibility. It could also highlight the difficulty in accommodating forbidden knowledge without domesticating that knowledge too far. These paradoxes of Greek education and knowledge are highlighted and explored in two of Shelley's early poems, *Queen Mab* and *Alastor*. Both the poems deal with the effect of an outside source of knowledge, gendered female in both cases, upon a static male world. They can be interpreted as studies in the role and importance of education; and they focus the various problems and possibilities of classical education for the liberal thinkers of the early nineteenth century.

QUEEN MAB

Queen Mab explores the possibilities for learning from the past. 'The Past, the Present, and the Future are the grand and comprehensive topics of this Poem', Shelley wrote to his bookseller, Thomas Hookham, while composing the poem.[50] Godwin had written of the educational power of history:

What species of amusement or instruction would history afford,
if there were no grounds of inference from moral antecedents to
their consequents, if certain temptations and inducements did
not, in all ages and climates, introduce a certain series of actions,
if we were unable to trace a method and unity of system in men's
tempers, propensities and transactions? The amusement would
be inferior to that which we derive from the perusal of a chronological table.[51]

History taught by its example of cause and effect. By studying the
past, the causes of the future could be ascertained in a mechanical
and reliable fashion. History forms the basic educational tool of
the poem, in that the fairy Mab reveals a vision of the past and the
present to the dreaming Ianthe so that she can learn to affect the
future. Mab explains the process to Ianthe, drawing upon
Godwin's language of cause and effect:

> The secrets of the immeasurable past,
> In the unfailing consciences of men,
> Those stern, unflattering chroniclers, I find:
> The future, from the causes which arise
> In each event, I gather.[52]

In keeping with the mechanistic view of history described by Mab,
the poem is structured rigidly. Mab moves strictly and chronologi-
cally through accounts of the past and the present to visions of the
future. The structure of the poem implies as much apparent confidence in the possibility of deriving unequivocal knowledge of the
future from the past as is taken for granted in Count Volney's *Les
Ruines* (1791). In that study, one of the main influences upon Shelley's work, the sight of the dilapidated town of Old Palmyra, leads
the writer to reflect upon historical change, the nature of society, the
role of religion. There is a logical link between the external, visible
world and the writer's reflections. Volney derives meaning unproblematically from his experience and assumes that because empires
have crumbled in the past, empires will continue to crumble in the
future. History repeats itself because events will always cause similar subsequent events. Human nature and causation do not change
but remain a reliable continuum for intellectual inquiry.

But this empirical view of history relies too much upon an assumption of the sameness of human nature and causation for

the contrasting and liberating effect of the ancient world espoused by the liberal thinkers, including Shelley. If the ancient world is to be perceived as the same as the contemporary world, subject to exactly the same processes of cause and effect, then the study of that world will not prove liberating but will merely enforce existing prejudices and opinions. The world becomes static with this perception and resists reform or alteration. 'Chains' of cause and effect link everything in the world, like Locke's chains of causation which require a first cause to initiate the process of causation but, once begun, continue with inevitable consequence.[53] Mab talks of the 'great chain of nature'.[54] And Shelley, in his prose note to the line about Necessity, mentions 'a chain of causes . . . which . . . make it impossible that any thought of his mind . . . should be otherwise than it is'. As well as Locke's 'chains' of causation, there are hints of the self-sufficient world promoted by Baron Holbach.[55] 'Motion', Holbach wrote, 'is produced, is augmented, is accelerated in matter, without the concurrence of any exterior agent . . . motion is the necessary consequence of immutable laws, resulting from the essence, from the properties inherent in the different elements.'[56] Such a world as Holbach describes produces the ultimate vision of conformity: 'We are obliged to admit that there can be no independent energy – no isolated cause – no detached action, in a nature where all the beings are in a reciprocity of action.'[57] This argument of logical sufficiency is picked up in Shelley's poem, in the description of the universe:

> No atom of this turbulence fulfils
> A vague and unnecessitated task,
> Or acts but as it must and ought to act.[58]

The Lockean or Holbachian world of Necessity, where everything 'acts as it must and ought to act' and there is no allowance made for 'independent energy', serves as an image of the conventional perception of Classical education. Just as for the necessitarian Godwin, a man is only 'a vehicle through which certain antecedents operate', so the schoolboy for educators like Vicesimus Knox was to imbibe uncritically the classical learning as it had been handed down for generations. There was no room for an independent voice, an 'independent energy', only a system of identical and unthinking atoms. The *Edinburgh Review* commented upon the claustrophobia within the Eton–Oxbridge established education system:

It is from [the fellows of King's College] that the masters of Eton
School were almost universally selected; and surely no system
was ever contrived with such singular infelicity. Bred in the
routine of Eton education, young men are sent to a college, in-
habited solely by Etonians, where all, or nearly all, study is
voluntary; and, after a few years, return to their old school to
teach the things they were themselves taught, in the place and in
the manner they had learnt them. If this *circulus vitiosus* is retained – if no attempt is made to pour some fresh blood into the
diseased frame of Eton, and renew its torpid life, we cannot hope
that evils which arise chiefly from the ignorance, the want of
enterprise, and the amiable prejudices of its governors, will be
abolished by those who have learnt no learning, and formed no
habits, but those of their own college.[59]

Shelley hints at a similar claustrophobia, a stifling world of tradition and incestuous corruption, within his poem. The chains of
cause and effect in *Queen Mab* are restricting, waiting to be broken:
they are 'the icy chains of custom' (I.23). What is needed is a
revolutionary, irrational force, the 'chainless winds' that Shelley
talks of in 'Mont Blanc', or 'the spirit of universal imperishable
love' for which he had longed, in a letter to Hogg, to relieve the
impersonal world promoted by Locke.[60] But the narrow world of
self-sufficient atoms and the unthinking rote-learning of the grammatical tools of 'dead languages' will not allow for such a force.
Significantly, just as Locke's first cause cannot alter the already
established chain of causation, so the power of Mab to change
history is an illusion. Her active verbs are merely ones of knowledge, revealing the pre-determined:

> The secrets of the immeasurable past
>   . . . I find:
> The future, from the causes which arise
> In each event, I gather.
>   (I. 169, 171–3)

The structure of the poem, which can map out the future before
Ianthe has done anything, suggests the powerlessness of man,
the imprisonment of the world within the *circulus vitiosus*. And
similarly, learning from history, if taught in the deterministic and
unchallenging way already described, can offer little enlighten-

ment for the future. With the past and the future so closely linked and structured in the poem, there is little apparent opportunity for the contrasting views and sudden alterations of opinion which Godwin and Hazlitt suggested were offered by classical education.

However, while the structure of *Queen Mab* suggests a mechanistic and logical view of history and a suffocating world of sameness, there are suggestions in the writing that this structure is being undermined from within. Shelley is certainly questioning the unproblematic relationship between past and present. The logical passage of time is disrupted by the confusion of tenses in the poem. Mab's description of the future, for example, moves from the past tense – 'Earth was no longer Hell' (VIII 14) – through the present tense – 'The habitable earth is full of bliss' (VIII 58) – to the future tense – 'spring's awakening breath will woo the earth' (IX 167). Time is unstable, apparently, containing both present and distant time in a single moment. The depiction of the past is also confusing. Mab describes one scene:

> Where Socrates expired, a tyrant's slave,
> A coward and a fool, spreads death around.
> (II. 176–7)

For a moment in the reading of this couplet, it is unclear to whom the epithet, 'a tyrant's slave', refers. Is it Socrates, or is it the 'coward and fool', the modern inhabitant of the ruins of Athens? In other words, are Socrates and the modern Greeks being contrasted or compared? It becomes clear in the reading. But the momentary uncertainty caused by the line structure serves to undermine confidence in the interpretation of history. A similar confusion occurs a little later where again a contrast or comparison is being drawn between the ancient world and the modern. Mab speaks:

> Where Athens, Rome, and Sparta stood,
> There is a moral desart now:
> The mean and miserable huts,
> The yet more wretched palaces,
> Contrasted with those antient fanes,
> Now crumbling to oblivion.
> (II. 162–7)

The cataloguing style, in which one phrase is juxtaposed with the next, makes the point of contrast unclear. Do the 'wretched palaces' belong to the ancient Greek civilisation or to the present? Does the contrast between the contemporary 'huts' and the 'ancient fanes' militate entirely in the favour of ancient society? The palaces and fanes, both symbols of wealth and oppression, become indistinguishable between the two cultures, and the 'contrasted' fails to make the distinction clear. Godwin had noted Shelley's fragmented style in the poem, criticising it for being 'wild, incoherent and abrupt'.[61] But Shelley's 'abrupt' style allows him usefully to question the relationship with the past, making it deliberately ambiguous whether the relationship with the past is one of kinship or contrast.[62]

The fragmentation of the link with the past all adds to the disruption of the inevitable pattern of predetermination. Reading the past becomes an unsettling matter of interpretation and confusion, rather than an uncritical and automatic absorption. As a result the fragmentation usefully exercises and broadens the mind in a way recently identified by Alan Richardson as distinctive of this period: 'One of the most compelling features of the Romantic critique of rationalist education is this defense of ruptures in the child's ordinary sense of self. Rather than seeking to infiltrate the child's mind, Wordsworth and Coleridge propose that the child be left by itself to confront gaps and limitations in its habitual thinking process.'[63] For the challenging of intellectual assumptions in Shelley's poem, the figure of Queen Mab herself is crucial. Mab combines many paradoxical characteristics. Her immanence and passivity as the Spirit of Nature permeating the world are contrasted with moments of external power, when she is able to 'rend/The veil of mortal frailty' (I. 180–1). The apparent weakness in her claims to knowledge and perception is reversed when the scene changes from present to future simply by the power of perception and, as a result, perception and knowledge gain a value in the poem. Yet this power to change the world through the alteration of opinion is brought about not through strict logical reasoning – as Godwin believed – but by Mab's conjunction of the logical, the scientific and the fictional. Certainly Mab's world is one of the scientific autonomy of spinning planets – Addison's 'spacious firmament on high' or, as Shelley puts it, a 'wilderness of harmony' – but within this world Mab sails on a magical chariot to a fantastic, oriental palace in the heavens, an 'independent energy', unaccounted for in the mechanistic world.[64] She combines the mechanistic and the human in her character, remaining as aloof and impersonal as the Holbachian spirit – 'Unlike the God of human error, thou / Requirest no prayers or praises' (VI. 199–200) – and yet also suffusing Ianthe with the warmth of human love. These shifts in Mab's identity, from scientific power to fictional fairy, from alien automaton to gentle mother, contribute to her difference, her magic.

But Mab's alterity is chiefly derived from her gender, from the fact that she is female. She recalls other great female magicians in contemporary literature, the witch in Southey's *Thalaba*, the later Moneta of Keats's *The Fall of Hyperion*. However, unlike these other female figures, Mab is not alone, exercising her female power in isolation. She communicates with Ianthe, another female figure. Thus their discourse is distinctly feminine, set apart from masculine discourse, and constitutes a representation of a particularly female form of education. Shelley is exploring the difference that the female principle – or, as Hélène Cixous has termed it, an *'écriture feminine'* – can make in a masculine world.[65] Cixous's 'feminine writing' is able to draw upon an 'impregnable language that will wreck partitions, classes and rhetorics, regulations and codes, . . . submerge, cut through'.[66] Accordingly Shelley's female discourse is one which renders unstable the clear distinction between the external world and the internal mind. This is apparent, for example, in the changes to the connotation of the word 'frame' in the poem. The 'unbounded frame' of the self-sufficient and logical Addisonian firmament becomes 'Ianthe's frame' later in the poem. The female mind is, it seems, its own place, free to absent itself from the mechanical operations of the established world. Again the fluidity of distinction between external and internal is apparent two lines later when Ianthe is described surveying the world: 'Moveless awhile the dark blue orbs remained / 'She looked around' (IX. 235–6). It is ambiguous here whether the 'dark blue orbs' refers to the spinning planets of the universe or to Ianthe's eyes. As Mab communicates her knowledge to Ianthe, the girl senses the change in a way that denies the masculine logic of cause and effect:

> The Spirit felt the Fairy's burning speech
> O'er the thin texture of its frame,
> The various periods painted changing glows.
>   (VI. 2–4)

The love and almost sexual charge of Mab's 'burning' speech and the 'mantling' sensation which Ianthe experiences, re-interprets the meaning of the traditional frame:

> For birth but wakes the spirit to the sense
> Of outward shows, whose unexperienced shape
> New modes of passion to its frame may lend.
>
> (IX. 155–7)

Cixous writes that in 'feminine writing' 'her libido is cosmic, just as her unconscious is worldwide: her writing also can only go on and on, without ever inscribing or distinguishing contours, daring these dizzying passages'.[67] By subverting established notions and circumventing the traditional empirical process of acquiring knowledge, Shelley's women can derive 'new modes of passion', a strikingly erotic discourse of education.

The subversion and circumvention is possible because Shelley's women are outside the established 'frame' of the world, not accounted for in any 'chain'. Their marginal status paradoxically has the potential to empower them. The world of the reader which Mab reveals, and which is the interest of the poem, is presented as a male world. The tyranny, deception and corruption are perpetrated by men, and the suffering is seen from a male perspective too. 'The poor man', Mab says,

> Whose life is misery, and fear and care . . .
> Who ever hears his famished offspring's scream
> Whom that pale mother's uncomplaining gaze
> For ever meets
>
> (V. 113–14, 116–18)

is the one who endures the suffering and upon whom the attention is focused. Ianthe is sent back to earth to try her feminine touch upon Henry, to convert him and thus convert the world. The message is that the difference which femininity signifies in a static world of sameness and masculinity can provide the 'independent energy' hidden within the 'frame' of the world. Ianthe's 'mantling' knowledge can offer Henry a new perspective. This looks forward to the perceived difference between Mary learning Greek and contemporary men learning it, such as her brother William at Charterhouse. Both William and Mary are presented with the same vision or texts, but one is within the system and just imbibes, while the other is outside the system with a different perspective, unaccounted for and so not safely incorporated. Ianthe (and Mary) can act upon this different perspective with newly enlightened views.

By these two strategies in the poem, the confusion over the relationship with the past and the feminisation of knowledge, Shelley unsettles the orthodox assumptions about education. Certainties are disrupted as the reader is compelled to reassess the sources of knowledge, the examples from history and the medium by which they are conveyed. The new way of thinking about education is ambiguous too, because it rests upon perception and interpretation rather than on obvious facts or definitions. The past, for example, becomes different only if one is compelled to rethink our relationship with it and to interpret difficult grammatical connections with it. There is no inherent and obvious difference about it. But if we accept the power of Mab, we realise the importance of perception and interpretation and its revolutionary role in changing the world for the better. So classical education, if reassessed and rendered problematic and exciting, can give 'men liberal views' which will alter radically their fixed opinions and prejudices. The optimistic spirit with which Shelley wrote *Queen Mab* is supported by the series of proselytising footnotes, advocating, *inter alia*, vegetarianism and atheism. The juxtaposing and questioning of the classical past with the contemporary present can apparently give rise to all sorts of liberating, positive new ideas.

ALASTOR

But later the picture darkens. While *Queen Mab* optimistically celebrates the possibilities of forbidden knowledge and unorthodox ways of deriving and directing that knowledge, *Alastor*, written three years later, explores the complications of knowledge, the difficulties of ascertaining it and the uncertainties over whether it is so unorthodox at all.[68] At first the Poet in *Alastor* sets out on a Rasselas-type search for knowledge and for the key to life. Having exhausted the classical texts of his childhood – 'all of great/Or good, Or lovely, which the sacred past/In truth or fable consecrates, he felt/And knew' (72–5) – he journeys abroad to learn like Volney and Ianthe from the ruined civilisations of the past:

> His wandering step
> Obedient to high thoughts, has visited
> The awful ruins of the days of old:
> Athens, and Tyre, and Balbec, and the waste
> Where stood Jerusalem, the fallen towers
> Of Babylon, the eternal pyramids.
>
> (106–11)

The Poet is dutifully imbibing the tradition here, 'obedient to high thoughts', following the conventional view of history and learning. But like Rasselas, he is particularly struck by the pyramids, mainly because, 'wild' and 'mute', they seem to offer the hints of mystery beyond customary wisdom for which he is unconsciously seeking:

> Among the ruined temples there
> Stupendous columns, and wild images
> Of more than man, where marble daemons watch
> The Zodiac's brazen mystery, and dead men
> Hang their mute thoughts on the mute walls around,
> He lingered . . .
>
> (116–21)

Later the Poet follows the course of a river, seeking to learn more about the human condition, both his own and that of civilisation in general. The river leads him from the base of the Caucasus, the traditional birthplace of civilisation, to the mouth, so that as he travels down he appears to follow the course of human history.[69] Contemplating the rocks at the base of the Caucasus is a similar process to lingering at the pyramids. Both constitute an attempt to confront the ancient origins of humankind and to consider the distance or connection between that time and the present for the possible epistemological benefits that might bring. But the river also symbolises self-knowledge as well as the appreciation of history. Thomas Taylor, the neoplatonist and author of the translations of Plato which Shelley read at Oxford, had written 'a river is the symbol of life', and Wordsworth in *The Excursion*, published the year before *Alastor*, makes his Solitary contemplate a river: 'Such a stream is human life'.[70] The Poet in *Alastor*, who echoes many of the lines and thoughts in *The Excursion*, cries in desperation 'Oh river, thou imagest my life'. The twisting course of the river articulates

the wanderings of the human brain, in a way which both beautifully mirrors the mind and yet refuses its symbolic and paradig-
matic role by its opaque qualities:

> Thy darksome stillness
> Thy dazzling waves, thy loud and hollow gulphs,
> Thy searchless fountain, and invisible course
> Have each their type in me.
>
> (505–8)

'Searchless', 'invisible' – such words render the river closed to
interpretation – like and unlike the mind – just at the moment when
it is being used most allegorically.

But the form which most tantalises the Poet, driving him to
seek further, is the vision of the woman. When she is considered
in the context of the pyramids and the river, it is clear that it is
her symbolism as another source of knowledge, and not simply
her state as an object of sexual desire, which attracts the poet.[71]
She offers knowledge which is at once familiar and mysterious.
In his 'Essay on Love', Shelley wrote that a woman should
ideally be 'a mirror whose surface reflects only the forms of
purity and brightness'. This picks up the image of the 'mirror'
which Shelley, drawing upon Addison's notion of the world reflecting and so teaching God's divinity, had used to describe the
process of deriving knowledge. In his notes on the difficulty of
analysing the human mind, he wrote that 'a mirror would be held
up to all the world in which they might behold their own recollections and, in dim perspective, their shadowy hopes and fears'.[72]
The woman comfortingly reflects the Poet's own concerns and
interests:

> Knowledge and truth and virtue were her theme,
> And lofty hopes of divine liberty,
> Thoughts the most dear to him, and poesy,
> Herself a poet.
>
> (158–61)

She fits understandably for the Poet into the tradition of learning,
sharing the same backgound of reading, a common heritage. But
like the pyramids that so fascinate him, she is also incomprehensible, as 'ineffable' as the ancient Egyptians are 'mute':

>   . . . her fair hands
>   Were bare alone, sweeping from some strange harp
>   Strange symphony, and in their branching veins
>   The eloquent blood told an ineffable tale.
>
>   (165–8)

Unlike the tales of his childhood education, which the Poet 'felt and
knew' exhaustively, the visionary woman's tale is tinged with the
strangeness and fascination of her femininity.

The problem lies in apprehending the strangeness, in approaching sources of knowledge which lie outside the accepted tradition.
The Poet's efforts to understand the woman result in an imprisoning stalemate, due to the imposition of himself upon her otherness.
In the effort to possess the Other, it is constructed as already part of
the Poet. The woman is an aspect of the Poet's self, 'herself a poet'.
Later when the Poet is pursuing his notion of his dream, it is
unclear whether he is indeed pursuing the woman or the inner
reaches of his own mind:

>   Startled by his own thoughts, he looked around.
>   There was no fair fiend near him, not a sight
>   Or sound of awe but in his own deep mind.
>
>   (296–8)[73]

The Poet's frustrated pursuit of the woman recalls Shelley's description of the frenzied and deceptive hunger of ambition, the
desire to know more and accrue more power:

>   It excites my wonder to consider the perverted energies of the
>   human mind . . . Yet who is there who will not pursue phantoms,
>   spend his choicest hours in hunting after dreams, and wake only
>   to perceive his error and regret that death is so near?[74]

This passage leaves open the careful balance between the necessary
and admirable desire to push knowledge further and the pessimis-
tic recognition that such searches beyond the self are always illu-
sory and impossible.

It is well acknowledged by critics that the Poet's quest results in
an extreme narcissism, a fact that is emphasised by the allusions to
the Narcissus myth.[75] The river, the mirror-still pools, the densely
overhanging trees with their 'network' of 'woven branches' all

reflect aspects of the Poet's self, in a way that is constricting and frustrating. The Poet literally stares at a reflection of himself in a pool, and learns of the ageing effects of his self-destructive pursuit; while the narcissi flowers echo his posture, also drooping over reflecting pools. This absorption in the self stems from the impossibility of apprehending adequately 'things foreign' to the mind. The comprehension cannot travel beyond the accustomed limits of its field of knowledge, and when it attempts to do so, it is forced to rely upon its usual resources and the sources of knowledge familiar to it, or as Michael O'Neill puts it, to brood 'over the fictionalising involved in knowing'.[76] Familiar sources of knowledge are seen to imprison the inquiring mind, to deceive the Poet in comforting but erroneous fictions. The frustrating whirlpool prevents the Poet's final discovery of the source of the river:

> the whirlpools and caves
> Bursting and eddying irresistibly
> Rage and resound for ever.
>
> (355–7)

And the whirlpool of his emotions and anxiety prevent him from embracing the visionary woman again, enveloping him in his solipsistic, constricting landscape. Despite the new form of quest and the apparent instability of the flowing river style, the world of *Alastor* is as claustrophobic and unchanging as the rational world *Queen Mab* presents.

Yet, again, as in *Queen Mab*, Shelley deconstructs this world of male construction and order. Behind the apparently imprisoning mirror which the male Poet projects on to the 'Other', on to everything beyond his comprehension and expression, there is some suggestion of an abundance of meaning and vitality. Behind the stagnant world of expression, lies a paradoxical wealth of the inexpressible. Many feminist theorists have sought to describe the bizarre position of the female, outside the realm of masculine discourse, masculine vision, masculine pleasure. Luce Irigaray writes that: 'The rejection, the exclusion of a female imaginary undoubtedly places woman in a position where she can experience herself fragmentarily as waste or as excess in the little structured margins of a dominant ideology, this mirror entrusted by the (masculine) "subject" with the task of reflecting and redoubling himself.'[77] Woman is the 'excess', the surplus, beyond the

expression of masculine discourse but destabilising the smoothness
of conventional linguistic structures. Behind the mirror image by
which the Poet constructs himself and the visionary woman in
Alastor is the inexpressible being of the woman which keeps
eluding him.[78] The scene of the dream encounter between the
poet and the woman illustrates well the dynamics of their relationship. The visionary woman commences as the mirror, reflecting
back the logical, articulate values associated with Man: 'Knowledge, and truth and virtue were her theme'. But as the passion
mounts, her difference, her inexpressible 'Other' nature, shows
through:

> Soon the solemn mood
> Of her pure mind kindled through her frame
> A permeating fire.
>
> (161–3)

'Permeating' like Queen Mab's 'mantling', the woman diffuses her
own sensual power through the existing 'frame' of the traditional
constitution. Her physical, exotic nature beyond the understanding
of the male poet – her 'ineffable tale' – builds into a crescendo until
the final union:

> Then, yielding to the irresistible joy,
> With frantic gesture and short breathless cry
> Folded his frame in her dissolving arms.
> Now blackness veiled his dizzy eyes, and night
> Involved and swallowed up the vision; sleep,
> Like a dark flood suspended in its course,
> Rolled back its impulse on his vacant brain.
>
> (185–91)

The male 'frame' is completely 'dissolved', and the poet's power of
expression, of knowledge and of sight overwhelmed. With the
disappearance of all the familiar realm of knowledge on which he
can rely, he becomes 'dizzy', recalling both the 'dizzy' of 'Mont
Blanc' – 'Dizzy Ravine! and when I gaze on thee / I seem as in a
trance sublime and strange / To muse on my own separate fantasy'
– and the 'dizzy' of Shelley's 'Essay on Life' – 'We are on that verge
where words abandon us and what wonder if we grow dizzy to
look down upon the dark abyss of how little we know.'[79] Cixous

writes of the woman's 'art of living her abysses, of loving them, of making them sing', celebrating the unknowability of the female concept.[80] The male epistemology becomes helpless and bemused when confronted with the alien, whether that is intimated by the far reaches of the mind or the alternative power of the woman. The woman's power in *Alastor* is unknowable for the poet, and he is left with the impression just of the shadowy imprints of her presence – 'blackness', a 'dark flood', a 'vacant brain'.

The power of the language in this passage holds a careful balance between the fullness and emptiness of meaning. What is important is the very indeterminacy of the term 'vacancy'. On the one hand, the blackness and vacancy which the poet experiences could signify the negation of meaning, the lack of intelligible existence for anything beyond his perception. In 'Mont Blanc', for example, Shelley ends with a negative concept of vacancy, which questions the epistemological dependence upon an external world:

> And what were thou, and earth, and stars, and sea,
> If to the human mind's imaginings
> Silence and solitude were vacancy?
>
> (142–4)

The conditional form of this closing sentence renders interpretation as tentative as the thoughts expressed, but the import is frightening and challenging. Perhaps beyond man's knowledge and expression there is nothing, no existence. On the other hand, there are hints in Shelley's work that 'vacancy' does hold more. The poet in *Alastor* appears to experience more when he derives knowledge from the study of the pyramids mentioned earlier:

> [He] ever gazed
> And gazed, till meaning on his vacant mind
> Flashed like strong inspiration, and he saw
> The thrilling secrets of the birth of time.
>
> (125–8)

Meaning 'flashe[s]' upon the poet, beyond language but full of secret, uncommunicable knowledge. Similarly in his 'Essay on Life', Shelley suggests the positive qualities of the 'vacant mind': 'Philosophy leaves what it is too often the duty of the reformer in political and ethical questions to leave, a vacancy. It reduces the mind to that freedom in which it would have acted but for the misuse of words and signs, the instruments of its own creation.'[81] In these examples, vacancy appears to signify for Shelley a condition of power and potential, a condition beyond language and familiar knowledge with all the errors and prejudices they bring. But the end of *Alastor*, when the poet dies, leaves the notion of 'vacancy' ambiguous. It is uncertain whether negation or plenitude is implied:

> But when heaven remained
> Utterly black, the murky shades involved
> An image, silent, cold, and motionless,
> As their own voiceless earth and vacant air.
> (659–62)

The poet leaves a world of 'vacant air', 'utterly black' like the visionary woman. While he breathes his last, he looks at two points of light in the sky, 'when two lessening points of light / Gleamed through the darkness' (654–5). These lights could be stars, lights from an un-human alien world; but on the other hand they could be the seductive eyes of the visionary woman, which have enticed the poet throughout his quest. There is a hint, then, that there is life beyond the poet, that the 'vacant air' and blackness do hold some impenetrable existence, that the eyes will continue to watch him after his death and that he is not so entirely alone or self-deluded in his quest. After all, the narrative which can speak of the poet's death denies the logic of his apparent solitude and solipsism, just as later in Mary Shelley's novel, *The Last Man* (1826), the narrative denies the logic of its account of the extinction of mankind by projecting, and reaching, a future reader. Implied but unstated in both the poem and the novel is a world elsewhere, a different time, which shapes and adds new frames of meaning and interpretation.

In both *Queen Mab* and *Alastor* the forbidden knowledge is not a question of facts and quantifiable knowledge so much as of perception. The sources of knowledge in the two poems – Mab and the visionary woman – cannot be articulated but are felt and diffuse themselves subtly. They disrupt and disturb, altering the minds of their pupils and, in the case of *Alastor*, driving the Poet to distraction and death. They eroticise the process of attaining knowledge, rendering it a matter of seduction and physical sensuousness rather than a logical routine of reading and learning from tradition. And they push back the boundaries of what can be considered the learning process, by appearing marginal and strange, and yet revealing such a powerful effect upon the world and their subjects. They serve therefore as images for the power of education and the possibilities of learning from Greek if guided in the right way. The power of the classics was also dependent upon perception. The same texts, history and culture of ancient Greece were shared with the conservative educationalists, but if approached differently, if perceived differently, they could change immeasurably the minds of liberal thinkers. For by recognising the foreignness of ancient Greece, the scholar could open up his mind to contrasting views and alternative ways of perceiving the world.

But that process is extremely difficult and ambiguous, and these poems, especially *Alastor*, highlight the difficulties. The solipsism of *Alastor* illustrates the difficulty of moving beyond familiar fields of knowledge and traditions of education. The traditional associations surrounding classics – in particular, its links with a certain social class and gender – were hard to break, and hard for scholars to diverge from, especially when no other alternative associations were established. The marginal status of both female sources of knowledge also raises the question of the relevance of classics and of such knowledge. While the feminisation of Greek studies by radical writers and intellectual women rendered them more exciting and subversive, it could also lead to the perception of the marginal importance of classics. Finally the frenzied egotistic pursuit in *Alastor* can serve as a dramatic metaphor for the problems in the liberal arguments about the classics. While the classics were perceived as 'foreign' as Hazlitt argued, they could give men 'liberal views'. But in the process of acquiring knowledge, even of this alternative kind, of the ancient Greek world, inevitably the alien world becomes a little appropriated, a little more familiar, a little 'fictionalised', and so is in danger of losing its power of contrast. Of course, *Alastor* offers an extreme depiction of a source of knowledge becoming appropriated to such an extent that it is indistinguishable from the 'human imaginings' of the scholar; but it poses the question of how far the classics could ever be interpreted as novel and exciting for long.

Yet, if *Queen Mab* and *Alastor* dramatise some of the problems and ambiguities of drawing upon the classics in the early nineteenth century, they also reveal why liberal writers such as Shelley chose to turn to the alternative sources of knowledge and literary subject matters which his new understanding of ancient Greece seemed to provide. The depiction of stale imprisoning worlds in the poems cry out for reform and alternative vision. These are provided by the sudden impact of a new force which is unaccounted for in the economy of those worlds. While appearing more or less accessible, and certainly extremely ambiguous and problematic, these new sources of knowledge nevertheless offer enlightenment, using the same visions, the same grammatical tools of language, but by offering a slightly 'foreign' perspective, disrupting and liberating the constricting and unreformed world. If educated to appreciate the subversive nature of ancient Greek culture, the poet could thus draw upon Greek subject matters to radicalise his writing and disseminate revolutionising views.

2

'The Common-hall of the Ancients': Democracy, Dialogue and Drama

> I further propose that the Athenian theatre being resuscitated, the admission shall be free to all who can expound the Greek choruses.
>
> Peacock: *Crotchet Castle*

In the early nineteenth century, Greece was an icon for people of all political persuasions. 'Il n'y a personne qui ne désire l'émancipation des Grecs', the conservative François René Chateaubriand announced in his *Note sur la Grèce*.[1] 'We are all Greeks', the radical Shelley claimed at the beginning of his poem of liberation, *Hellas*. The model of Greece was the same and yet it could be appropriated by two very different political factions. As was illustrated in the last chapter, ancient Greece could be seen in two ways. It could be seen as the *same*, endorsing the British *status quo* by offering an uninterrupted historical line, imbibed by generations of schoolchildren. Or it could be perceived as *different*, challenging the understanding to comprehend a remote, old culture. The idea of Greece as the same was comforting to conservative writers, while the idea of it as different was attractive to liberal writers. With these two conflicting interpretations, Greece amounted to a particularly ambiguous metaphor for the political writer. In drawing upon the metaphor, the writer was faced with an underlying concern that the opposing association of Greece would be suggested to the reader, that the radical would be tamed, tinged with vestiges of conservatism, or vice versa.

The problem of misinterpretation was aggravated by the climate of political repression in the first few decades of the century. This was particularly intense in the years after the end of the Napoleonic War, the peak years of Shelley's literary career.[2] In 1817 the Lord

53

Liverpool government passed the Seditious Meetings Act and sus-
pended the Habeas Corpus Act. Three years later, the 'Six Acts'
were passed, restricting the freedom of the press and the right to
hold political meetings.[3] Spies and *agents provocateurs* were reputed
to be everywhere and fear was increased by the severity with which
any dissension was crushed. Most notorious in this period was the
Peterloo Massacre in 1819. Eleven people were killed after yeo-
manry, armed with sabres and cutlasses, attacked a huge gathering
of men, women and children meeting in peaceful protest in Manchester. Reform – political and social – was most needed and most
bitterly opposed.

The repressive measures of the postwar government drove the
literary writers underground. Writers or publishers of seditious
works could be imprisoned without trial, as Richard Carlile, the
publisher of Paine's *The Age of Reason*, discovered to his cost.[4] But
the attitude and behaviour of the government and the Establishment that supported it required criticism and challenge. The
extremity of the situation provoked extreme responses in return.
Radicals, stung by governmental refusals to reform parliament in
any way, went further by demanding universal suffrage, annual
parliaments and the rejection of all moderation. Popular cheap
journals, such as William Cobbett's *Political Register* or Richard
Wooler's *Black Dwarf*, sprang up to voice these demands. So there
was a great need for a political response to public events from
so-called literary writers. And yet attack and resistance were becoming increasingly difficult because of government repression.
Direct criticism was impossible; only subterfuge and covert attacks
were available to the writer. From 1815 onwards, poets turned
increasingly to mythical subjects as political opinions had to be
disguised. A wide range of writers, from the radical to the moderately dissenting, were forced into allegorical writing, into writing
about classical subjects in order to express heterodox views. This
therefore complicates the simple dichotomy, depicted by Olivia
Smith, between the sophisticated writing of 'those who were within
the civilised world', who were educated in the classics and anxious
to maintain cultural hegemony, and the plain style of 'those who
were entirely outside', the radical writers who were uneducated
in the classics and resisted established authorities of power and
learning.[5] For those who sympathised with the radicals also drew
upon the classics, upon the same models shared by conservatives.
This naturally resulted in general confusion over the proliferation

of images and the problem of interpretation. Distance from the reading public, necessitated by the need for disguise, and the misappropriation of images by other political groups, added to the confusion.

The ambiguity of the political implications of Greece and the classics at this time is particularly highlighted by Shelley's politics and Hellenism. During the 1980s, Shelley was re-established by critics as a political writer. Paul Foot led the way with his passionate monograph *Red Shelley*, which laid claim to Shelley as an early socialist and feminist.[6] Since Foot's work, Paul Dawson and Michael Scrivener have pointed out in more detail the radical political qualities in Shelley's poetry and prose.[7] However, these critics, provoked by the apolitical interpretations of Shelley's work which predominated earlier in the century, have perhaps gone too far in their description of Shelley as an unequivocal radical. Critics are now beginning to question this radical, political interpretation. For example, in his book on Romantic reading audiences, Jon Klancher has described the difficulty of all liberal, political writing during the post-Napoleonic war period in view of the multiplying and fragmenting audiences and the problems of direct communication.[8] More recently, Stephen Behrendt has examined the prefaces to Shelley's poems to consider the uneasy relationship he held with his readers and the British public, exiled as he was for most of his writing career in Italy.[9]

At once more radical and more marginal than most political writers of the period, Shelley exemplifies the difficulties of writing visionary and revolutionary poetry as an aristocrat at a time of great turbulence and change. In the next two chapters, I will examine how the metaphor of Greece affected and articulated the visions and difficulties of the educated radical writer. There were two aspects of Greece which were particularly amenable to political appropriation, and which dominated radical discourse. First, Greece was perceived to be the first democracy, a free republican state. Second, Greece represented a pagan, Arcadian world of pleasure and licence, an alternative to the orthodox system of rules, order and oppression. The politics of this pastoral Arcadia is explored in the next chapter. But in this chapter, I will consider the ways in which political discussion was focused through the metaphor of democratic Greece and through aspects of Greek culture most associated with democracy – discussion, dialogue and drama. This will lead to a reading of what are arguably two of Shelley's most democratic works, his translation of *The Cyclops* and *Swellfoot the Tyrant*.

DEMOCRATIC DIALOGUE

Unlike Rome, Greece was associated with republicanism and freedom. The controversial implications of this association could be diluted to a general appreciation of the patriotism and courage of the Greeks, a sentiment in which all could share. In the various enthusiastic poems which appeared around the time of the Greek War of Independence, all ancient Greeks without discrimination were represented as bold and freedom-loving. 'Ye sons of the brave!', a poem ran in the *Gentleman's Magazine*, 'once again shall that freedom be thine / Which mankind first learned of thee'.[10] More frequently, however, the democracy of Greece was accorded political significance. The political constitution of ancient Greek states was perceived to reflect upon the contemporary situation in Britain. This can be seen in the extreme polarity between histories of Greece written at the time. Thomas Paine, the advocate for the American and French revolutions, portrayed Athenian democracy in a very attractive light, emphasising its direct participatory basis: 'Simple democracy was no other than the common-hall of the ancients. It signifies the form, as well as the public principle of government.'[11] Athens, for Paine, was the model for the new American system: 'What Athens was in miniature, America will be in magnitude. The one was the wonder of the ancient world; the other is becoming the admiration and model of the present.'[12] But conservative historians portrayed Athens very differently. John Gillies set out his views bluntly in the preface to his *History of Ancient Greece*:

> The history of Greece exposes the dangerous Turbulence of Democracy and arraigns the Despotism of Tyrants. By describing the incurable evils inherent in every form of republican policy, it evinces the inestimable benefits of well-regulated monarchy.[13]

William Mitford also countered Paine's vision of the spread of Athenian democracy to America and France by describing the chaos in the ancient world which resulted from the export of Athenian democracy to other states:

Throughout Greece, as we have seen, Lacedaimon was the patroness of oligarchy, Athens of democracy. When a struggle between the two parties in any republic, came to a crisis, application was commonly made to one or both of those states. . . . In all republics therefore, where Athenian influence now extended, a form of government was established, tending at least to democracy . . . the democratical party gained the superiority; numbers of the noble and wealthy, with their forward adherents, were banished; the partizans of democracy, raised to powers and riches under the patronage of Athens, became thus, through interest, attached to Athens. . . . Through such circumstances Greece always swarmed with exiles; and those unhappy men were perpetually on the watch for opportunities to effectuate a revolution. . . .[14]

As Mitford implies here, conservative historians frequently made a pointed comparison between democratic Athens and the austere, oligarchical regime of Sparta. 'Such a constitution of society seems the highest elevation and grandeur to which human nature can aspire', Gillies described ancient Sparta.[15] And Mitford conceded that only his beloved Sparta was capable and educated enough to sustain a democratic constitution: 'If democracy was a form of government desirable for any people that ever existed, the Lacedaimonians must have been above all others competent for it.'[16] The fact that the wise Lycurgus 'deemed it unfit' even for the incomparable Spartans proved for Mitford the unattractive qualities of the democratic system. Earlier in the eighteenth century, unorthodox thinkers such as Rousseau had expressed admiration for Sparta, because of what they saw as the primitive simplicity of Spartan life, which resisted the sophistication of the metropolis and hegemonic centres of authority.[17] Now in the 1790s depictions of Sparta were influenced by politically polarised representations, by the contrast of democratic and revolutionary America and France.[18] In his study *A Review of the Governments of Sparta and Athens* (1794), Sir William Drummond participated in this debate by openly acknowledging the sharp political divisions inherent in the contrast between Athens and Sparta, and examining the political consequences for the reader if he were to follow one or other model:

Those who admire the order, the union, and the regularity which reign in monarchy; who think tranquility preferable to a false notion of liberty . . . will probably prefer Lycurgus to Solon.

Those, on the other hand, who believe the people to be the best
judges of their own happiness; who admire the arts, the eloquence and the philosophy of Athens ... will think it just to
transfer the laurel from the brow of the Lacedaimonian to that of
the Athenian lawgiver.[19]

Drummond himself chose to remain sceptical, disposed only to
praise the moderation and mixed constitution which he considered
to be exemplified by the contemporary British government. Despite
his liberal credentials, he was wary of unchecked praise for
Athenian democracy:

The impartial reader will probably take a middle course between
these two extremes. He will admire, in the Athenians, the virtues
of a free, a learned and enlightened people; but he will condemn
that liberty which often bordered upon licentiousness, that vola-
tility which generally proceeded from caprice.[20]

The political interpretation of Athenian democracy presented by
such writers as John Gillies and William Mitford meant that, for the
radical writer around the turn of the century, allusions to Greek
democracy were seen as challenging and provocative. Greek
democracy was lifted from its historical context and perceived as
relevant to contemporary polemical debate. Shelley certainly
seemed to believe this. In the register at his hotel in Chamonix in
1816, and in another at Montavert, he entered his occupation as
'Δημοκρατικός, Φιλανθρωπότατος, και Αθεος' (Democrat, Philan-
thropist and Atheist). These three words, given even more shocking value by being phrased in ancient Greek, were the three most
rebellious adjectives Shelley could conceive. It is probable that the
'φιλανθρωπότατος' was inspired by Prometheus, whom Shelley and
other contemporaries considered one of the great mythical political
rebels.[21] At any rate, the degree of outrage which this statement had
the potential to cause can be gauged from the fact that even the
liberal Lord Byron, discovering one of Shelley's entries a few
months later, endeavoured to delete it in order to clear his friend's
name.[22]

Shelley significantly associated democracy with atheism, for it
was the cultural licence to challenge orthodox opinion, a licence
which was perceived to emanate from the Athenian democratic
system, which appealed to the subversive writers of the late

eighteenth century. This licence was considered particularly advantageous in the challenge to the authority of the Christian church which was bound up with the government and with central political control. By revealing the similarities between eastern and Christian myths or between modern and ancient customs in the challenging, Greek, open manner, the authority of the western Christian church could be undermined. Elinor Shaffer explored the controversial effect of comparative mythology in the late eighteenth century in her book *'Kubla Khan' and the Fall of Jerusalem*, arguing that alternative myths either necessitated greater syncretism and flexibility or mounted a challenge to the old centres of authority.[23] Through the discovery of other cultures and beliefs, she suggests, Christianity could no longer claim to be the earliest or the unique source of truth. This meant that the centralised power previously exercised by the ideological force of Christianity was fragmented and challenged. To challenge Christian cultural hegemony was the implicit purpose behind such enterprises as William Payne Knight's *A Discourse on the Worship of Priapus* (1786) or Erasmus Darwin's *The Botanic Garden* (1791).[24] These works celebrated the pagan myths of the classical world, with their obvious delight in luxurious nature and sexuality, in order to highlight the contrast with the gloomy and authoritarian stories from the Christian Bible.

Following in the same pattern was Shelley's 'Essay on the Devil and Devils' which he wrote around 1819. By comparing the way different cultures account for the existence of evil in the world, Shelley undermines the definitive account posited by Christians and exposes it as a constructed myth. Significantly, he compares the Christian explanation with the Greek: 'The Greek philosophers abstained from introducing the devil. They accounted for evil by supposing that what is called matter is eternal and that God in making the world made not the best that he, or even an inferior intelligence would conceive; but that he moulded the reluctant and stubborn materials ready to his hand.' But the early Christians could not rely upon this explanation because it suggested that God is less than omnipotent, and 'like panic-stricken slaves' they searched for a solution which would combine God's benevolence with his omnipotence. So 'the Christians therefore invented or adopted the Devil to extricate them from this difficulty'.[25] The narrator of the essay purports to be deeply pious and to be shocked by the possibility of anyone disbelieving the Christian story: 'Depend upon it, that when a person once begins to think that there is no

Devil, he is in a dangerous way.'[26] But the ironic tone adopted throughout the piece serves a similar purpose to the alternative myths. It wittily destabilises the supposed authority of the typical ecclesiastical scholar, by exposing it to alternative, implied meanings.

Challenge to established beliefs could be derived not only from comparative myths but also from philosophy. David Hume grounded the controversial sceptical views first expressed in his *A Treatise of Human Nature* in the classical tradition of philosophical inquiry, in the pagan atmosphere of the first pre-Christian philosophers. He acknowledged admiration for the clarity and lack of distorting prejudice in the work of these ancient Greek thinkers:

> Several moralists have recommended it as an excellent method of becoming acquainted with our own hearts ... to recollect our dreams in the morning, and examine them with the same rigour, that we wou'd our most serious and deliberate actions. Our character is the same throughout, say they, and appears best where artifice, fear and policy have no place, and men can neither be hypocrites with themselves nor others. . . . In like manner, I am persuaded, there might be several useful discoveries made from a criticism of the fictions of the antient philosophy.[27]

William Drummond, another Scot, followed Hume's example in his *Academical Questions*, tracing philosophical strands of thought from the Greeks to the present day and culminating in an agnostic conclusion. 'Who, that possesses any taste at all, will deny their charms to the arts of poetry and eloquence, or hesitate to acknowledge, that the most brilliant models in both are to be found in the antient languages of Greece and Rome?', he wrote in the preface.[28] And he went on to link that 'eloquence' with political freedom: 'Philosophy, wisdom and liberty support each other; he, who will not reason, is a bigot; he, who cannot, is a fool; and he, who dares not, is a slave.'[29] The study of philosophy – and the study of Greek philosophy in particular, it was implied – led to a sceptical position which resisted the dogmatic beliefs of the Church and threatened the certainties of established culture.

The most favoured stylistic form of these democratic works of comparative mythology and sceptical philosophy was the dialogue. Paine termed democracy the 'common-hall of the ancients', and the dialogue best conveyed the sense of the 'common-hall' of voices, where discussion and dissent were permitted and welcomed and no single voice dominated. Joseph Spence, for example, whose work of comparative mythology *Polymetis* (1747) was to become one of the most important influences upon Leigh Hunt,[30] explains the dialogue form of his work by arguing that it makes the reading more entertaining and circumvents the problem of the obtrusive personal pronoun.[31] It is clear that the dialogue form is intrinsic to the book's message. The study of alternative stories is for Spence iconoclastic, aimed at undermining the centrality of church power and replacing it with a flexible spirit of inquiry and receptiveness to other ideas. Along with the dismissal of the church goes the abandonment of the monolithic 'I'. A dialectic form apparently is the most appropriate for a dialectic spirit.

The ultimate source for the dialogue form was, of course, Plato, whose dialogues allowed his readers to experience an appropriate sense of confusion and 'aporia' when the interlocutors failed to solve a problem, and subsequently to grasp an answer through an inductive method of inquiry. Plato, however, was scarcely read in the eighteenth century because, as Peacock's Rev. Dr Folliott puts it, 'in our Universities, Plato is held to be little better than a misleader of youth; and they have shown their contempt for him, not only by never reading him ... but even by never printing a complete edition of him'.[32] As a result, the predominant model for the eighteenth-century dialogue was Cicero. His *Academica* consciously alluded in its title to Plato's Academy, a school of philosophy founded upon his dialogues which set a precedent for other writers to express their philosophical ideas in dialogue form. In its sceptical exploration of the different traditions of philosophy current at the time and its Greek atmosphere, Cicero's work was heavily imbued by Plato, and it constituted one of the main sceptical sources (as opposed to the neoplatonic) by which Plato's ideas were disseminated. The *Academica*, then, lay directly behind Drummond's *Academical Questions* and behind Hume's *Dialogues Concerning Natural Religion* which were so controversial that they were published posthumously. Unlike Cicero, Hume's *Dialogues* adopts Greek names for the interlocutors – Cleanthes, Philo and Demea – but conveys a similar atmosphere of enlightened discussion and freedom. The dialogue form helps to convey this freedom: 'Any question of philosophy', Hume wrote, 'which is so obscure and uncertain, that human reason can reach no fixed determination with regard to it; if it should be treated at all; seems to lead us naturally into the style of dialogue and conversation.'[33]

The influence of Hume's *Dialogues*, and Drummond's *Academical Questions*, which Shelley read in 1815, can be seen in the Socratic dialogue, 'A Refutation of Deism', which Shelley wrote around the same time as *Queen Mab*. The Greek names of the characters, Eusebes and Theosophus ('pious' and 'godlike in wisdom'), ironically set the tone for a piece questioning all degrees of belief in a god and allowing only the rationality and independence of atheism. A choice emerges in the discussion between the exercise of reason and the dependence upon faith.

> Suppose, however, it were admitted that the conclusions of human reason and the lessons of worldly virtue should be found, in the detail, incongruous with divine revelation, by the dictates of which would it become us to abide? Not by that which errs whenever it is employed, but by that which is incapable of error; not by the ephemeral systems of vain philosophy, but by the word of God, which shall endure forever.

The exercise of reason is actually incompatible with faith in God. Theosophus's attempted compromise in deism is disproved as illogical by Eusebes, thus confirming the stark choice he is offering Theosophus. The two men end up asserting arguments which they do not really believe because the flow of the discussion, itself sinful because rationally conducted, leads them there. Both characters are, as Eusebes puts it, 'unsettled' by the discussion. And the reader is unsettled too because while both characters resist the power of atheism to 'seduce' them, Shelley has in the speech of Eusebes put forward strong and reasoned arguments for the nonexistence of God and the self-sufficiency of the world without a creator.

Shelley's later major dialogue work, *Julian and Maddalo: A Conversation Poem*, also explores the subversive impact of reasoned discussion and argument, if in a less direct way. Instead of confronting the issue in argument, the poem reveals the challenging power of reason through allusions to other texts. Hume had written of the social dimensions of dialogue: 'the book carries us, in a manner, into company, and unites the two greatest and purest pleasures of human life, study and society'.[34] This light side of dialogue is evident at the beginning of *Julian and Maddalo*, as the two rebels, one a 'complete infidel and scoffer at all things reputed holy', converse:

> So as we rode, we talked; and the swift thought,
> Winging itself with laughter, lingered not,
> But flew from brain to brain – such glee was ours,
> Charged with light memories of remembered hours,
> None slow enough for sadness.[35]

But later the conversation moves from banter to serious philosophical inquiry:

> Our talk grew somewhat serious, as may be
> Talk interrupted with such raillery
> As mocks itself, because it cannot scorn
> The thoughts it would extinguish – 'twas forlorn,
> Yet pleasing, such as once, so poets tell,
> The devils held within the dales of Hell
> Concerning God, free will and destiny:
> Of all that earth has been or may yet be
> Of all that vain men imagine or believe,
> Or hope can paint or suffering may achieve,
> We descanted, and I (for ever still
> Is it not wise to make the best of ill?)
> Argued against despondency.[36]

The narrator Julian, who tends to be optimistic, does all he can to resist a sceptical position, arguing 'against despondency'. But ultimately he recognises the inevitability of scepticism, as he reveals in such phrases as 'all that vain men imagine or believe' or 'Is it not wise to make the best of ill?'. Most significant here is the allusion to the devils conversing. This refers to *Paradise Lost*, Book II, and the devils' activities after the meeting called by Satan:

> In discourse more sweet
> (For eloquence the soul, song charms the sense)
> Others apart sat on a hill retired,
> In thoughts more elevate, and reasoned high
> Of providence, foreknowledge, will and fate,
> Fixed fate, free will, foreknowledge absolute,
> And found no end in wandering mazes lost.
> Of good and evil much they argued then

> Of happiness and final misery,
> Passion and apathy, and glory and shame,
> Vain wisdom all and false philosophy.[37]

The devils engage in the 'false philosophy' of pagan thinkers, of
Plato and Cicero, and endeavour to do without the true teaching of
the Christian God. Thus Julian and Maddalo are behaving like
rebellious devils by conversing about the nature of life instead of
obediently believing the Bible. Like the devils, they are situated in
a 'Paradise of exiles' (57). The devil allusions only confirm the
demonic, subversive nature of the conversation poem and the radical implications of dialogue.

But not all dialogues of the period seem intrinsically radical in
form. Walter Savage Landor's *Imaginary Conversations of the Greeks
and Romans* is one example. Certainly Landor's interest in the
ancient Greek world was influenced by his enthusiasm for republicanism and liberty. He was an early supporter of Napoleon whom
he saw as a heroic champion of ancient republicanism. Later, after
Napoleon had become Consul for life and seemed to be deserting
the cause of republicanism, Landor followed the examples of
Aeschylus and Pericles by actually dropping his pen and metaphorically picking up his shield, marshalling a few troops together
with the intention of fighting for his country in the Peninsular War
campaign.[38] These qualities of patriotic action, enthusiasm for liberty, and honourable austerity are what he chooses to emphasise in
ancient culture in his *Imaginary Conversations*. The conversation
between Pericles and Sophocles illustrates his perception of Greek
culture as pervaded by freedom and duty:

> *Pericles*: Hither come the youths and virgins, the sires and
> matrons; hither come citizen and soldier.
> *Sophocles*: A solecism from Pericles! Has the most eloquent of men
> forgotten the Attic language? has he forgotten the language of all
> Greece? Can the father of his country be ignorant that he should
> have said hither *comes*? for citizen and soldier is one.[39]

Yet while the content of the *Conversations* promotes a revolutionary
way of life, imbued with the perceived values of fifth century
democratic Athens, the form in which they are written is very
different. Rather than subvert as *Julian and Maddalo* does, they seem
intended to convert. Values are propounded to exemplify an

admirable way of life rather than to unsettle and fruitfully perplex. 'Many nations, O Xerxes, have risen higher in power, but no nation rose ever to the same elevation in glory as the Greek', Artabanus begins his conversation with Xerxes, and this sentiment is not disputed.[40] Indeed, rather than characters disagreeing and disputing provocatively, there is a remarkable meeting of minds, even across time and place. Achilles and Helen, divided by war and enemy lines in Homer, are depicted by Landor in sympathetic conversation. Plato and the notoriously misanthropic Diogenes are depicted in harmony. Even Solon and Pisistratus, who were absolutely polarised in political opinion, discuss the constitution of the state amicably. The implication is that there is a simple and single quality of republican Greekness – the 'language of all Greece' – which is unequivocal and can be shared by everyone. The *Imaginary Conversations* reveal not the democratic allowance of differences but rather, in Keith Hanley's terms, the 'homogeneity' of Greece which binds all the speakers, and audience and writer, together.[41] In the zeal of conversion, Landor imbibes this quality of Greekness and then imparts it without evidence of doubts or differences. And crucially, he writes it without any hint of humour.

For dialogues could be funny. Indeed humour itself was perceived as Greek and subversive. The *Examiner*, for example, referred to the ability of the Greeks to 'laugh with Aristophanes and the satirists at what deserved greater respect'.[42] The dialectic incongruity of language and rhymes lies behind the anarchic and iconoclastic verses of Byron's *Don Juan*. The juxtaposition of disparate thoughts and registers in Byron's poem leads to a continual comical debunking, which is not possible in Landor's earnest 'homogeneity'. It also evokes a cosmopolitan atmosphere, the 'common-hall' market-place of different voices. Indeed Byron invites the reader to determine whether more cantos will be written by his purchasing power, perhaps the first literary demonstration of democratic capitalism.[43] Byron's cosmopolitanism and debunking humour are also shared by Peacock. Apparently more confident of certainties than Byron, Peacock structures his dialectic novels around stereotypes and soundbites. Each character is given a suitable name, a typical viewpoint, and a repeated characteristic phrase, in an exaggeration, and possible parody, of the Humean model. In *Headlong Hall*, for example, the pessimist who believes that the world is in decline, Mr Escot, is opposed by the optimist, Mr Foster, who believes everything is getting better, and the

novel pivots around their polarised views.[44] Other suitably named
eccentrics include Mr Cranium, who believes that character is
determined by the anatomy of the skull. Character and beliefs in
the novel are determined by nomenclature, and are unswayed
by external considerations. As Cranium says, 'you know his own
system is of all things the dearest to every man of liberal thinking
and a philosophical tendency'. But the novels actually highlight the
dichotomy between 'systems' and 'liberal thinking'. While the
assembled characters each promote their beliefs, the hosts invari-
ably are jovially impartial, reflecting the liberal author behind the
conversations. Squire Headlong invites the promoters of different
'systems' to his house because of the fashionable success of attracting so many different types of city people to one's country
residence. 'It now became his chief wish to have them all together
in Headlong Hall, arguing over his old Port or Burgundy, the
various knotty points which had puzzled his pericranium.'[45] The
'old Port or Burgundy' phrase beautifully undercuts the seriousness of the discussion described here. For the 'liberal thinking', and
the humour in Peacock's work, stem not from the disputations
themselves but from the undercutting of those dialogues, from the
lacunae and from the momentary interruptions of bizarre action.
One of the most memorable moments of *Headlong Hall*, for example,
occurs when the sight-seeing Mr Cranium is blown up accidentally
in the tower, by the enthusiastic Mr Milestone, anxious to effect his
schemes for landscape improvement. The mutually conflicting
'systems' of the two men, which form some of the discussions of the
novel, are thus ridiculed and subverted by the absurdity of the
book's plot.

   While debunking humour provides the subversive edge in
Peacock's novels, however, there is a danger that the humour can
lose its polemical force and become simply comforting and banal.
The hosts in Peacock's novels, who entertain with port and
burgundy, reduce all radical discussion to the level of dinner-party
conversation, warming to the soul but not worrying to the mind.
Headlong's 'old Port or Burgundy' recalls Peacock's admission to
Hogg that 'tea, Greek and pedestrianism constitute the *summum
bonum*'.[46] The 'tea' could be thought either to clash provocatively
with the 'Greek', or to contain it, to reduce it to the level of a
placebo. Benjamin Robert Haydon's recollection of a dinner party
with Wordsworth, Keats and Charles Lamb sounds similar to one
of Headlong's gatherings:

It was indeed an immortal evening. Wordsworth's fine intonation as he quoted Milton and Virgil, Keats's inspired look, Lamb's quaint sparkle of lambent humour, so speeded the stream of conversation, that in my life I never passed a more delightful time. All our fun was within bounds. Not a word passed that an apostle might not have listened to.[47]

The speakers differ in tone and content, but blend together under the atmosphere or 'bounds' of the dinner table. Dialogue, it seems, can be subversive when different viewpoints are aired and disputed, but only within certain 'bounds', certain settings. Peacock's characters oppose one another, but in the end the tone of the novel is one of harmony and cheerfulness, a boundary of conviviality which renders the internal disputes safe. The safe boundary is certainly highlighted when it is momentarily disrupted at the end of *Crotchet Castle*. While Mr Chainmail is holding a medieval-style banquet, a crowd of machine-breakers arrive, clamouring for support and arms. Faced with the interruption of the 'real' world, the so-called men of 'liberal thinking' attack and disperse the crowd, their democratic aspirations shattered.

Democratic dialogues thus represented 'common-halls' of voices but within a controlled space. Outside forces like machine-breakers could threaten that space, and shed light upon the fragility and the deceptiveness of the dialogue form. The conversation in Shelley's *Julian and Maddalo*, for example, is thrown into confusion by the interruption of a voice of despairing madness; while 'A Refutation of Deism' was deliberately priced out of the reach of the 'multitude' because of its possible disruptive effects. Shelley admitted in the preface: 'The mode of printing this little work may appear too expensive, either for its merits or its lengths. However inimical this practice confessedly is to the general diffusion of knowledge, yet it was adopted in this instance with a view of excluding the multitude from the abuse of a mode of reasoning liable to misconstruction on account of its novelty.'[48] And Landor's *Imaginary Conversations* become so precious in the face of the threatening outside world that they read like cold marble monuments preserved in spite of death into an alien age. Landor intensified this sense of alienation and anachronism through his publication of poems in Latin, his retreat to his ramshackle country mansion, and his general asserted obliviousness to his lack of readership.

He was anxious to escape to the imaginary world of the conversations away from the real 'common-hall' voices.[49]

One of the main 'common-hall' voices was that of William Cobbett. He promoted himself as the spokesman for the people with various pamphlets and his popular *Political Register*, and in many ways he shaped the working-class consciousness in the early nineteenth century. His *Grammar of the English Language*, which he published in 1818, was intended to furnish the people with the means to voice their grievances, since mastery of language, he thought, could bring power. But in contrast he maintained a strong stance against classical education and what he termed the 'learned languages'.[50] The plainness of his style was as politically determined as his opinions.[51] He believed in unequivocal opposition, in encouraging the masses to rebel by emphasising their hardship, in being unafraid to demand change and in simplifying and polarising different groups in society. Simplicity of style, with its semblance of artlessness, spontaneity and transparency, accentuated and articulated these views. Allusion, scepticism and witty humour, which have been identified as characteristic of the dialogue, were therefore necessarily inimical to him. He became a further force of division, an outside voice which disrupted liberal conversation.

Shelley's liberal contemporaries held William Cobbett in much suspicion and distrust, both for his opinions and his style. Lord Byron acknowledged his instinctive contempt for such men as Cobbett and Orator Hunt:

> If there is to be a scene in England to which all seems approaching – by the violence of the political parties – you will probably see me in England in the next spring but I have not yet decided the part I ought to take. . . . I am not democrat enough to like a tyranny of blackguards – such fellows as Bristol Hunt are a choice of evils with Castlereagh – except that a Gentleman scoundrel is always preferable to a vulgar one.[52]

Likewise, Leigh Hunt maintained a virtual campaign against Cobbett in the *Examiner*. On 5 October 1817, he summed up his case: '[Cobbett] has done a great deal of good by disseminating the knowledge of constitutional freedom, in a style, upon the whole, of pure and rigorous English; but it is doubtful, whether he has not done almost as much harm to the cause by the strong sense there prevails of violence on both sides.' Hunt's dislike of Cobbett was founded primarily on his contempt for his paltry education and literary accomplishments: 'He has no imagination, or the power which carries a man out of the sphere of his own grosser experience. . . . A little acquaintance with the "learned languages" which he abuses so much, might have assisted him in this respect.'[53]

Shelley also made pointed references to Cobbett's humble background, describing his 'horror of the sanguinary commonplaces of his creed'.[54] However, it seems that Shelley, in contrast with the others, was torn between intellectual endorsement of Cobbett's political aspirations, his call for parliamentary reform, and instinctive dislike of Cobbett's 'commonplace' background and education. Since Cobbett identified himself with the people, Shelley's relationship with him can be thought to represent his general attitude towards the British masses. He was fascinated by Cobbett in many ways. He ordered the *Political Registers* to be sent out to him in Italy, declaring that he longed to meet their author.[55] He admitted to Peacock in a letter: 'Cobbett still more and more delights me. . . . His design to overthrow Bank notes by forgery is very comic.'[56] Yet he also expressed some dislike of Cobbett's character. He wrote to Peacock in 1819: 'What a pity that so powerful a genius should be combined with the most odious moral qualities.'[57] His comment recalls his acknowledgement of the innate prejudice born of his aristocratic upbringing which appears in his great political tract of 1820, 'A Philosophical View of Reform': 'Though at bottom it is all trick, there is something magnificent in the chivalrous disdain of infamy connected with a gentleman.'[58] In his uncertainty over Cobbett, Shelley was also revealing his uncertain relationship with the British people.

Shelley's distrust of the leaders of popular dissent around 1820 was not exclusively personal. He was not distanced from Cobbett, William Hone and 'Orator' Hunt only by class and education. He was also uncertain, as were many of the second-generation Romantics, about the arguments and the methods for achieving reform put forward by the new political campaigners. After the Peterloo Massacre, Cobbett had called for mass insurrection: 'Things cannot long remain in the state of 16 August. Our foes must give us our rights; or all law must be laid aside; and the country must then go on, as long as it can, under a system of open force-military.'[59] Shelley was similarly incensed by the massacre. He wrote to

Charles Ollier: 'The same day your letter came, came news of the Manchester work and the torment of my indignation has not yet done boiling in my veins.'[60] But despite his continual call for revolution, and his depiction of social upheaval in *The Revolt of Islam*, he was in fact concerned about the consequences of a People's revolt, a demand for 'rights' on a mass scale. He was all too aware of the similarities between the feelings aroused by the Peterloo Massacre and the circumstances of the French Revolution thirty years before. 'The tyrants here', he wrote to Peacock, 'as in the French Revolution have first shed blood. May their execrable lessons not be learnt with equal docility.'[61] He toned down his call for universal suffrage in 'A Proposal for Putting Reform to the Vote', fearing that to offer the vote to every male citizen 'would be to place power in the hands of men who have been rendered brutal and torpid and ferocious by ages of slavery.'[62] In a sentence, later cancelled, in an earlier draft of this pamphlet, he acknowledged his lack of political courage: 'and who is bold enough to say that he would abolish the Lords and pull down the King, careless of all the ruin and bloodshed that must ensue'. Shelley feared, like many others at the time, that long-term oppression rendered its victim brutal and vicious in retaliation, inexperienced in the art of reasoned dissent.

Shelley's later dialogues represent indirect responses to these other alternative voices, to the increasingly popular voice of Cobbett. While writing democratic dialogues, Shelley was anxious to resist the seduction of what he perceived as the demogogue preaching the excesses of violence. The dialogue form was required to offer licence but not licentiousness. What was demanded was licence, but not licence to kill. The give-and-take of drama offered Shelley the most appropriate form in which to explore the possibilities of licence and control in democratic writing. Fifth-century drama was itself inextricably linked with the democratic political system which inspired it.[63] Shelley wrote ecstatically in the 'Discourse on the Manners of the Ancient Greeks': 'What was the combination of moral and political circumstances which produced so unparalleled a progress during that period in literature and arts ... are problems left with the wonder and conjecture of posterity.'[64] Drama and comedy articulated the possibilities and difficulties of democratic political writing and the fragility of the relationship between the political writer and his public which Shelley's uneasy relationship with Cobbett epitomised.

CYCLOPS

One of the main texts in which Shelley explored some of the questions about democratic revolutions and the threat of violence is his translation of Euripides' *Cyclops*, which he undertook in 1819 just after the Peterloo Massacre. For many readers, the *Cyclops* appears a strange choice of drama for translation. Why did Shelley not translate one of Euripides' major canonical tragedies? Why did he choose this lesser-known satyr play? The answer lies in the political possibilities and questions which Euripides' text offers the reader and which Shelley uncovered and highlighted. Hunt had written of the subversive implications of Greek laughter, laughing 'with Aristophanes and the satirists at what deserved greater respect'. The satyr play, performed after the tragic trilogy at the Great Dionysia dramatic festival, laughed at tragedy, the most important institution in Athenian cultural life. According to Sir Arthur Pickard-Cambridge, 'it seems probable that one of the essentials of the satyr play was that characters indistinguishable from the figures of tragedy were exposed to the disruptive incursion of a satyr chorus'.[65] The satyr chorus, like Peacock's machine-breakers, interrupt the 'mythological situation where, properly speaking, they had no business'.[66] The potential of the satyr play to interrupt or to disrupt offered Shelley the possibility of disturbing or resisting institutions of power.[67]

The satyr's licence is derived from wine and the intoxicating freedom it induces. The satyrs serve Dionysus, the god of wine, rather than the major Olympian king, Zeus. They follow an alternative centre of authority and subvert the traditional narrative thrust of myths with their 'disruptive incursions'. The desire for immortal fame and cult-hero status, which motivates the conventional heroes of tragedy, is subverted by the satyrs' love of wine beyond all other things. The wine stimulates games, free playfulness, the display of sexuality. This intoxicated licence to replace conventional myth with Dionysiac enjoyable drinking is evident in Shelley's translation. The satyr chorus are able to maintain their lightheartedness even in the employment of the monstrous Cyclops.[68] When Ulysses first lands on the island of the cyclops, for example, he appears to have arrived not at a monster's cave but 'at the blithe court of Bacchus' and sees 'a sportive band of Satyrs'. At the satyrs' first entry they sing a joyful chorus, despite their servile position and temporary separation from their lord, Bacchus: 'An Iacchic melody / To the golden Aphrodite / Will I lift'. Their spirit seems irrepressible, whatever the uncivilised conditions in which they live; and it is rendered all the more playful after Ulysses' gift of wine: 'I bring no gold but Bacchic juice'. After drinking and letting out an inarticulate whoop of delight – 'Papaiapax!' – Silenus is completely released from rational conversation: 'Babai! Great Bacchus calls me forth to dance! Joy! joy!'

But the gift of wine is equivocal; men should beware the Greeks bearing gifts. For Silenus's release through wine and the service of Bacchus renders him not only free from traditional myths and the authority of Zeus but also free from responsibility. His character is taken over, overwhelmed by wine, and he is utterly unreliable. After attempting to strike a bargain over the Cyclops' food in return for the wine, Ulysses is betrayed by Silenus as soon as the Cyclops appears. Later, the satyr chorus express eagerness to assist Ulysses in escaping from the Cyclops' clutches, but at the critical moment they retreat in fear and Ulysses is forced to rely only upon his trusty crew of the conventional Homeric story. The licence which wine offers becomes drunken licentiousness. Thus by implication, the satyr play, in ridiculing and subverting conventional myth and drama, is in danger of creating anarchy, of going beyond acceptable limits when it mocks without control or responsibility. Just as the satyr play offers the attractive release desired for political expression, so it reflects the dangers of political release, the dangers of the intoxicating rhetoric of popular revolution.

That the drunken anarchism in the play is particularly relevant to political anarchism is made plain throughout Shelley's translation. Shelley accentuates and draws out political references in the text. The cyclops, for example, lives in a democracy. Ulysses demands to know the political constitution when he first arrives:

Ulysses: Obeying whom? Or is the state popular?
Silenus: Shepherds: no one obeys any in aught.[69]

Despite their occasional cannibalism, which is required by the myth, the cyclops race appear to live an exemplary abstemious life, virtually vegetarian and certainly teetotal. Whereas tyrants are normally monstrous flesh-eaters in Shelley's writing, the vegetarian cyclops appear positively liberal and attractive, politically egalitarian.[70] But, on the other hand, the Cyclops is also tyrannical when he does eat flesh, when he suffers a schizophrenic revolution in character. Shelley's translation alters the apolitical monstrousness of the Cyclops' behaviour into something significantly political. The chorus sing:

> . . . and so, for all delight
> Of Bacchic sports, sweet dance (lithe) and melody
> lawless giant's wandering flock[71]
> We keep this ~~monstrous Cyclops sheep~~

Shelley's deliberate alteration of the original Greek is emphasised by the fact that he actually erased his original closer translation in his manuscript version, 'this monstrous Cyclops' sheep', in order to replace it with the alternative political version, 'this lawless giant's wandering flock'. The democratic freedom which the Cyclops enjoys can be exploited and rendered threateningly violent. Abolishing oppressive laws can result in 'lawlessness' and the creation of an equally oppressive and fearful 'lawless' tyrant.

Through our alternating sympathies for the Cyclops or for Ulysses during the course of the play, we are compelled to confront questions about the nature of political oppression and revolution. Both Ulysses and Cyclops become victims at different points in the play and respond with violence. Shelley and Mary were creating various portrayals of victims at this time. In Shelley's *The Cenci*, Beatrice, driven to madness by her father's intolerable tyrannical treatment of her, retaliates with violence and murder. In Mary Shelley's *Frankenstein*, the monster only resorts to his devastating pursuit of destruction after he has been rejected by the De Lacey family in the cottage next door and later disowned by his creator and parent, Frankenstein. These portrayals are influenced by the experience of the French revolutionary mob and the subsequent fear of revolutionary crowds, released and suddenly empowered after centuries of oppression and brutality.[72] In Shelley's *Cyclops*, the representation of the dangerous victim offers a similar equivocal picture of the oppression and the violence which can result from brutal treatment. The Cyclops reacts with cannibalistic violence after Ulysses has supposedly stolen his food. Ulysses responds with blinding cruelty after he has been imprisoned in the Cyclops' cave and some of his crew have been consumed. But after the blinding, Ulysses fears violent retaliation again from the monster. He addresses the chorus who are preparing to

blind the Cyclops after the monster has collapsed in a drunken
stupor:

> Be silent ye wild things – nay hold your peace
> And keep your lips quite close – dare not to breathe
>   e'er   the monster
> Or spit or ~~even~~ wake, lest ~~Calamity~~ ye should waken
> Calamity – until the Cyclops eye
> Be tortured out with sight destroying fire.[73]

The previous victims – the crew – reciprocate with extreme cruelty,
with 'sight destroying fire'. They are now the revolutionary mob,
'ye wild things'. But most significant is the term 'Calamity' which
we know, from Shelley's alterations in his manuscript version, was
a deliberately chosen word, decided upon after some thought.
'Calamity' carried political connotations. Shelley used the word in
his description of the French Revolution in 'A Philosophical View
of Reform':

> Then the oppressed, having been rendered brutal, ignorant, ser-
> vile, and bloody by long slavery . . . arose and took a dreadful
> revenge on their oppressors. Their desire to wreak revenge to this
> extent, in itself a mistake, a crime, a *calamity*, arose from the same
> source as their other miseries and errors. [My italics][74]

The calamity of the violence in the French Revolution was due to
the previous oppression, the 'long slavery'. The Cyclops, if
provoked, could retaliate with equal violence, stung into action by
the pain of his torture.

Thus the Cyclops and Ulysses and his crew are locked into a
strange relationship of mutual victimisation, mutual violence,
where boundaries and distinctions have become blurred. The analogy with the possible violence of an uncontrollable mob is clear.
Cobbett's rhetoric was in danger of unleashing the ferocity of such
victims. In the light of this depiction of violence during the play,
the ending of the drama is disturbing. The Cyclops, lonely now and
crippled, shouts violent defiance impotently from the shore, evinc-
ing our sympathies more like Theocritus's monster than Homer's:

> Not so, if, whelming you with this huge stone,
> I can crush you and all your men together;

I will descend upon the shore, though blind,
Groping my way adown the steep ravine.

(713–16)

But the chorus replies with cruel merriment:

And we, the shipmates of Ulysses now,
Will serve our Bacchus all our happy lives.

(717–18)

'Serving Bacchus' is now revealed to be less a matter of innocent
tipsiness and rural cavorting and more a terrifying release of drunken violence and lawlessness. Such 'happiness' demands control,
education, leadership. The *Cyclops* dramatises the dangers of the
revolutionary mob and the difficulties of writing subversive democratic verse; yet it does not offer any solutions. The satyr play form
articulates the difficulties and offers the comic release for their
exploration but cannot provide any obvious limits to the licence.
Of course, like the philosophical dialogue, drama or comedy
cannot by its very nature provide answers or conclusively close
off discussion. But Shelley did move on to consider the balance
between comic licence and the need for leadership more explicitly
in his *Oedipus Tyrannus; or Swellfoot the Tyrant*, written the following year.

SWELLFOOT THE TYRANT

Swellfoot the Tyrant is the funniest poetic work Shelley ever wrote.
The whole drama is a study in the comic puncturing of pomposity
through the translation of Sophocles' *Oedipus Tyrannus* into Aristophanic comedy. Mary Shelley described Shelley's inspiration for
his study of comic 'disruptive incursion' in her 1839 notes to the
poem:

We were then at the baths of San Giuliano. A friend came to visit
us on the day when a fair was held in the square, beneath our
windows: Shelley read to us his *Ode to Liberty*; and was riotously
accompanied by the grunting of pigs brought for sale to the fair.
He compared it to the 'chorus of frogs' in the satiric drama of
Aristophanes; and, it being the hour of merriment, and one

ludicrous association suggesting another, he imagined a political-satirical drama on the circumstances of the day, to which the pigs would serve as chorus – and *Swellfoot* was begun.[75]

Aristophanes can be appropriated to puncture the high art of Sophocles, just as the frogs, in Aristophanes' play, interrupt with hilarious vulgarity the serious discussion of Dionysus and his slave as they journey down to the underworld. Comedy debunks idealistic but possibly misplaced political aspiration.

The pomposity begins early, in the opening preface. In writing reminiscent of Swift's *Tale of a Tub*, Shelley displays ludicrous false learning and pedantry. The play is said to be translated 'from the original Doric'. In the attempt to dazzle the reader, the preface is littered with complicated, often coined words and apparently learned references. Shelley explains the term 'triad' in a long-winded manner, before confusing the reader with a series of Latin tags and quotations: 'The tenderness with which he treats the PIGS proves him to have been a *sus Boeotiae*; possibly *Epicuri de grege porcus*; for, as the poet observes, "A fellow feeling makes us wondrous kind".'[76] A Parthian shot hints at the tedious possibilities of sequels to the work: 'Should the remaining portions of this Tragedy be found, entitled, *Swellfoot in Angaria*, and *Charite*, the Translator might be tempted to give them to the reading Public' (p. 390). Amid all this posing pomposity, the grunting bathos can be detected only in the irony with which the whole preface is written. One is scarcely in the mood to receive *Oedipus* seriously after being informed that 'The word Hoydipouse (or more properly Oedipus) has been rendered literally SWELLFOOT, without its having been conceived necessary to determine whether a swelling of the hind or the fore feet of the Swinish Monarch is particularly indicated' (p. 390). Nothing can be understood to have been translated 'literally' in the play, except by a comic literalness *ad absurdum*.

In this ironic, debunking atmosphere *Oedipus* does not last long. The title is immediately transformed into a literal translation – 'Swellfoot the Tyrant' – which is comic and which carries overtones of greed, excess, overweening power, quite different from the suffering history behind Sophocles' hero's name. The initial scene, in which Swellfoot confronts the chorus of grunting pigs begging for more food, recalls the opening scene in Sophocles, where Oedipus responds to the chorus's demands for an end to the plague which is afflicting them. But Shelley's Swellfoot is more tyrannical in the modern sense of the word, contemptuous of the chorus and unperturbed by their suffering. The oracles, which feature so importantly in Sophocles, are dismissed by Swellfoot and his court. As all tyrants do, Swellfoot manipulates the oracles to suit his affairs and to console and deceive the clamorous pigs:

> *Purganax*: O, would that this were all! The oracle!!
> *Mammon*: Why it was I who spoke that oracle,
> And whether I was dead drunk or inspired,
> I cannot well remember; nor in truth,
> The oracle itself!
>
> (I.i.108–12)

But the frightening tyrannical power of Swellfoot, which is itself a biting comment upon the power of George IV and his ministers, is hilariously deflated by the fact that he is a pig. In the preface, Shelley expresses mock concern that he does not know which feet were swollen, the fore feet or the hind ones, thus emphasising the swinish form of his hero. And when Swellfoot is at his most tyrannical, calling for butchers to kill a few of the complaining pigs and admiring himself in the mirror, it is his fat pig proportions of which he is most proud:

> These graceful limbs are clothed in proud array
> Of gold and purple, and this kingly paunch
> Swells like a sail before a favouring breeze,
> And these most sacred nether promontories
> Lie satisfied with layers of fat.
>
> (I.i.2–6)

The Orwellian vision of a republic of pigs offers Shelley the possibility of examining familiar political arguments in an unfamiliar setting.[77] But the main contribution of the pig characters is comic. The false pomposity of following one's stomach around – 'this kingly paunch swells like a sail before a favouring breeze' – is derived from Aristophanes. Indeed the line reads like a parody of a bad translation from Aristophanes, where one is repeatedly confronted with the bizarre conversion of language into physical objects. The dramatists in the *Frogs*, for example, physically weigh words in a pair of scales to determine their moral weight. So too Swellfoot's political greed and excess are transformed into his

physical corpulence. Laoctonos, one of Swellfoot's henchmen, has
a name which means 'people killer'; he duly proceeds to butcher a
few pigs. The pigs, when killed, are converted into their physical
constituents, sausages and bacon; and the economy is run, not
through the symbolic circulation of money, but through the literal
export of the city's only resource, pork:

> The failure of a foreign market for
> Sausages, bristles, and blood puddings,
> And such home manufactures, is but partial.
> (II.i.18–20)[78]

The contrast between the bureaucratic language here and the
bizarre physical subject matter is a further example of the puncturing of pomposity.

Shelley even mocks his own conventional style, just as he enjoyed
the fact that the grunting pigs interrupted his *Ode to Liberty*.
Purganax imagines the imminent arrival of Iona in language which
recalls Shelley's 'Ode to a Skylark', only for the allusion to be
punctured by an irreverent comment from First Boar (obviously the
pun is intended):

> *Purganax*: But like a standard of an admiral's ship
> Or like the banner of a conquering host,
> Or like a cloud dyed in the dying day,
> Unravelled on the blast from a white mountain;
> Or like a meteor, or a war-steed's mane,
> Or waterfall from a dizzy precipice
> Scattered upon the wind.
> *First Boar*: Or a cow's tail.
> (II.i.98–104)

First Boar's remark brings Purganax's lyricism down to earth, and
also points out the pointlessness of the endless abstract similes.
Similarly, later, Mammon's Gothic imagination is punctured by
Swellfoot:

> *Mammon*: I hear a crackling of the giant bones
> Of the dread image, and in the black pits
> Which once were eyes, I see two livid flames.
> These prodigies are oracular, and show

The presence of the unseen Deity.
Mighty events are hastening to their doom!
Swellfoot: I only hear the lean and mutinous Swine
Grunting about the temple.

(II.ii.61–8)

Mammon's lines look forward to Shelley's other visions of revolutionary apocalypses in *Prometheus Unbound* and *Hellas*, but while in those poems they are depicted in all seriousness, here they are undermined by Swellfoot's subversive literalness.

The comic undermining in *Swellfoot*, then, is earthy and parodic. The sense of ludic release, the freedom it gives to write about physical details like eating and farting, serves a similar purpose to that found in Aristophanes. But debate continues to rage among critics over how far Aristophanes is actually subversive and so what purpose is served by the ludic release.[79] Since Aristophanes mocks centres of power, like the lawcourts, could he be interpreted as radical? Since he frequently attacks leading political figures in the democracy, could he equally be seen as conservative? Ideas about carnival, to which Aristophanes is closely indebted, are similarly divided. Bakhtin argues that the transformation of the world and the direct inversion of traditional hierarchies of power which take place in carnival have a subversive effect, because they offer a temporary glimpse of how the world can be ordered with no binding guarantee that the old system will be restored at the end of the day.[80] But later critics have seen the carnival purely as cathartic, an offering by the establishment to satisfy the people and relieve tensions so that they will behave for the rest of the year.[81] Simon Goldhill complicates the picture of Aristophanes as carnival by arguing that since the comedies were produced at the same festivals and performed in the same theatres as the tragedies they parodied, the relationship between the two was more ambiguous. Tragedy, according to Goldhill, was itself both a cultural institution and a challenge to the city's institutions. As a result, he prefers to think that Aristophanes 'negotiates as well as celebrates the possibilities of transgression'.[82]

Shelley was in a similar political predicament. First, *Oedipus Tyrannus*, the drama being mocked, was perceived as radical. A drama written at the time of the most ideal political circumstances should not be mocked. And *Oedipus* in particular was politically risqué because of its depiction of incest.[83] Secondly, his own political writing was being debunked in the drama. Mary Shelley's anecdote does not inform us what Shelley thought of his 'Ode to Liberty' after the pig-grunting episode, but it cannot exactly have enhanced the poem's ability to inspire the listeners to political activity as originally intended. If visions of ideal utopias and the destruction of evil regimes are to be systematically debunked, what does that tell us about the politics of the debunker or the debunking medium? Comedy is perhaps dangerously out of control, taking its licence to licentiousness, if nothing, not even political aspiration, is sacred any more.

This perhaps is the reason why there is more than a hint in *Swellfoot* that Shelley considered comedy, despite its democratic associations, as degenerate. Mary Shelley certainly expresses a degree of embarrassment about the piece, admitting that 'hesitation of whether it would do honour to Shelley prevented my publishing it at first' but ultimately defending it as 'a mere plaything of the imagination'. Shelley voiced dislike of comedy in his 'Defence of Poetry', perceiving it to be the product of a degenerate age:

> But in periods of the decay of social life, the drama sympathises with that decay. . . . Comedy loses its ideal universality: wit succeeds to humour; we laugh from self-complacency and triumph instead of pleasure; malignity, sarcasm and contempt, succeed to sympathetic merriment; we hardly laugh but we smile. Obscenity, which is ever blasphemy against the divine beauty in life, becomes, from the very veil which it assumes, more active if less disgusting: it is a monster for which the corruption of society for ever brings forth new food, which it devours in secret.[84]

Comedy appears here to release the worst aspects in people. It encourages their 'self-complacency' and their voracious appetite for 'obscenity'. In its monstrousness it is like the 'lawless' Cyclops or the ungoverned satyrs, violently destructive and uncontainable.

Ironically, the concept of the degenerate nature of comedy is supported by the model of *The Frogs* from which *Swellfoot* is derived. The 'plot' of *The Frogs* is based around the idea of the degeneration of Athenian drama: since the death of Euripides, no good plays have been written; all the great playwrights are dead. Dionysus, god of theatre, ventures down to the underworld to resurrect a dramatist to restore Greek theatre to its former glory and to boost morale. Aristophanes is thus suggesting that he is a belated Greek dramatist, living after the time of the theatre's golden age. So the fetching of Iona Taurina to rescue the pigs' fortune is a little like Dionysus's eventual decision to take Aeschylus back with him as the Athenian saviour. But Iona is a far more ridiculous figure than Aeschylus, the most respected dramatist, and the echo must be seen as a further parody of a parody. If Aristophanes is belated, Shelley is hopelessly belated and far more degenerate. Not only his chorus but even his heroes are pigs, and they act accordingly.

The belatedness of Shelley's play is further accentuated by its Theban and Boeotian setting. Of course Thebes is the city of Oedipus and the Sophoclean tragedy is placed in Thebes, while Oedipus reaches the outskirt of Athens in *Oedipus at Colonus*. Thebes is often the site for tragedy because it offers the playwright the freedom to explore disturbing issues in the 'other' city which would prove too unsettling if set in Athens. But for Aristophanes, the colloquial response to Thebes and the region of Boeotia in general was as relevant as the tragic presentation of the city. In *Olympian VI*, Pindar offers an insight into the common argot of Athenian insults about Thebes: 'Rouse your comrades, Aineas, and sing first of Hera Parthenia, and then say whether by our words we thrust that old insult *Boeotian sow* aside.'[85] Pindar's reference to the Greek insult of the Thebans as pigs suggests Shelley was also thinking of him, as well as Edmund Burke's *Reflections on the Revolution in France*, when he referred to the 'swinish multitude'.[86] So the Greeks seem to have portrayed Boeotia as a dull backwater with semi-literate inhabitants. Shelley's aristophanic play is set then in a fallen Athens, an Athens fallen as a consequence of political corruption and degeneracy. These ideas must lie behind the comment in the preface that the play 'was evidently written by some learned Theban, and, from its characteristic dulness [sic], apparently before the duties on the importation of Attic salt had been repealed by the Boeotarchs'. The play is dull because it has not been spiced up by any influence from the more civilised and sophisticated Athenians. Dullness here, as in Pope's *Dunciad*, equals political corruption. Shelley's world is even more outrageous and more unattractive than Aristophanes' belated Athenian world. Swinish democratic comedy has unleashed a horrifying picture of obscenity and baseness.

The fear of how far this degeneracy will go leads to a desire for leaders. The people are thoroughly unattractive in their piggish behaviour. After Burke had referred to the people as the 'swinish multitude' in his *Reflections*, radical writers had been responding with celebratory and attractive depictions of pigs. But Shelley's pigs are more ambiguous. While they are sympathetic in their state of oppression, they disgust the reader with their noisy grunting and eating; and later, like many representations of deprived people, they resort to fighting each other in their struggle for physical survival. Yet Shelley's choice of a leader to guide and control this 'swinish multitude' seems equally ambiguous. Swellfoot – George IV – and his ministers are ridiculed and eventually outtricked in the true spirit of democratic satire. But the heroine of the piece and the leader to whom the pigs flock, Iona Taurina, bizarrely symbolises Queen Caroline, the estranged wife of George, behind whom the liberal press were rallying in her battle against her husband's order of banishment. Shelley had abstained from the popular mourning for Princess Charlotte three years before. When even Leigh Hunt had edged his *Examiner* of 7 November 1817 with black to indicate the public grief at the premature death of the princess, Shelley had written a strong pamphlet rejecting public interest in the monarchy and mourning rather the wrongful execution of the three Pentridge conspirators condemned to death for allegedly agitating for reform. He had contrasted the interest among the ancient Greeks in those who truly served the public with the British interest in the monarchy: 'The Athenians did well to celebrate with public mourning the death of those who had guided their republic with their valour and their understanding, or illustrated it with their genius.'[87] In *Swellfoot*, however, it is a monarch who becomes the representative of the people and upon whom the interest is focused. Although Caroline has not distinguished herself in any way nor revealed any popular or liberal concern, yet she is the figure around whom the opposition gathers. Indeed Shelley continues the Burkean allusions by appearing to echo Burke's idealising description of Marie Antoinette in his portrayal of Iona. She appeals to the sense of chivalry Burke acknowledged in his treatment of the French queen:

> Gentlemen Swine, and gentle Lady-Pigs,
> The tender heart of every Boar acquits
> Their QUEEN, of any act incongruous

With native piggishness, and she, reposing
With confidence upon the grunting nation,
Has thrown herself, her cause, her life, her all,
Her innocence, into their Hoggish arms.

(II.i.157–63)

While these lines could be interpreted ironically as a parody of
Burke's famous passage, yet the echo in Iona's name of the Io of
Aechylus's *Prometheus Bound* and her similar fate, suffering the
repeated stings of a gadfly, suggest that Iona must be viewed
sympathetically.

The climax of the play particularly highlights the troubling side-
lining of the people and the resort to problematic leaders. The stage
directions read:

> The image of FAMINE thus arises with a tremendous sound, the
> PIGS begin scrambling for the loaves, and are tripped up by the
> skulls; all those who EAT the loaves are turned into BULLS and
> arrange themselves quietly behind the altar. The image of FAMINE
> sinks through a chasm in the earth, and a MINOTAUR rises.[88]

The chorus of pigs, the oppressed and starving people, are reduced
to an unattractive and inconsequential rabble. They are only interested in personal nutrition, instant gratification, and then they
remove themselves to the margins of the action. The more important political dealings and discussions about long-term settlements
are undertaken by the aristocratic figures, Iona, Famine, Purganax.
Indeed there is an attempted deal between the *deus ex machina* and
the government agency, between Liberty and Famine, before the
crucial 'Green Bag' test brings the crisis to a head. Liberty desperately tries to hold on to the possibility of peace before the critical
revolutionary act of emptying the bag over Swellfoot and destroying him:

> By thy dread self, O Famine!
> I charge thee! when thou wake the multitude,
> Thou lead them not upon the paths of blood . . .
> . . . those radiant spirits, who are still
> The standard-bearers in the van of Change.
> Be they th' appointed stewards, to fill
> The lap of Pain, and Toil, and Age!

(II.ii.89–91, 95–8)

The main enemy for Liberty and Famine is not a tyrannical monarchy, but the fear of a violent, uncontrollable people if ever the system is fragmented. Stewards are required to guide the People, for without them they are swine-like, 'brutal and torpid and ferocious'. The attempted reconciliation recalls the speech of Athene at the end of the *Oresteia* which attempts to pacify the Furies after they have lost the battle over Orestes. The 'multitude' has lost out in this battle between aristocrats and can only threaten potential violence. But significantly Liberty's attempted reconciliation fails. It is nearly drowned in any case by the grunting of the Theban pigs in a possible echo of the interrupting of Shelley's 'Ode to Liberty' by the grunting of Italian pigs. And Iona Taurina ignores all the advice. After her successful overthrow of Swellfoot, she drops her Marie Antoinette disguise and becomes a Circe figure, whipping up her swinish followers in a frenzy of hatred and revenge:

> Give them no law (are they not beasts of blood?)
> But such as they gave you. Tallyho! ho!
> Through forest, furze, and bog, and den, and desert,
> Pursue the ugly beasts! tallyho! ho!
>
> (II.ii.125–8)

Greece was still associated with democracy and the ability to 'laugh at' the establishment. The continuing controversial reputation of Greece is evident from the fact that this work, like most of Shelley's, was censored and withdrawn by the publishers after only a brief circulation. But the allusions to Aristophanes and Sophocles are not used here to appeal to a wide range of readers who would interpret the openness of Greek democracy as a metaphor for the accessibility of literature for the masses. Instead, the play is aimed at an elite, those who could understand Greek and therefore appreciate the jokes, those who might perhaps tend to sympathise with the rulers rather than with the ruled. The Pig chorus is excluded from the discussion at the end of the play. Likewise, the liberal debate was being kept from the mass of the people.[89] It could also be said that, as a result, liberal thinking was becoming less relevant. The question of the relevance of Greek drama to contemporary British politics is whimsically acknowledged in the allusions to Greek legend made by Purganax while he is speaking about Iona Taurina's circumstances (II.i.59–71). Legends suggest Iona's crime – adultery – while conveniently avoiding the necessity of spelling out the unmentionable details. But how far can the experience of Pasiphae or Europa ever offer a sufficient parallel for the behaviour of Iona Taurina? Again the question of relevance is posed in the final speech of the play. The Minotaur speaks:

> I am the Ionian Minotaur, the mightiest
> Of all Europe's taurine progeny –
> I am the old traditional Man-Bull;
> And from my ancestors having been Ionian,
> I am called Ion, which, by interpretation,
> Is John; in plain Theban, that is to say,
> My name's JOHN BULL:
>
> (II.ii.103–9)

Word play makes the connection between Greece and Britain. There is no intrinsic point of connection between Ion and John, or between the Minotaur and the traditional British bull symbol. So what, then, is the connection between Greek republicanism and British politics?

The open, democratic association of Greece, which challenged and liberated, was no longer viable after Shelley's early years. The repression of the government, the violence of the revolution – these both conspired to make naive hopes of liberty and democracy far more problematic. Political positions became divided and extreme, with the consequences of any political action appearing, after the Revolution, more dramatic, more dangerous. Both the *Cyclops* and *Swellfoot the Tyrant* reveal the difficulty of maintaining any entrenched political position in the chaos of revolution or unleashed mob rule. The use of a Greek model, particularly in *Swellfoot*, highlights the discrepancy between the ideal of Greek libertarian democracy and the real political dilemma for a poet in the turbulent post-Napoleonic war years. That discrepancy, that distance, was crucial. In his recourse to Greece, Shelley was to question the relevance of his poetical subject matter to the political and social needs of the time. This debate was focused upon the role of Greek pastoral for political thinking.

3

'A Flowery Band': Pastoral, Polemic and Translation

I wonder none of you stray to the Elysian climate, and like the sailors of Ulysses, eat the Lotus and remain as I have done.

Shelley: letter to Hogg

In his 'Discourse on Pastoral Poetry' (1709), Alexander Pope argues that the pastoral genre was originally derived from the lazy life-style of shepherds in warm climates: "'Tis natural to imagine, that the leisure of those early shepherds admitting and inviting some diversion, none was so proper to that solitary and sedentary life as singing; and that in their songs they took occasion to celebrate their own felicity.'[1] Keats describes the typical landscape in which those shepherds might be supposed to have lived:

> Some shape of beauty moves away the pall
> From our dark spirits. Such the sun, the moon,
> Trees old, and young, sprouting a shady boon
> For simple sheep; and such are daffodils
> With the green world they live in; and clear rills
> That for themselves a cooling covert make
> 'Gainst the hot season.[2]

Both writers consciously create a stereotypical *locus amoenus*, which crucially depends upon simple qualities and pleasures. Shepherds 'sing', rivers are 'clear' and the world is 'green'. The enjoyment of the landscape is intensified by its contrast with the supposed complication of everyday life. Keats describes pastoral as 'a flowery band' which is cherished 'to bind us to the earth, / Spite of despondence, of the inhuman dearth / Of noble natures, of the gloomy days, / Of all the unhealthy and o'er-darkened ways'.[3] Although neither Pope nor Keats actually believes that the countryside really appears as they describe, each creates an idyllic unselfconscious world which is indebted to the traditional pastoral topos of simplicity.

In writing about the Romantic interest in Greek pastoral, however, critics have been guilty of confusing the simplicity inscribed within the stereotypical pastoral world with one supposedly inherent in the writer's engagement with his pastoral subject. As a result, the writing of Greek pastoral in the second decade of the nineteenth century has been interpreted either as a simple disengagement from contemporary politics or social concerns or as a simple allegory conveying, through the politics of style, a covert message. Timothy Webb has observed that 'Shelley often turned to Greek writers for spiritual solace' and that Greek literature constituted 'something beautiful and therapeutic'.[4] Greek pastoral, according to Webb, is an attractive and unproblematic world to which the author can temporarily retreat when life, and more serious literary matters, become too stressful and difficult.[5] In order to resist this interpretation, Marilyn Butler has argued that the writing of Greek pastoral represented a covert discourse for the game of oppositional politics. For her, the detailed contents of the pastoral world are unimportant. The pastoral constitutes a package to be appropriated by the writer for his political interests.[6]

But these accounts fail to address the complications and ambiguities inherent in pastoral. William Empson observed that there are almost as many versions of pastoral as there are writers of pastoral; and one of the principal difficulties of writing pastoral is in ensuring that the correct version is recognised by readers.[7] The ambiguity is noted by Leigh Hunt in his preface to *Foliage* (1818): 'I need not inform any reader acquainted with real poetry that a delight in rural luxury has ever been a constituent part of the very business of poets as well as one of the very best things which they have recommended, as counteractions to the more sordid tendencies of cities.'[8] Hunt plays here with the opposing concepts of 'rural luxury' and the 'business of poets'. For the contradictions he points out between apparent pastoral laziness and poetic activity highlight the essential ambiguity of pastoral, founded in its 'perceivable distance between the alleged and the implied'.[9] The writer of pastoral is faced with the problem of breaching or exploiting that distance, in his attempt to fix or tease interpretation.

Moreover, the simplicity within the pastoral topos is itself highly problematic. In many ways pastoral is figured as a nostalgic genre, always looking back to an original moment of perfection and unity but itself unable to match the model. So by never actually appearing as perfect and unified as intended, pastoral works always break the expectations of the genre even as they try to fulfil them. While Raymond Williams and John Barrell have confronted the division within pastoral by suggesting that it is a repressive genre and one which constantly attempts to silence these failures or indeed the disruptive forces of history in its effort to attain perfection, Judith Haber has contended recently that the divisions and awareness of incompletion are inherent within the genre itself.[10] Pastoral, throughout history, has remained 'a mode that worked insistently against itself, problematising both its own definition and stable definitions within its texts'.[11] The original model of perfection which pastoral works might yearn to recover has been further questioned recently with Simon Goldhill's elegant analysis of the framing devices and 'self-contradictory' nature of the poetry of Theocritus, the supposed father of pastoral.[12]

As a result, the relationship between pastoral and politics is problematic and teasing. Since the traditional pastoral topos is in fact fragmented and ambiguous, it leaves uncertain the message being conveyed by the political appropriation of the pastoral genre. Moreover since the approaches to pastoral vary widely, the directness of communication with an audience demanded by polemic is compromised and questioned. And yet this problematic relationship was ideally suited to articulate the problems of distance inherent in political writing in the early nineteenth century. The previous chapter traced the growing distance between the ideal model of democratic Greece as open, common and egalitarian, and its portrayal in texts increasingly divorced from common readers. The discussion of pastoral takes up once more the question of distance – which is essential to the pastoral genre – and considers whether the distance of author to subject matter can be interpreted polemically or whether it highlights the problems of attempting to imply political relevance by alleging irrelevance and lack of concern. This problem was of course more acute for Shelley, who was anxious to convey strongly-held political views but who could be perceived as unconcerned, living as an exiled aristocrat in the pastoral world of far-off Italy. Shelley's pastoral writing highlighted the problem of distance even more acutely since it appeared usually in the form of translations from the Greek. If pastoral opens up the gulf between the writer and his imagined pastoral world – like Keats's 'green world' that exists apart from his world of 'despondence' – then translation of those 'green world' texts first created by distant writers opens up the gulf immeasurably. Shelley's translations of the *Homeric Hymns* and his free 'translation' of *Adonais* pose questions about the opportunities or the problems in acknowledging the two discrete worlds of author and text. But before examining these translations, I will explore the potential of pastoral writing for simple political allegory in the early nineteenth century. This demands consideration primarily of what Marilyn Butler has termed the 'Marlow Manifesto', the noticeable increase in pastoral subjects in the writing of the Shelley circle after 1817, and Butler's claims about the politics of style.

MARLOW MANIFESTO?

In her writing about the politicisation of myth in the second decade of the nineteenth century, Marilyn Butler has argued forcibly that Greek literature, and particularly what she sees as the light, cheerful pastoral form, was interpreted by readers as subversive. She has inverted the arguments about the evasive, escapist nature of Romantic Greek pastoral, so suggesting that the mythmaking, while seeming apolitical, was precisely at the centre of political debate. The qualities associated with pastoral – pleasure, paganism, sexuality and sociality – were designated as southern by Madame de Staël in her essay *De l'Allemagne* and placed in direct contrast to the northern qualities epitomised in German literature – melancholy, Christianity, repression and loneliness.[13] Staël herself was banished from France because of the perceived radicalism of her essay, which dared to mount a defence of Germany during the hegemony of Napoleonic France. But soon the introverted nature of German literature, identified by de Staël, proved attractive to reactionary and apostatic writers such as Coleridge, because it provided a suitable expression of their retreat from politics. With the politicisation of German melancholy literature, radicals quickly adopted the alternative literature of the south in an oppositional political battle, a rhetorical politics of style. Butler goes further and argues that the choice of southern Greek subjects for poetry occurred at a specific place and time. The moment for the Greek revolution happened in Marlow, where Shelley was temporarily living near Peacock, in 1817, at a time of harsh government repression. Thus she terms the interpretation of Greek Arcadia by the radical writers – Shelley's close circle – the Marlow Manifesto.

A political group is defined both by external reception and by self-perception. The pagan interests of Shelley and his friends were certainly perceived by others – especially the contributors to contemporary journals – as politically motivated. The conservative reviews were typically hostile, suggesting that the critics were provoked by the polemical nature of the new work. John Taylor Coleridge, writing in the *Quarterly Review*, was wary of the political implications of the pleasure depicted in the Marlow poems:

> It may seem a wild apprehension to talk of the systematic revival of Epicureanism amongst us in this age of the world; yet something very like it both speculatively and practically, and that too in its most dangerous because least offensive form, seems to be inculcated in all the writings we have alluded to. Lucretius is the philosopher whom these men profess most to admire; and their leading tenet is, that the enjoyment of the pleasures of the intellect and sense is not to be considered as the permitted and regulated use of God's blessings, but the great object and duty of life.[14]

Most notorious among the reactions of reviewers was that of John Gibson Lockhart, who wrote a series of articles for *Blackwood's Edinburgh Magazine* entitled 'On the Cockney School of Poetry', a series provoked primarily by Hunt's *Rimini*, which was published in 1816 before Butler's posited date for the new writing. The articles claimed that there was a new London group of writers, comparable to the Lake school, led by Leigh Hunt. Their poetry was marked by moral depravity, presumption and vulgarity, characteristics inspired by the city landscape in which Hunt lived. The artificiality of their rendition of Greek pastoral, Lockhart argued, was mirrored in, and probably inspired by, the pseudo-country air of suburban Hampstead. What is most surprising is the attack on Hunt for his lack of Greek learning: 'He is a man of little education. He knows absolutely nothing of Greek, almost nothing of Latin, and his knowledge of Italian literature is confined to a few of the most popular of Petrarch's sonnets.'[15] In his attack on Hunt, Lockhart is motivated as much by social snobbery as by politics. 'Mr Hunt cannot utter a dedication, or even a note, without betraying the shibboleth of low birth and low habits', he continues. It could be argued, of course, that this attack on Hunt's background is made for covert political ends but it is noticeable that Byron and even Shelley were exempt from the full extent of the fury. The article on Hunt in *Blackwood's* expresses horror that Hunt should have had the presumption to dedicate his *Rimini* to Byron. Reaction to the Marlow group was tinged with snobbery as well as political outrage and indeed class-consciousness and politics become hard to disentangle.

There are many indications that the members of the Shelley circle were conscious of some sort of political programme behind their work, binding them together. The correspondence of the Marlow period of Shelley's life, 1817–18, has been collected by W.S. Scott under the title *The Athenians* and reads like the intimate letters of some private club, led apparently by Thomas Jefferson Hogg.[16] The spirit in the letters is one of frivolity and performance as Greek reading and Greek names are paraded and boasted. This ostentatious and playful display of Greek gives the impression that more is being conveyed than a simple love of scholarship and learning; that these are in fact the hallmarks of a private code, a code which, according to Butler, necessitated the manifesting of Greekness. For example, Hogg wrote to Peacock:

> I have in no respect bettered my condition as an Athenian, but my mind's boat has remained moored just above the falls of All-evil's weir under the arch of Great Idleness bridge unpainted, unswept and untrimmed. . . . If I have been in practice less loyal to Greece than usual I am not without this apology, that in my heart I am more Grecian than ever.[17]

Hogg's rhetoric here playfully enjoys the paradoxes of pastoral. He has presumably not been as busy reading Greek literature as he should have been – not 'bettering' himself 'as an Athenian' – and yet his idleness has rendered him 'more Grecian than ever' because that is the lazy condition of Greek shepherds and poets. Being 'Grecian', then, is an easily adopted pose that requires little work or reading but is a question of style and motivation. Peacock replies with a name-dropping list of pastoral and comic poets:

> I have been inebriating myself with curious draughts of classicopoetical punch of which Theocritus has been the sweet,

Aristophanes the acid, Pindar the spirit and Homer the water, on
the principle of 'αριστον μεν ὑδωρ'. Pindar has grown into favour
with me.[18]

The interest in Greek was also apparently put into practice by the
group, although the ironic allegorising rhetoric of the letters of the
'Athenians' must not be interpreted too literally. But Hogg's
remark to Hunt about pagan rituals, 'I hope you paid your devo-
tions as usual to the Religio Loci, and hung up an evergreen', is
corroborated by rumours circulating at the time that Shelley had
erected an altar to the pagan god Pan and was acting the part of an
Arcadian devotee, while Keats apparently received a laurel wreath
– the traditional reward for ancient poets – from Leigh Hunt.[19]

While the Shelley circle displayed and performed their Greekness
within the private letters in Marlow, their published writing was
also infused with pastoral subjects and pagan values. The change in
Peacock's work around this time is striking. He abandoned his
dialogue-based novels and launched instead into poetry, publishing *Rhododaphne* in 1818, a strange mythical tale set in Thessaly,
recounting the dilemma of the hero, emotionally torn in his attraction to two different women, and bound less by the dictates of
conventional morality than by the strong force of sexual desire.
The literary departure for Peacock is consciously alluded to at the
beginning:

> Among those gifted bards and sages old
> Shunning the living world, I dwell, and hear,
> Reverent, the creed they held, the tales they told.[20]

Peacock contrasts the 'living world' now 'shunned' with the alternative world of magic, which he has now entered and preferred as
the fitting subject for poetry. Shelley stressed the alternative
qualities of the new poetry in his review: 'It is a Greek and a pagan
poem. In sentiment and scenery it is essentially antique. . . . There
is here, as in the songs of ancient times, music and dancing and the
luxury of voluptuous delight.'[21] Leigh Hunt, who was always renowned for his indefatigable cheer and good humour, added a
sense of social commitment and political motivation to his cheer in
the preface to *Foliage*: 'It is high time for them, and for all of us, to
look after health and sociality; and to believe that although we
cannot alter the world with an *ipse dixit*, we need not become

desponding, or mistake a disappointed egotism for humility.'[22] The opening poem in the *Foliage* collection, like Peacock's *Rhododaphne*, overtly asserts itself as a new type of poetry in programmatic terms:

> For a new smiling sense has shot down through me,
> And from the clouds, like stars, bright eyes are
>   beckoning to me.[23]

Leigh Hunt's espousal of cheer in fact lasted his lifetime, and was more than a year's 'voluptuous delight' inspired by Marlow theories. For example, his *Examiners* frequently call upon their readers to revive ancient customs and bring back the traditional Christmas.[24] But in a much later work, *A Jar of Honey from Mount Hybla*, which relates pastoral tales connected with Sicily as a suitable comforting gift for Christmas, Hunt gives a hint of the possible political reasons behind his good humour:

> Poetical expression, in humble life, is to be found all over the south. In the instances of Burns, Ramsay and others, the north has also seen it. Indeed, it is not a little remarkable that Scotland, which is more northern than England, and possesses not even a nightingale, has had more of it than its southern neighbour. What that is owing to, is a question: perhaps to the very restrictions of John Knox and his fellows, and Nature's happy tendency to counteract them.[25]

The joy of poetry, like the singing of nightingales, is here made political through its opposition to the centralised power bases of church and state: 'Nature's happy tendency to counteract them'. Leigh Hunt appears to be espousing a political interpretation of pastoral here just as he had years before, in 1817.

There are indications, then, that the Marlow writers were conscious of themselves as a group with a political purpose. But there are problems with this simple description and to maintain it dogmatically is to ignore the complications which are inherent in the very nature of pastoral. First to complicate the picture is the fact that the group were far less unified and cohesive then Marilyn Butler has argued. Shelley, for one, seemed set apart from the others. Hogg and Peacock tended to converse together about the situation at Shelley's house, rather than to correspond directly with Shelley. Indeed Hogg, in keeping with the competitive 'Athenian' spirit, was quick to point out Shelley's perceived late membership of the group: 'When you did not esteem the Classics (*pace vestra*, let me use so impious an expression that there was once a time when you preferred the ghost seers of Germany to the Philosophers of Greece) I was anxious that you should see your error.'[26] Outsiders also treated Shelley differently. Lockhart criticised him but acknowledged that he was separated from the iniquitous Cockney School by class and, in consequence according to the magazine, by talent:

> Mr Shelley is devoting his mind to the same pernicious purposes which have recoiled in vengeance upon so many of his contemporaries; but he possesses the qualities of a powerful and vigorous intellect, and therefore his fate cannot be sealed so speedily as theirs. He is also of the 'COCKNEY SCHOOL', so far as his opinions are concerned; but the base opinions of the sect have not as yet been able entirely to obscure in him the character, or take away from him the privileges of the genius born within him.[27]

For his part, Shelley did not allow the new enthusiasm for Greek pastoral to take over the whole of his intellectual life. It is noticeable that it is only in his correspondence with Peacock, Hunt and Hogg that the display of Greek is evident. In his letters to William Godwin, to Lord Byron, and to Mary while he was in London, Shelley made no mention of Greece or of a new political programme.

The other loose cannon was Keats. It was Keats's *Endymion* which evinced the great attack from the *Quarterly* and which provided extra target-practice for Lockhart at *Blackwoods*. Closely associated with Hunt in Hampstead and daring to write about Greek subjects without the correct educational background or politics, Keats represented the typical Cockney School writer for these critics and they duly hounded him, so Shelley thought, until his death. Yet Keats seemed detached. He never travelled down to Marlow and he disagreed with Shelley on literary style and conventional politics, expressing shock, for example, at Shelley's anti-monarchical views.[28] Moreover, his *Endymion* raises more questions about pastoral and beauty than it answers, and conveys more than a simple oppositional politics of style. The division, or what has been termed 'faulture', between private and public was more subtly posed by Keats than by the other Marlow writers.[29] The privileging of beauty at the beginning of *Endymion* – 'A thing of beauty is a joy for ever' – provokes questions about the nature of beauty and its relationship with the social world. Perhaps beauty is to be taken as a challenge to our conventional concerns and thus can be understood to be subversive, testing morals and moralising institutions.[30] But perhaps it is to be understood at face value, apolitical and unashamed. The ambiguity itself is challenging, and the confusion it causes in Keats's readers has been described recently as a prime example of 'solecism'.[31] While Keats may be interrogating and experimenting with political discourse in his writing of the beauty of the Greek pastoral world, he is definitely not manifesting Greekness simply for political statements nor is he writing through some kind of manifesto.

The second difficulty with Butler's manifesto is the fact that the so-called Marlow writers were not the exclusive visitors of pastoral. Others composed pastoral poetry from without the group, men who revealed very different political beliefs. One of the main influences on Keats's and Shelley's conception of pastoral was Walter Savage Landor, who, the last chapter revealed, constituted a highly ambiguous and mysterious political figure. His poem *Gebir* describes the colonising mission of Gebir, the Iberian king, to the semi-magical world – complete with shepherds and streams – of Charoba, Queen of Egypt. Expectations are raised by the queen's confidante Dalica – and by the readers – that the mission will be unsuccessful. It is assumed that the magical pastoral world and the martial world of reality do not – and cannot – mix, and Dalica determines to resist any reconciliation. Clara Reeve, Landor's source for the story, had depicted a powerful queen resisting dramatically the imperial advances of the western king.[32] But Landor subverts expectation. Charoba falls in love with Gebir, and although Dalica succeeds in killing him, he dies with the knowledge of Charoba's undying attachment: 'O Gebir! best of monarchs, best of men.'[33] The love in the poem is ostentatiously posited as pastoral, framed and perhaps mirrored by Tamar's love for the Nymph. Yet it is very different from the carefree, sensual and promiscuous emotion which Butler identifies. It is tinged disconcertingly with the attractions of colonial power; and it carries a tragic intensity which derives from an appreciation of the aching distance between the pastoral and the real world. Landor, of course, further stressed the un-openness of his pastoral world by reissuing the poem in Latin five years later.[34]

The third main difficulty with the idea of an organised and co-hesive Marlow group is the inconsistency of the political opinions which emerge from their writing. While Peacock's determination to 'shun the living world' can be interpreted as an implicit determina-tion to contrast that living world with an alternative preferable and highly relevant one, there are hints in his writing that it could be just the consequence of his general dissatisfaction with contempor-ary literature:

> The life, the intellectual soul
> Of vale, and grove, and stream, has fled
> For ever with the creed sublime
> That nursed the Muse of earlier time.[35]

This is the same mood of despair about current trends in literature which two years later provoked Peacock's *The Four Ages of Poetry*, in which he asserted that poetry was no longer relevant to the modern world of industry and machines. So the relevance of Pea-cock's poetry to the contemporary world is not clearly analysed or stated. Indeed his lifelong scholarly interest in Greek, regardless of the political circumstances, is reconfirmed by his letter to Lord Broughton, over twenty years after Shelley's death:

> I have turned my corner of the railway carriage to account by making a strict vow to read nothing in it this summer but Greek. And in this way I have lately read through the Iliad, the Odyssey and Aeschylus: the result of which confirms me in the opinion that the march of Mechanus is one way and the march of Mind is another.[36]

The reading of Greek offers Peacock an escape from the onset of industrial mechanisation, from the new railway and the city of his work. This need to escape, confessed in 1843, seems no different from the sentiments Peacock expressed in 1817 and 1818.

Similarly Hunt appears not to have considered all the implica-tions of a politicised Greece. He adopts aspects of Arcadia, the happiness and the concentration upon physical pleasures and beauty, but he ignores the more controversial issues, the political egalitarianism and the advocation of free love. The 'Nuptial Songs of Julia and Manlius' closes the *Foliage* collection, and endorses the celebration of marriage:

> Venus without thee can plan
> No right pleasure: but she can
> Thou consenting. . . .[37]

Hymen, or marriage, is essential for the pleasures of Venus according to this poem. Hunt seems unconcerned by the acceptance of social hierarchy in the poem. Marriage is happily celebrated because it ensures children sprung from the guaranteed aristocratic stock:

> Take thy joy: and let us see
> Shortly a fair progeny,
> For a name so old as thine
> Must not be without its line.[38]

Although Hunt's *Rimini* had caused a stir among critics with its depiction of the incestuous love of Francesca for her husband's brother, there is no consistency behind Hunt's work. *Foliage* promotes marriage, and thus a meditated, political purpose behind Hunt's work seems less likely.

In comparison with the writing of Peacock, Hunt and Hogg, Shelley's treatment of pastoral is at once more sharply political and more ambiguous. More than a simple politics of style, ranged against the northern allegiance of the first-generation Romantics, Shelley's interpretation of pastoral reaches for something intrinsically radical, in tune with his fervent political beliefs, within the constitution of the pastoral world. But, on the other hand, his writing also reveals a subtlety, an acknowledgement of the dangerous seductiveness of Greece, which does not trouble the other writers. The seductiveness is both attractive and dangerous – attractive perhaps because dangerous. He wrote to Leigh Hunt that the 'Greek plays are perpetually tempting me to throw over their perfect and glowing forms the grey veil of my own words'.[39] This half-playful admission can be interpreted in two ways. On the one hand Greek literature distracts the reader from his true course of study just as a beautiful woman can seduce the male observer. Thus it is suggested that Greek literature constitutes an escape and a substitute for serious and important reading. On the other hand Greek literature offers subversive liberation, which troubles the reader just as the naked and perfect female statues embarrass the censorious reader who attempts to cover them up. It is in rebellion against these oppressive and unattractive readers that Shelley commented in his notebook while viewing the Hellenistic statues in the Uffizi gallery: 'Curse these figleaves! Why is a round tin thing more decent than a cylindrical marble one?'[40]

Shelley deliberately poses the question of the extent of subversiveness in the celebration of beauty. Greece as seductive, teasing woman occurs in another image in his letters. When Hogg was urging him to use a dictionary when reading Greek poetry, Shelley replied that by using a dictionary, he might 'lose the end while busied about the means; and exchange the embraces of a living and tangible Calypso for the image of a Penelope, who, though, wise, can never again be young'.[41] Hogg would attempt to fix the concept of Greece, so that its connotations of scholarship, antiquity and wisdom could be depended upon as unproblematic. The image of Greece for him remains unambiguous and simple, just as the Greece of Hunt and Peacock is a dependable realm to which they can escape. Shelley, in contrast, articulates the greater sophistication of the Greek metaphor, arguing that it cannot be fixed by a dictionary and that to attempt to do so would be to alter and falsely simplify the concept. It is as a seductive, dangerous Calypso that he would prefer to think of Greece. Calypso's reputation as a dangerous *femme fatale* implies the radical nature of Greece. But the contrast Shelley draws with Penelope is significant and makes problematic Calypso's attraction for him. Penelope, who is wise, would apparently keep Shelley too alert and thinking, while the young and beautiful Calypso, and the distant pastoral world of Greece she represents, tempt him, as they do Keats, with the possibility of sensual forgetfulness.

An acknowledgement of the erotic sensuousness of the pastoral world is evident in Shelley's representation of the hellenised Italy where he lived in exile. In a remark to Hogg, when he was attempting to persuade his friend to come out to visit him in Italy, he drew out the soporific effects of the pastoral world: 'I wonder none of you stray to the Elysian climate, and like the sailors of Ulysses, eat the Lotus and remain as I have done.'[42] Like the lotus, the pastoral world traps the reader till he is so drugged that he is unable to return to his proper destination and yet it is also pleasurable and indeed 'Elysian'. Italy is constructed as a substitute paradisical Greek island, the island of the Lotus-Eaters. Mary Shelley wrote, in her notes about the writing of *Prometheus Unbound*, that 'Italy enchanted Shelley; it seemed a garden of delight placed beneath a clearer and brighter heaven.' Shelley was particularly struck by southern Italy, originally colonised by the Greeks and named Magna Graecia before the Roman expansion. The landscape around Pompeii was described in Greek pastoral terms, with its blue skies and 'hypaethric' temples.[43] And yet Shelley repeatedly criticised the inhabitants of modern Italy and felt uncomfortable in their company: 'In Italy it is impossible to live contented; for the filthy modern inhabitants of what aught [*sic*] to be a desert sacred to days whose glory is extinguished, thrust themselves before you forever.'[44] Shelley would prefer the imaginative space of an idealised Italy, without the irritating distraction of contemporary inhabitants. John Barrell's argument that the pastoral genre represents country life within certain aesthetic 'constraints' and masks the genuine, historical condition of rural peasants is sadly apposite here.[45] In his imaging of Italy as a substitute pagan Arcadia, Shelley was in danger of suggesting by implication that the Greece of his poetry and imagination represented a retreat, a Lethean diversion from real political issues and social concerns.

HOMERIC HYMNS

Shelley's exploration of the expectations and assumptions surrounding Greek pastoral can be seen in his translation of the *Homeric Hymns*, started in his notebooks while at Marlow in the years 1817–18. It is significant that it is in translation that Shelley chose to explore pastoral. In his essay 'A Defence of Poetry', he argued that a complete transmission of poetry from one language to another was impossible. 'It were as wise to cast a violet into a crucible that you might discover the formal principle of its colour and odour, as seek to transfuse from one language to another the creations of a poet' was his famous line.[46] Rather than magical and unproblematic correspondence between one author and another or between the original text and the eventual translated text, translation depended crucially upon the decisions made by the translator. A contemporary translator, Charles Abraham Elton, in the preface to his translations from the classics, summed up the permutations well:

Some critics, even in the present day, appear to think that a translator has only to render the letter of his author, without adding or omitting; while others allow the latitude, not merely of consulting the genius of a modern language by synonymous or circuitous expressions, but of running a sort of rivalry with the original: improving the author where he is judged susceptible of improvement, and modifying his faults, and supplying his deficiencies, where he is judged faulty or deficient.[47]

Elton has identified the deception inherent in translation. It can be interpreted either as offering the possibility of absolute sameness or as proving so impossible that the translator is given full licence to render the text how he wishes, to assert power over the text. The deception can be seen to be similar to that found in the pastoral genre. In pastoral, as already discussed, there is a similar ambiguity over the distance between the author and his subject matter, over the dynamics of power between writer and text. An appreciation of the general implications of pastoral and of translation enhances a reading of Shelley's *Homeric Hymns*.

In many ways Shelley's *Homeric Hymns* are acutely political and engaged. His translation deliberately emphasises and draws out the political possibilities in the Greek texts. The mythical subjects of the poems – phenomena of nature such as the sun, the moon and the earth – are used to express the joyful celebration of the physical world. The moon, for example, is personified and the poem recounts the story of her typical day, beginning with her washing her limbs in the sea at dawn. This joy in itself could be interpreted politically, because of its freedom from moral comment. But Shelley also highlights the slight political comments in the poems by his choice of vocabulary. For example, the sun shines for everyone. The Greek expresses this as 'φαίνει θνητοίσι και' αθανάτοισι θεοίσιν' ('who gives both mortals light and all the immortals', George Chapman translates). But Shelley translates this as 'alluming the *abodes* / Of mortal men and the eternal gods'.[48] The addition of the word 'abodes' points out a connection between the men and the gods: they all live in 'abodes', and so share the light regardless of hierarchy. Similarly Shelley's translation of the 'Hymn to the Earth, the Mother of All' extends the simple catalogue in the Greek of all the things that are nourished by the earth – 'έκ σέο δ' εύπαιδές τε και εύκαρποι τελέθουσι' – with rich adjectives emphasising the abundance of earth for all of life:

All things that fly, or on the ground divine
Live, move, and there are nourished – these are thine;
These from thy wealth thou dost sustain; from thee
Fair babes are born, and fruits on every tree
Hang ripe and large, revered Divinity!⁴⁹

With the addition of *'every* tree' and 'ripe and large' fruits, a vision
is conjured up of the unlimited beneficence of earth bestowing gifts
regardless of distinction or the petty rules imposed by mankind. In
these poems, Greece offers the possibility of an open and democratic world.

Further politicising of the *Hymns* is evident in Shelley's translation of the 'Hymn to Venus'. About thirty years earlier, the 'Hymn
to Venus' had been presented in such a way as to suggest at least its
political possibilities, if not its actual political content. Isaac Rittson, schoolmaster and promising classical scholar, translated the
hymn in 1788 and published it with Joseph Johnson, the radical
London publisher. His notes to the translation point out the contrast between repressive Christianity and the liberal Greek culture
found in the poem:

It is true that the prevalence of stubborn custom, of particular
situation and of rigid authority, have produced (however paradoxical it may seem) more serious alterations, more sects and a
greater tenacity with regard to opinions, than the lax and supple
temper of Paganism was capable of.⁵⁰

The present establishment, intimately bound up with Christian
institutions, was 'stubborn' and 'rigid'; the ancient Greek world
was 'supple' and accommodating. To write about the Greek world,
symbolised in the figure of Venus, was in some way to oppose the
contemporary institutions. Venus in particular became a more subversive figure after the publication of Godwin's *Political Justice*,
which advocated the abolition of marriage as one more oppressive
institution which restricted the freedom of the individual.⁵¹ Free
love, promoted by Venus, was therefore a political act of rebellion
against all institutions.

Shelley's translation of the 'Hymn to Venus' manipulates the
depiction of love in the poem to make it more attractive and desirable. The figure of Venus is idealised while all who oppose her
are represented as hardened and cruel. In the Greek, Venus is

constructed as cunning, using tricks to capture her victims in love: 'οὐ γάρ οἱ εὔαδεν ἔργα πολυχρύσου'Αφροδίτης' ('whom all the gold of Venus never can tempt', according to Chapman's translation). But in Shelley's version, Venus is admirable. Her persuasion is tender but unnoticed: Minerva will not 'heed thy gentle flame'.[52] Vesta's renunciation of Venus's offer of love is made far more unnatural in Shelley's version. Where the Greek observes that she merely rejects marriage ('ἄντι γαμοιο'), Shelley translates 'for such gentle ties / Renounced'.[53] Venus becomes gentler and more beautiful, while the other goddesses who reject her love seem fiercer. They symbolise all the obstacles that threaten love – war, cruelty, institutional chastity. Diana's interest in 'φόρμιγγές τε χοροί τε διαπρύσιοί τ' ὀλολυγαι'('lyre music and dances and shrieks of delight') is completely erased from Shelley's picture, and he concentrates only on her hunting attributes. The manuscript version reads:

> . . . the shadows green
> Of the wild woods, the bow, the . . .
> And piercing cries amid the swift pursuit
> Of beasts among waste mountains, – such delight
> Is hers . . .[54]

The innocent 'ὀλολυγαι' of Artemisian festivals is here converted into the 'piercing cries' of the hunt, while the lyre and dances disappear in the textual hiatus. Similarly Minerva's 'fierce war and mingling combat' seem a cruel option when compared to Venus's 'gentle flame'. Even Vesta is wrong to renounce Venus when she chooses her chaste and isolated way of life: 'A virgin would she live mid deities divine'. The original Greek describes Vesta herself as divine; but Shelley has reversed the word order in his translation so that the goddesses who accept love and are liberated are divine, while Vesta who resisted is just a single word, a sterile virgin.[55]

Shelley's exaggeration of the depiction of sexual love in the 'Hymn to Venus' seems to convey an underlying political message that opposes the repressive measures of the government and the narrowness of Christian morality promoted by the politically powerful Church of England. Yet there is in Shelley's translation an ambivalence about the power of that female love. The uncertainty Shelley shows in his depiction of Venus reflects a general

uncertainty about the distance between the Greek pagan world
and the ordinary, public world. Venus makes claims about her
power.

> The laughter-loving Venus from her eyes
> Shot forth the light of a soft starlight smile,
> And boasting said, that she, secure the while,
> Could bring at will to the assembled Gods
> The mortal tenants of earth's dark abodes,
> And mortal offspring from a deathless stem
> She could produce in scorn and spite of them.[56]

Shelley translates the Greek 'φιλομμειδής' as 'laughter-loving' and
extends the Greek phrase 'ἡδὺ γελοιήσασα' (smiling sweetly) to
'from her eyes shot forth the light of a soft starlight smile'. While
'φιλομμειδὴς ζ traditionally denotes the sensual and inferior qualities
of Venus compared to those of her male colleague deities, Shelley
emphasises the attractive qualities of the epithet by this extended
image in the second line.[57] But then, immediately afterwards, his
Venus becomes more dominant and less caring. 'Φιλομμειδὴς' is
also the epithet given to the pre-Olympian Aphrodite, recalling her
origins as a pre-Olympian dawn goddess, in order to contrast her
with her later role as Olympian goddess and establishment figure,
denoted by the epithet Dios Thugater (Daughter of Zeus). Shelley's
presentation of Venus's assertiveness in the second half of this
passage apparently questions the lightness of 'φιλομμειδὴς by alluding to the powerful establishment qualities of the unstated 'Dios
Thugater'. After boasting ('ἐπευξαμένη' in the Greek), Venus is
then 'secure', a word which Shelley frequently used, along with
'serene' and 'safe', to connote an ease which stems from lack of
concern about the world, an ease like that of the Lotus-eaters drawn
to a pastoral paradise.[58] Venus's lack of concern is revealed in her
evident dismissal of mortals. To her, the greatest harm a god can
suffer is to be polluted by a proximity with the mortal inhabitants
of the world. Rather than a breaking of hierarchy noticed in the
'Hymn to the Sun', there is an accentuation of hierarchy here, a
hauling-up of the drawbridge under the tyrant Venus's withering
'scorn'.

   Venus's power over the world is similar to that of the Earth, in the
'Hymn to the Earth'. Shelley admittedly stresses the rich fertility of
the earth in this hymn, and a contrast is drawn between pagan

abundance and Christian austerity to make a political point about
the oppression of contemporary post-Napoleonic-war hardship:
'from thee / Fair babes are born, and fruits on every tree / Hang
ripe and large, revered Divinity!'[59] Yet Shelley also accentuates
the description in the Greek of the absolute control which
Earth exercises over the People – 'πότνια, σεῦ δ' ἔχεται δοῦναι
βίον ἠδ' ἀφελέσθαι / θνητοῖς ἀνθρώποισιν' – and extends it to two
full lines:

> The life of mortal men beneath thy sway
> Is held; thy power both gives and takes away![60]

The power of the gods in the Hymns is echoed in the power of
the translator over his text. On the one hand the power is enabling.
The distance from the original Greek text allows Shelley to present
his own interpretation, his own words. He is aware of his ineluct-
able difference from the Greek poet – like the difference between
immortal and mortal – and this gives him the power to act inde-
pendently, almost to write a new poem which in a sense liberates
the radical potential in the original. In the same way, Castor
and Pollux, in the 'Hymn to Castor and Pollux', intervene in
the mortal world to save some sailors struggling in a storm. Yet
the power is repressive. Shelley, in altering words and inserting
additional phrases, is attempting to impose his notion of Greece
upon the original poem, to assert control and to fix the text, to
'throw over' the 'grey veil' of his own words. Derrida has written
in *Dissemination* that translation stabilises meanings which are
admirably fluid and ambiguous in the original.[61] So in noticing
possible radical overtones – for example in the original description of Venus's treatment of other goddesses – and then emphasising these in the manipulation of language, Shelley has fixed
the ambiguous meaning as oppressively as Venus is in danger
of acting. Jenny Strauss Clay has argued that each of the *Homeric
Hymns* is concerned about 'the acquisition or redistribution of
timai within the Olympian cosmos' and that while power is chaoti-
cally distributed throughout the world before the *Hymns*, by
the end of the poem power has been ordered and stabilised
within the figures of the various deities.[62] Shelley's translation,
it seems, attempts to forestall that process and to stabilise
and appropriate power much earlier in his interpretation of the
poems.

THE BANQUET

The distance between the gods and the real world of mortals, which Shelley uncovers in his translations of the *Homeric Hymns*, articulates his concern over the distance between the poetry of Greek pastoral, however politically motivated, and the affairs of the 'real' world of the early nineteenth century. Shelley reveals the danger together with the excitement afforded by liberating paganism. He expresses the need constantly to renegotiate the relationship with Greek Arcadia, just as he was always re-examining his political position with Thomas Love Peacock and their different ideas about reading audiences and the role of poetry. One attempt to bridge the gap between Greece and the contemporary world was his translation of Plato's *Symposium*, which he undertook shortly after the first six *Homeric Hymns*, again with the interest in the political implications of Greek love.

The propagandist preface to the translation, 'A Discourse on the Manners of the Ancient Greeks', which in fact was never published, claims that the translation will reveal the real Greece uncensored, unaltered, so that it may be accessible to the general public, including the Greekless reader: 'There are many to whom the Greek language is inaccessible who ought not to be excluded by this prudery to possess an exact and comprehensive conception of the history of man.'[63] By this bid to appeal to all classes – regardless of their education and knowledge of Greek – Shelley sought to breach the inaccessibility and distance associated with Greece. He attempted to avoid the 'prudery' and to give his readers direct access to Greece by acknowledging the fact that the love discussed in the *Symposium* is homosexual love, the closest emotional bond in ancient Greek society. Whereas other translations, notably the translation by Floyer Sydenham recently edited by Thomas Taylor, substituted original references to male partners with descriptions of female partners, complete with all the additional accoutrements of female dress and behaviour, Shelley followed the Greek original and depicted a world of love between men.[64] But he could not bring himself to translate the passages describing casual sexual encounters between men and representing the possibility of male bonds based purely on physical attraction and relationship. For him, the Greeks were the most pure civilisation, the model for his political programme of liberation and paganism, and they could not be portrayed as victim to emotionless sexual drives. He defended his interpretation in the preface:

> We are not exactly aware . . . what the action was by which the Greeks expressed their passion. I am persuaded that it was totally different from the ridiculous and disquieting conceptions which the vulgar have formed on the subject.[65]

Shelley's expectations of Greek society altered his translation. Lovers who 'συγκαιακειμένοι και συγκειμενοι' ('sleep together and make love') are described more 'platonically' by Shelley. They are said to be 'delighted with the intercourse and familiarity of men'.[66] Similarly χαρίσασθαι', the Greek term for the sexual gratification of a lover, becomes an emotional rather than a physical bond for Shelley, translated vaguely as 'devotion': 'if indeed the devotion of a lover to his beloved is to be considered a beautiful thing'.[67]

Shelley's alterations of the text reveal the extent to which the Greek pastoral world of love and paganism is constructed by the nineteenth century writer as a means of negotiating the impossible distance of that world. Shelley's translation is radical in its effort to confront the homosexuality of Plato's world and to share this knowledge with a wide audience. But it is revealing that even in a translation which flaunts its grainy realism and documentary objectivity, elements of authorial censorship and bowdlerisation are evident. The facts of Greek homosexuality are too startling and alien to be transmitted in translation. The strange customs have to be ameliorated through understanding, through parallels with contemporary cultures. The male bonds are rendered more like understandable nineteenth- century male friendships, based upon the familiar concept of sympathy, and thus the distance between Shelley's world and the Greek world is bridged.

'HYMN TO MERCURY'

The questions raised about the translator's construction of a text in Shelley's *Banquet* seem barely conscious. The alterations of the text are made almost despite Shelley's best intentions to translate faithfully and objectively as he urges so passionately in the preface. But his 'Hymn to Mercury', written a couple of years later, is a far more self-conscious and sophisticated piece of translation. The poem raises more complicated questions about power and the relationship between a translator and his text than those raised in either the earlier hymns or the *Symposium*. Primarily it acknowledges a more plural, multiplicit pastoral world in the original text than is allowed in the earlier hymns. The earlier hymns presented a beautiful pastoral that could be interpreted either as escape or allegory. But the 'Hymn to Mercury' hints also at the dark side of things within pastoral, or, as Judith Haber might term it, the self-contradiction of the genre. The figure of Mercury is particularly ambiguous, a bizarre mixture of innocence and cruelty. Shelley points out this contrast in Mercury's treatment of the tortoise:

> . . . grasping it in his delighted hold,
> His treasured prize into the cavern old.
>
> Then scooping with a chisel of gray steel,
> He bored the life and soul out of the beast. –
> Not swifter a swift thought of woe and weal
> Darts through the tumult of a human breast
> Which thronging cares annoy – nor swifter wheel
> The flashes of its torture and unrest
> Out of dizzy eyes – than Maia's son
> All that he did devise hath featly done.
>
> (47–56)

'Delighted' and 'cavern old' are words added by Shelley to accentuate the romance of Mercury's world. The contrast between this romance and Mercury's killing of the tortoise is dramatic, accentuated as it is by Shelley's metaphor, which includes references to 'torture and unrest' in addition to the original Greek which simply described the speed of thought.[68]

Mercury is most alarming because he does not care about anything. His killing of the tortoise produces the first lyre, which plays such beautiful music – 'joyous and wild and wanton – such you may / Hear among revellers on a holiday' (70–1) – that the cruelty on which it is based is forgotten. Similarly, after the great sacrifice of Apollo's oxen, which the vegetarian Shelley overtly describes as 'butchery', Mercury jumps back into his cradle and 'lay innocent as a new-born child'. There is no moral framework in the poem, no clearcut oppositions between men and gods, between ethical choices. There is only Mercury's whimsical power, which even the

more stable god Apollo fears and propitiates. Mercury's power
seems to be like his lyre's music, necessarily based upon cruelty,
powerful because of its wildness and fluidity.

   This ambiguity of pastoral, which is both light and dark, innocent
and cruel, is reflected in the plurality of voices used in the translation. Mercury raises the issue by his questioning of the nature of
truth in his mendacious speech to Jupiter:

> Great Father, you know clearly beforehand
> That all which I say to you is sooth;
> I am a most veracious person, and
> Totally unacquainted with untruth.
>
> (485–8)

Shelley rhymes 'sooth' and 'untruth' here in a way which suggests
that they are interchangeable rather than polar opposites. It
becomes increasingly hard to tell in the magical confusion of the
poem what is truth and what is not, and where the standard of
meaning lies. Multiple voices jostle together, all apparently with
equal validity. Sometimes Shelley asserts lines as popular clichés.
'There he lay innocent as a new-born child, / As gossips say'
(198–9) occurs when Mercury is disclaiming knowledge of Apollo's
cows. 'Though it has been said / That you alive defend from magic
power' (42–3), Mercury says when he is persuading the tortoise to
sacrifice its life to make the lyre, thus hiding behind the narrative
frame of popular tradition. At other times Shelley appears to pastiche other discourses, the romantic, the sentimental, the pompous
language of institutions. This, for example, is the first description of
the tortoise:

> The beast before his portal at his leisure
> The flowery herbage was depasturing,
> Moving his feet in a deliberate measure
> Over the turf.
>
> (28–31)

This is reminiscent of Ezra Pound's *Homage to Sextus Propertius*,
which uses pastiche to distance ironically the translator from his
text and from what Pound saw as the tyrannical tradition of translation.[69] And in Shelley's translation here, something similar is
going on. Like mosaic pieces, the different voices are layered in the

poem dialogically, but the translator himself is hard to place.[70] It is worth noting that this is the one Greek poem which Shelley translated where both Latin and Greek names are used, so that even Mercury sometimes becomes Hermes. The translator has no apparent moral commitment or designs upon the text, but hides behind an endless array of voices and framing devices. He is as liberating as Mercury, but also as unreliable.

The translation of these poems, which are themselves about the allocation of power within the cosmos, thus throws light upon the dynamics of power involved in the writer's relationship with another culture, with a text from the past. The problems of distance and relevance, which both pastoral and translation pose and which the *Homeric Hymns* press most acutely upon the political writer, are confronted by textual alteration and manipulation, by allusion, pastiche, bricolage.[71] Far from being a retreat to Eden, to a world of beautiful and unproblematic gods, or a quick notebook exercise to join the political fashion of his friends, these translations by Shelley represent an experimental negotiation of the distance between his nineteenth-century world and the archaic Greek texts. They can be seen as a tentative but brave embrace of an extremely fiery and unpredictable Calypso, an exploration of the difficult relationship between poetry and politics.

ADONAIS

The *Homeric Hymns*, distant as they are, hold some immediate relevance to the contemporary world, since they describe the power of the gods (or poets) to intervene in human situations. *Adonais* is far less overtly political. The most extreme form of the personal pastoral poem, the pastoral elegy, it is perhaps least suited to form part of a political manifesto. But when put beside these earlier poetical experiments, the same issue of the immediacy or difference of the Greek pastoral world for contemporary concerns and feelings is evident. The poem is most obviously about death. Shelley was prompted to write it by the news of Keats's death from tuberculosis in Rome and he composed it consciously in the elegiac tradition, alluding in the form to the lament poems of Theocritus, Bion, Moschus and Milton. Shelley considered death a state to be both envied and abhorred. In Keats, he saw a symbol of death and at the same time the shadowy image of himself and his own condition. Keats the public poet to be lamented and Shelley the private poet lamenting become difficult to disentangle in the course of the poem, since the descriptions of them as sensitive poets hounded to death by an unsympathetic and unappreciative crowd are so similar. Indeed Shelley has been said to have 'consumed' Keats in his writing of *Adonais* by recognising what he perceived to be weaknesses in his own poetic persona and projecting them on to his recreation of Keats's life, thus resisting similarities between the two poets and obliterating or consuming Keats's separate, independent identity.[72] But while there are elements of resistance within the constructed relationship between the two poets in the poem, there is also a strong hint of envy. Keats has moved to a state where harsh reviewers cannot touch him and this Lethean state is highly attractive. Feelings of envy for Keats's condition motivate Shelley to stress the similarity between the two poets and hence the strong possibility that he will achieve the same state of 'forgetfulness'. Death is therefore presented as accessible and attractive. But death also involves the physical process of dying and the graphically described decomposition of the body. This abhorrent death is extremely alien to the living poet, causing a recognition not of the accessibility but of the mystery of death. Shelley is then compelled to stress, and to wish for, the dissimilarity between himself and Keats.

This dual response to death and to Keats the epitome of death, this envy and abhorrence, is similar to the ambiguous attitude towards the temptation posed by pastoral Greece explored earlier in the chapter. Death becomes at once tempting with the promise of liberation from care and yet also alarmingly destructive and powerful. Death is deceptively accessible to the understanding and yet also alien and incomprehensible, as alien indeed as the Greek pastoral world seems to the nineteenth-century poet. Jerrold Hogle has argued that writing about death is always bound up with 'the "stress" of transference' because death itself 'is always perceived as the "shadow of a likeness given" '.[73] In other words, death is represented by signs such as the tombstone or even the dead body, because the referent itself is absent, distanced, inexpressible. Writing about death is a form of translation, constructing the incomprehensible in the language of the comprehensible.

The language of the comprehensible for death is the formalised tradition of pastoral elegy. Ellen Zetzel Lambert, continuing the misapprehension of the simplicity of pastoral, has written that pastoral elegy 'offers us a vision of life stripped not of pain but of complexity'.[74] Yet if we acknowledge that the language of elegy depends upon a process of constructing a different world and of lamenting an empty body or sign, then pastoral elegy becomes as ambiguous and complicated as the pastoral translations already discussed. Elements of language might appear simple but the process of reaching that 'vision of life', of negotiating the relationship between life and death, or between this world and the imaginary Greek pastoral world, is highly problematic. Translation is a metaphor for the process, but the process is also achieved through translation, through the mediation of the elegiac tradition, other lamenting texts. Shelley's *Adonais*, therefore, must be read through the ideas of pastoral and translation and, in particular, through his translations of the elegies attributed to Bion and Moschus.

Shelley's translation of Bion's 'Lament for Adonis' eroticises the text. The poem already has elements of necrophilia within it, narrating as it does the grief of Aphrodite for her dead lover, Adonis. Unlike the elegies of Moschus or Milton, the poem explores the intensity of heterosexual love, as well as the pain of loss. Bion's version places that love and grief within the context of the cycles of nature and the developing rituals of mourning. Love is as natural as the attractions of one season to the next, even if, with the allusions to the legend of Persephone, that nature itself contains hints of sadness. But in Shelley's version there is something even more intense and unsettling in the love which is displayed in response to death:

> . . . . . Aphrodite
> With hair unbound is wandering through the woods,
> 'Wildered, ungirt, unsandalled – the thorns pierce
> Her hastening feet and drink her sacred blood.
> Bitterly screaming out, she is driven on
> Through the long vales; and her Assyrian boy,
> Her love, her husband, calls – the purple blood
> From his struck thigh stains her white navel now,
> Her bosom, and her neck before like snow.
>
> (16–24)

In the original Greek Adonis's blood stains his own navel, not Aphrodite's, in an isolated tableau. But Shelley's version suggests that now the lovers mingle their blood where before they mingled kisses. There is a Swinburnian sensuousness in the final lines, which juxtapose Adonis's blood with Aphrodite's beauty, his 'purple blood' and her 'white navel'.[75] Indeed the 'sacred blood' of Aphrodite, mentioned several lines before, is altered by this later image so that it becomes associated with death, with the 'sacredness' of the spilt blood of the Crucifixion. Here Shelley is 'half in love' with a very uneaseful death.[76]

Moschus's 'Lament for Bion' has a more formal and formulaic structure than Bion's 'Lament for Adonis'. The elegy is now not for a mythical hero but for a poet, and thus to a certain extent the poem has become self-referential, a poem about the composition of an elegiac lament or about poetry in general.[77] Shelley's translation emphasises and questions the ornamental construction of the poem even further. For example, while the Greek calls simply on the plants to mourn, Shelley accentuates the anthropomorphising of nature:

> Let every tender herb and plant and flower,
> From each dejected bud and drooping bloom,
> Shed dews of liquid sorrow, and with breath
> Of melancholy sweetness on the wind
> Diffuse its languid love.
>
> (4–8)

The accentuated anthropomorphic nature in Shelley's version highlights the artifice of elegiac writing, the extent to which the connection between nature and mortal life, which is designed to console in the elegiac tradition, is in fact created and determined by human desire. For there are hints in Shelley's translation that he perceives the connection to be problematic and unreliable precisely because it is not a natural connection but determined by human language. 'Augment your tide, O streams, with fruitless tears' (2), the poem begins, the 'fruitless' crucially being Shelley's addition to the original text. A few lines later the old consolations, myths such as are found in Ovid's *Metamorphoses*, prove to be of little comfort:

> . . . and thou, O hyacinth,
> Utter thy legend now – yet more, dumb flower,
> Than 'ah! alas!' – thine is no common grief.
>
> (10–12)

The Greek is content to recall the legend, considering the mythical lament of the hyacinth to be sufficient in Bion's case. But Shelley requires more than 'Ah! Alas!' and recognises the futility in expecting any kind of sufficient response from what is after all only a 'dumb flower'.

The descriptions of terrifying ritual and the formal self-referentiality in Bion's and Moschus's poems give the lie for ever to the notion that pastoral is simple or ideal, even at its origins. But Shelley's translations further accentuate the problematic elements within the poems. The pastoral elegy, through his rendition, becomes a site in which desires for similarity and anxieties about unalienable difference are played out. These translations inform the even more free translation of *Adonais*. For example, the erotic treatment of death found in Shelley's translation of Moschus features again in *Adonais*. The description of Keats's burial place is sensuously beautiful, as Shelley admits – quoting Keats – in the preface: 'It might make one half in love with death, to think one should be buried in so sweet a place.' Death is 'the amorous Deep' who refuses to release Keats after his successful seduction. Keats is feminised here in his refiguration as Persephone snatched by husband Death, and thus the envy which Shelley feels for his deathly state is further tinged with erotic attraction. But the seduction of death is not only based upon sexual attraction but is conveyed by the tempting possibility of sameness.[78] Death, it is implied, shares the same conditions as Nature. For the first half of the poem Keats's death is mirrored by the withering of plants and flowers and various natural phenomena as they supposedly mourn for him. They mourn in human terms. Morning, for example,

> .... sought
> Her eastern watchtower, and her hair unbound,
> Wet with the tears which should adorn the ground,
> Dimmed the aerial eyes that kindle day.
>
> (120–3)

The perfectly explicable events of a wet morning, when the sun never emerges from behind dark clouds, are imagined here in human terms as signs of mourning. Thus it is implied that if death and nature share similarities and that nature acts in human terms, then logically death and the human condition are similar, closely allied.

But there are hints that this relationship of sameness is not natural but constructed. In stanza 10, one of the morning Dreams is shown to be deceiving herself about the nature of death. She calls out to the others:

> 'Our love, our hope, our sorrow, is not dead;
> See, on the silken fringe of his faint eyes,
> Like dew upon a sleeping flower, there lies
> A tear some Dream has loosened from his brain.'
> Lost Angel of a ruined Paradise!
> She knew not 'twas her own.
>
> (84–9)

For a moment Keats is imagined to be alive and sharing in the grief of nature. But this is the Dream's own construction of this vision, signified by the fact that the tear which she spots is not that of Keats but her own, dropped upon his dead body.

Anthropomorphised flowers and dreams assert the closeness and human qualities of death but prove to be deceptive attempts to hide the hideousness of death beneath. Keats's poems are said to be 'like flowers that mock the corse beneath' in the second stanza. By implication the 'flowers' or the standard topoi of the elegiac tradition similarly mock the 'corse beneath' or the task of consoling through the myth of the closeness of death.[79] Flowers and ritualised grief cannot penetrate to Keats's impervious condition: 'O, weep for Adonais! though our tears / Thaw not the frost which binds so dear a head!' (2–3) Again and again the poem contrasts the activity of the living flowers with the 'cold' or 'icy' condition of the dead Keats. Keats is cold and secure: 'that unrest which men miscall delight, / Can touch him not and torture not again' (354–5). His distance from contagion recalls the security of Venus, in Shelley's translation of the Hymn, whose distance from mortal contagion we argued proves problematic and ambiguous.

With the acknowledgement of the difference of death, something which nature cannot hide, there emerges the recognition of the divided fragmented condition of the pastoral elegy. Within the ornamentation of the traditional elegy lurks the physical condition of death:

> The leprous corpse touched by this spirit tender
> Exhales itself in flowers.
>
> (172–3)

The macabre shock of death within the elegiac description undermines the consoling feeling of the closeness of death. Shelley draws
upon his early Gothic interests for phrases like 'cold hopes swarm
like worms within our living clay' (351) and the 'Invisible Corruption' (67) which begins the process of decomposition while the
body is still warm and beautiful. The 'corruption' is invisible and
also significantly inexpressible. Death, despite the illusions of rituals and elegy, is impossibly alien and unknowable. The apprehen-
sion of death is possible only through the bizarre juxtapositions in
Shelley's poem, which suggest a black hole of meaning in the
interstices of language. This must account for the shocking juxtapositions, for example, in his description of the Protestant cemetery
in Rome:

> Go thou to Rome – at once the Paradise,
> The grave, the city and the wilderness;
> And where its wrecks like shattered mountains rise
> And flowering weeds and fragrant copses dress
> The bones of Desolation's nakedness
> Pass . . .
>
> (433–8)

Rome, the city of paradoxes and ruins, epitomises here the ambiguous state of death, known to us through the curious combination of
'fragrant copses' and 'Desolation's bones'.

   The subverting of expectation afforded by the occasional glimpses at the Otherness of death allows Shelley to re-read Keats and
his treatment of pastoral. Keats's Endymion becomes Actaeon, the
supposed Shelleyan figure – 'one frail form' – who joins the mour-
ners:

> . . . he, as I guess,
> Had gazed on Nature's naked loveliness,
> Actaeon-like, and now he fled astray
> With feeble steps o'er the world's wilderness,
> And his own thoughts, along that rugged way,
> Pursued, like raging hounds, their father and their prey.
>
> (274–9)

Keats's Endymion manages finally to achieve a successful union
with the Moon goddess, albeit in an insubstantial way, unsupported

by much conviction in the language. Shelley's Actaeon figure, in contrast, is forever severed from the divine world, having only once 'gazed upon Nature's naked loveliness'. The Actaeon figure thus highlights poignantly the gulf separating mortal and immortal or the poet and the pastoral realm of the imagination, a gulf which Keats optimistically bridges. Similarly Keats's 'cold pastoral' in his 'Ode on a Grecian Urn' becomes even more distanced and unsettling in Shelley's rewriting:

> One from a lucid urn of starry dew
> Washed his light limbs as if embalming them;
> Another clipt her profuse locks, and threw
> The wreath upon him, like an anadem,
> Which frozen tears instead of pearls begem.
>
> (91–5)

Keats's urn poses the problem of writing about Greece because of its silence and inscrutability. He is compelled to draw upon a lengthy imaginative ekphrasis, rather like Shelley's 'fragrant copses' dressing the bones of the dead, in order to compensate for the silence of the urn. Here, however, the urn itself becomes part of the mocking ritual, used to cover the dead body with 'starry dew'. It cannot penetrate to the 'frozen' state of the dead but becomes part of the sinister embalming process, turning that pastoral still colder.

The temptation and the abhorrence of death, which are juxtaposed in *Adonais*, replicate the ambiguous relationship of the poet to Greece. The pastoral world of Bion and Moschus, like that of the *Homeric Hymns*, confuses with its possibilities of nearness and its alienating distance. It is also used in an attempt to mediate that distance, to console and translate the terrifying shock of death. But the consolation is deceptive. Pastoral flowers mock rather than contain the 'corpse beneath'. Translation, while attempting to negotiate distance, opens up the gulf still wider. Moschus's formality throws new light on the chaos of death which no formality can reach. And so, in the final stanzas of the poem, Shelley departs from the elegiac tradition, the language of consolation and sympathy, and moves rather to the language of inspiration, as he is physically carried off in his boat, 'darkly, fearfully, afar'. Critics have described the end of the poem as an apocalyptic 'rebirth' or a religious 'apotheosis', but it seems more

1: 'Comparing the opposite customs of Europe and Asia': The Erechtheum, James Stuart

2: 'Pure, simple and sublime': View of the Pnyx and Acropolis at Athens, William Haygarth

4: 'De Grekes were godes!': The Artist in Despair over the Magnitude of Ancient Fragments, Henry Fuseli

3: 'Mid deities divine': The Hymn to Venus, Bodleian Shelley Manuscripts e.12.

5: 'The Cross against the Crescent': The Massacre of Scio, Eugene Delacroix

6: 'The idea of Greece which keeps us together': The Shelley Memorial. Onslow Ford

uncertain than that.[80] Shelley abandons the deceptive mediation of Bion and Moschus for the ambiguous and fitful inspiration of Plato and Pindar.

Plato famously banished poets from his Republic because they produced in art only a copy of a copy and so were thrice removed from reality. His qualms about art were derived from an unease about the distance between poetry and the subject being described. These qualms were confronted further in the *Ion*, which Shelley translated. In the *Ion*, writing was no longer a question of imitation but of inspiration: 'beautiful poems are not human nor from man but divine and from the gods', according to Shelley's translation.[81] The final lines of *Adonais* appropriate the Platonic ideas of inspiration and a transcendent ideal world to invest with additional force some of the Pindaric metaphors of sailing or being blown for the writing of poetry.

> The breath whose might I have invoked in song
> Descends on me; my spirit's bark is driven,
> Far from the shore, far from the trembling throng
> Whose sails were never to the tempest given.
> (487–90)

The wildness associated with Pindar's writing style is combined with the transcendence of Plato in order to suggest the possibility of reaching the other world of Keats, death and the pastoral. 'Breath' is no longer dependent upon imitation or closeness for successful description, but can achieve great imaginative leaps through its own divine sources.

But inspiration or breath is unpredictable and fragile, and so the ending of the poem is left open-ended and uncertain. Pindar's poems carry always the dark undertones of the transience of all human life and endeavour, which put in perspective the creativity of the narrating poet. Plato's attitude to Ion is ambiguous and possibly ironic. Can such divine madness be trusted? Certainly it seems that Shelley's Platonic transcendence is based upon faith and human will rather than on the logical dialectic grounding advocated by Plato. And if transcendence is based only upon faith and hopes, can it be depended upon to last, to be sustained?[82] Shelley's other translation of sailing to an unknown, distant world – a sonnet by Dante – appears to reach a comforting escapist world of timeless communion with past spirits:

> Guido, I would that Lapo, thou, and I,
> Led by some strong enchantment, might ascend
> A magic ship, whose charmed sails should fly
> With winds at will where'er our thoughts might wend,
> So that no change, nor any evil chance
> Should mar our joyous voyage; but it might be,
> That even satiety should still enhance
> Between our hearts their strict community.[83]

Shelley wills a closeness of connection here between himself and
the Dantean text, between his modern position and the idealised
pastoral world, although the tenuousness of the will is implied by
the optative 'I would that' at the beginning. But *Adonais* does not
deceive with notions of comfort, consolation or closeness. The deed
is done: 'my spirit's bark is driven'. Either the distant, pastoral and
untranslatable world of death has been reached by the daring of
Shelley's inspiration, or he has arrived at obliteration, at the finality
of expression.

    Shelley's pastoral texts, whether describing the first beautiful
dawn of the world when the divine roles were only just being
allocated or relating the traditional mourning rituals for a dead
friend, articulate generally the problems of the distance between
the pagan Greek world and early-nineteenth century Britain with
its pressing political concerns. The distance is both celebrated and
resisted, according to the need to write allusively or directly to the
readership. In the next chapter, I will explore more specifically one
of the key ways in which Greece was constructed positively as
distant and different – namely in its orientalisation.

4

'Hope beyond Ourselves': Orientalising Greece

Savages are distressed at the waning of the moon and attempt to counteract it by magical remedies. They do not realise that the shadow which creeps forward till it blots out all but a fragment of the shining disc, is cast by their world. In much the same way we civilised people of the West glance with pity or contempt at our non-Western contemporaries lying under the shadow of some stronger power, which seems to paralyse their energies by depriving them of light.

A.J. Toynbee, *The Western Question in Greece and Turkey*, 1922

Thou demandest what is Love. It is that powerful attraction towards all that we conceive or fear or hope beyond ourselves when we find within our own thoughts the chasm of an insufficient void and seek to awaken in all things that are, a community with what we experience within ourselves.

Shelley: 'Essay on Love'

One of the most arresting moments in Euripides' play *The Bacchae* is the first entry of the chorus of Bacchic women. Whooping their way across the stage, the women appear wild and uncontrollable. Smelling of wine and the untamed countryside outside the city walls, they are liberated from formal constraints. More crucially, they have been orientalised, overwhelmed by the god Dionysus who has returned from Asia where he introduced his dances and rites. The women's rituals are typically eastern and mysterious, at once seductive and barbaric. Pentheus the king resists the new religion as a threatening import from foreign lands, while at the same time recognising its attractions. As he prepares his disguise so that he can watch the women undetected, it is unclear whether he is adopting the alien women's attire or whether he is releasing the latent femininity within him, a femininity evident in Dionysus's ambiguous identity. In Pentheus's confrontation of the Bacchic women and subsequent seduction by them, the play dramatises the polarities between male and female, between west and east. Pentheus's defence of his city against the external female threat seems a classic case of the western Greek *polis* against eastern barbaric hordes.[1] Yet once Pentheus has yielded to the suggestions of Dionysus, he opens up eastern characteristics previously repressed in himself and loses his fixed sense of identity. The tearing apart of his body by the frenzied Maenads dramatises literally the fragmenting of identity Pentheus has experienced under the pressure of the clash and indistinction of cultures.

Edward Said cites Euripides' *Bacchae* in his *Orientalism* as a prime example of the western domination of the east.[2] Ancient Greece, Said argues, provides one of the earliest examples of the desire of western nations to influence and exercise 'authority over the Orient'.[3] According to Said, Pentheus typifies western man's ability to subjugate Asia. Yet Pentheus, besides being far from victorious, is hardly certain of his western identity. Indeed the clearcut polarities between self and other, familiar and unknown, are completely undermined in the play and torn apart. Within the microcosm of the play, it is possible to see a wider battle for the identity of Greece. While Said argues that Greece is unequivocally western, there are as many indications in the play that she could be considered eastern, that she indeed feared and resisted her eastern qualities.[4]

The instability of the Greek image has already been noted in previous chapters. The distance between the nineteenth-century writer and the world of ancient Greece, it was argued in Chapter 3, rendered it difficult to maintain control over the appropriation and interpretation of the Greek world. The present chapter considers how the resulting instability was in part articulated in the confusion over whether Greece was to be considered as west or east, whether she was 'one of us' or 'one of them'. Was Greece to be used as a confirmation of western values? Or did she challenge with her eastern difference? How could the politically liminal position of Greece be expressed in terms of Orientalism, of cultural difference?

Traditionally, studies of Hellenism or Orientalism have viewed the relationship between different cultures as benign and non-political. Raymond Schwab's extensive study of the influence of the Orient on western literature was content to describe the influence 'enriching' for the west and unproblematic.[5] But now any study of the relationship of different cultures must take account of Said's arguments in *Orientalism* that the process of gaining influence from and knowledge of other cultures cannot be benign, but participates in an undeclared, subconscious strategy of manipulation and control. Schwab's Oriental Renaissance marks, for Said, the emergence of the British imperialistic dominance over the east. Said's work, politicising cultural relations, has been as enlightening as the feminist studies of the last two decades which have politicised the relationship between the sexes and the representation of women. Indeed, in the last few years, the study of cultural relations has been drawing closer to feminist criticism. In an article updating his *Orientalism*, Said has admitted, 'we can now see that Orientalism is a praxis of the same sort, albeit in different territories, as male gender dominance, or patriarchy, in metropolitan societies'.[6] Said advocates linking his work on the construction of the east by the west and the politicisation of orientalism with what he sees as similar work undertaken by feminists and Black studies critics on the manipulation of the weak by the strong. Among feminist critics, Gayatri Chakravorty Spivak has pioneered the movement to extend the application of the term 'the Other' – which has been adopted by French feminists to refer to the feminine – to the wider meaning of the dispossessed and controlled, whether that means women, the poor, the East or other ethnic groups.[7]

In this chapter I wish to draw upon the new vocabulary of cultural and gender difference in order to explore the complexity of the difference which Greece presented to Shelley and his contemporaries. The inclusion of some feminist approaches in this study of the orientalising of Greece serves to illuminate more fully the challenge to the poetic self which Greece poses. Pentheus's identity and fixed knowledge of himself disintegrates under the seductive power and chaotic violence of the eastern Bacchae. In a similar way, many of the certainties of Romantic poetry – the creative poetic mind, the desire for unity – are questioned when confronted by a different, resisting subject such as a foreign country or a strange woman. Some recent work on Shelley's orientalism has focused upon his use of mythology, and his interest in Eastern religions and stories.[8] My concern is rather with the question of relationship which the study of orientalism raises and with the metaphorical impact of cultural difference upon the writing of poetry. The work in which Shelley explored the complicated epistemological problem of relationship most fully was *Epipsychidion*. So after examining the general confusion over whether Greece was to be represented imaginatively as occidental or oriental – a confusion which focused the general anxiety about the relationship with the ancient world, assumptions of self identity, and latent hopes for a world 'beyond ourselves' – I will concentrate more specifically upon Shelley's response to a culturally destabilised Greece, considering in particular his most seductive and orientalising work, *Epipsychidion*.

ORIENTATION

When Romantic period writers wished to express the western orientation of Greece, they often contrasted it precisely with the east. For example, William Robertson's *An Historical Disquisition concerning the Knowledge which the Ancients had of India*, which Shelley ordered from his bookseller in 1812, recounted the Greek conquests of the east and suggested that the subsequent trading links were dependent upon this early dominance. While contrasting Greece with the east, writers also endeavoured to align it with Britain and with perceived western values. Greece was constructed as the important origin of western civilisation, and for this reason its childlike qualities were emphasised.[9] Schiller re-claimed a value for the 'naive' – 'its pure and free strength, its integrity, its eternity' – identifying it as a childlike quality exhibited by the ancient Greeks.[10] Like the children in Wordsworth's poems, the classical Greek age was constructed as the innocent childhood of western civilisation. 'Greece was as a hermit-child', Shelley wrote in *Hellas*; and earlier, corresponding with a friend in 1819, he considered what would have happened to western civilisation if the unruly adolescent years of the Roman empire had not intervened:

> Were not the Greeks a glorious people? Who knows whether under the steady progress which philosophy and social institutions would have made (for in the age to which I refer their progress was both rapid and secure,) among a people of the most perfect physical organisation, whether the Christian religion would have arisen, or the barbarians have overwhelmed the wrecks of civilisation which had survived the conquests and tyranny of the Romans – What then should we have been?[11]

If the historical conquests and spread of religion had not happened, Shelley argues, the relationship with Greece would have been continuous and unproblematic. Greece is mythical and timeless, available for iconic appropriation, while the historical reality of Rome interrupts the natural continuum.[12] Significantly this passage reaches a climax with the question of what 'we should have been'. Greece is chiefly important to Shelley here for its potential contribution to western culture and 'our' nature.

The occidental Greece was lent further Britishness by the imposition in its construction of certain characteristics which Said designates as traditionally western, characteristics such as chastity, purity, perfection, logic, restraint. Incidentally, these qualities are the masculine qualities which Hélène Cixous has identified in her analysis of the gendered polarisation of the world.[13] Greece represented the highest pinnacle of western achievement, the 'ideal prototype of everything excellent and lovely'. *The Monthly Magazine* gave voice to the widely-held view of the excellence of Greek literature: 'The Perfection of the Writings of the Ancients has been a universal theme of admiration. The works of the Greek and Roman are truly looked upon as Models of Perfection, as miracles of Genius, and as efforts of god-like minds.'[14] The poet William Haygarth went further, representing Greece as the haven of the literary muses, the guardians over national literature in English. Haygarth's poem, *Greece* (1814), which was written 'in the country it attempts to delineate', reads like a homecoming, with all the familiar names and places from Classical literature remembered.[15] But significantly, in order to achieve this sense of a literary *nostos*, he dismisses the eastern aspects of the Greek landscape, and emphasises instead the purity and restraint of the countryside:

> ... Nature here
> Wears not a smile upon her lips to lure
> Pleasure's soft vot'ries, they would scorn her chaste,
> Her mild enjoyments; they, in fragrant groves,
> And flow'ry meads, and shady bow'rs, may hold
> Their frantic orgies; but she calls the sons
> Of Virtue, those whose spirits soar beyond
> The narrow prison of their earthly frame,
> To scenes more glorious; those whose souls are sooth'd
> With more than human visions, them she leads
> Amidst her solitudes, till all their thoughts,

Refin'd by contemplation of her works,
Become, like her, pure, simple, and sublime.[16]

Haygarth's description seems to be part of the widespread alteration at this time of the southern Greek landscape into a chaste
northern scene identified by Martin Bernal in *Black Athena*.[17] The
aspects of landscape associated with warm climates, and so the
stereotypical east, have been repressed in his poem in favour of
the bracing northern virtue which makes the scene appear British,
just as his metre eschews the fashionable ornamentation of rhyme
for the restraint of blank verse, adopted by 'the greatest masters
of English poetry'.[18] Winckelmann also seemed to be thinking of
a northern climate blown on to the southern Greek landscape
when he articulated his belief in the surpassing beauty of the
Greeks:

> The most beautiful body of ours would perhaps be as much
> inferior to the most beautiful Greek one, as Iphicles was to his
> brother Heracles. The forms of the Greeks, prepared to beauty, by
> the influence of the mildest and purest sky, became perfectly
> elegant by their early exercises.[19]

Winckelmann denies the hot exotic climate of Greece and prefers
the more obviously western, and northern, 'mildest and bluest
sky'. Wordsworth re-imagined the ancient Greek climate, writing in the *Excursion* of the 'lively Grecian' living 'in a land of hills /
Rivers and fertile plains, and sounding shores / Under a cope of
sky more variable', a description which provoked a wry comment
from Byron about Wordsworth's lack of knowledge of the real
Greece.[20] Shelley's description of the Greek colonial city of Pompeii
also offers a westernised climate, and a sense of the infectious
quality of beauty and purity prevalent in Greece, which he
must have gleaned from reading Fuseli's translation of Winckelmann:

> This scene was what the Greeks beheld. (Pompeii you know was
> a Greek city). They lived in harmony with nature, and the inters-
> tices of their incomparable columns were portals as it were to
> admit the spirit of beauty which animates this glorious universe
> to visit those whom it inspired. If such is Pompeii, what was
> Athens?[21]

Shelley's conception of the Greek climate was drawn from the ancient Greek colonies in Italy, and in this he was not unusual. The traditional Grand Tour of the young British gentleman did not reach as far as Greece, but gathered its classical experience from Italy.[22] The model for Josiah Wedgwood's classical vases derived from Italy and his pottery works near Manchester were named Etruria. The artist for the designs of the Greek figures on Wedgwood's vases, John Flaxman, spent seven years studying the art in Rome as part of the Fuseli neo-classical circle. It is noticeable in Flaxman's lectures, which he delivered to the Royal Academy from 1810 till his death in 1826, that he preferred the late, Roman Hellenistic statues – such as the Laocoön and Niobe – to the classical Greek statues of Phidias and Praxiteles.[23] Goethe likewise drew inspiration for his Greek-influenced poetry from his travels in Italy, where Greek culture had been imported by the Romans secondhand. And Winckelmann was also drawn to Rome, writing his famous theories about Greek art after studying Roman copies in Italy rather than Greek originals in Greece.[24] Thus Italy, which had been the central source for European culture ever since the Renaissance, was adopted as a symbol of westernised Greece. It acted as a mediator between the west and Greece, to assert the connection. It is true that Italy itself was increasingly being considered as different from Britain, France and Germany, from the centres of Romanticism.[25] As observed in the previous chapter, Madame de Staël's polarisation of European culture into the Latinate south and the Romantic north influenced the conception of Italy as different. Continuing Staël's account, the Swiss J.L. Sismondi analysed Italian literature in his work *A Historical View of the Literature of the South of Europe*, while promising a sequel on Northern literature, mainly from Britain and Germany.[26] The fashionable distinction between north and south is brought out in de Staël's novel *Corinna*, in which Italy is not incorporated within the British, western tradition, but constantly contrasted with it. It is warm, exotic, uninhibited and even described as 'Oriental.'[27] As a result, the use of Italy to harness the even more exotic nature of Greece was itself far from unproblematic. And yet the qualities which Shelley attributes to Italy are western. For him, the inhabitants were alien but the country itself radiated the light and purity which his contemporaries most admired.

Greece, however, was also perceived to be eastern, different and unattainable. It was represented as exotic and mysterious.

Much was acknowledged to be left to the imagination through lack of knowledge.[28] Often the mystery of Greece was exemplifed by the description of the eastern custom of keeping women indoors away from the prying eyes of men. Tales set in Greece, as in India, often involve descriptions of royal harems. Ida is sent to a harem briefly in Sydney Owenson's novel set in Greece, *Ida of Athens*.[29] One of the stories in Thomas Moore's *Lalla Rookh*, 'The Veiled Prophet of Khorassan', describes a harem in which one woman from each of the conquered kingdoms in the prince's empire is imprisoned, thus emphasising the epistemological link between gender and culture in which hidden women symbolise distant countries.[30] But as well as appearing hidden and mysterious, Greece also appeared to be physically beautiful, exuding presence. Just as the feminine principle for feminist critics traditionally is represented by the body and material concerns – and the masculine principle is represented by the mind and abstract concerns – so Greece and the east were associated with uninhibited, erotic beauty. Shelley wrote to Hogg of 'the bowers of Greek delight', echoing the 'bowers' of Haygarth's poem, which Haygarth had dismissed as not characteristically Greek, and so suggesting that Greece is an exotic place of physical pleasure.[31] Byron's *Oriental Tales* also rejected the Haygarthian depiction of Greece as a land of restraint and purity. His tales, set in Greece, depict a world of primitive values of love, violence and revenge, a world in which eastern passion is more important than western decorum.

Greece's eastern qualitites were attractive not only because they were different and unwestern but also because they suggested an asylum for escape. Greece became associated with an ideal eastern paradise, an original Eden, appearing more ideal because, like the Orient, it was distant and inaccessible.[32] Shelley depicts a Greek paradisic island in his *Epipsychidion*: 'It is an isle under Ionian skies / Beautiful as a wreck of Paradise.'[33] Byron, despite what critics have considered his greater sense of realism, associated Greece with an eastern paradise too, and emphasised the distance and inaccessibility this denoted:

> I shall leave England for good . . . I shall find employment in making myself a good Oriental scholar. I shall retain a mansion in one of the fairest islands, and retrace at intervals, the most interesting portions of the East.[34]

One of Byron's acquaintances, Robert Dallas, in his *Recollections of the Life of Lord Byron, 1810–1814*, locates Byron's 'fairest island' more specifically: 'He would frequently talk of going to reside at Naxos, in the Grecian Archipelago, to adopt the eastern costume, and to pass his time in studying the Oriental languages a bit.'[35]

As well as constructing a general so-called eastern atmosphere, writers in the period sought to express Greek cultural difference through accounts of what were perceived to be specifically eastern beliefs or customs. Much of the purpose behind William Jones's work is to prove that the ancient Greek and Indian religions were closely linked, that there were many similarities between their deities and myths.[36] His studies of Hindu culture pioneered a general move towards syncretic mythology, the task of establishing parallels between mythological systems to suggest unity behind all religions. Similar efforts were made to find parallels in literature. Richard Hole pointed out the similarity between eastern and Greek literary tales in *Remarks on the Arabian Nights*.[37] And in his eastern gothic tale *Vathek*, William Beckford made explicit parallels between what was to him the mildly horrifying custom of applying make-up in India and that in Greece:

> It was an ancient custom in the East, and still continues, to tinge the eyes of women, particularly those of a fair complexion, with an impalpable powder, prepared chiefly from crude antimony, and called formah. . . . This pigment, when applied to the inner surface of the lids, communicates to the eye (especially if seen by the light of lamps) so tender and fascinating a languor, as no language is competent to express. Hence the epithet ΙΟΒΛΕΦΑΡΟΣ, attributed by the Greeks to the Goddess of Beauty.[38]

Beckford glides here from Indian custom to Greek custom without comment as if there were no difference between them. For him, the seductive, feminine, peculiar behaviour is characteristic of all eastern culture. Significantly, Madame de Staël also commented on the custom of painting the eyes in her description of Italian Orientalism. She is faintly dismissive of the custom, which can only deceive when observed under candlelight.

While Greece was imaginatively conceived as both west and east, the historical and geographical reality behind this image cannot be ignored. Since the war against Persia in the early fifth century BC, Greece had fluctuated between conflict and uneasy integration in its relation with Asia. The fortunes of war dictated whether the country was to be considered European or Asian. Byron summed up the situation:

> Where Greece was – No! she still is Greece once more.
> One common cause makes myriads of one breast,
> Slaves of the East, or helots of the West.[39]

Greece's geographical location on the boundary of Europe and Asia allowed it to serve as the measure of the clash between east and west. The late-eighteenth century historian, John Gillies, in his history of Greece, pointed this out, describing it as 'the happy position of the country which, forming, as it were, a frontier of Europe with Asia, is divided only by a narrow extent of sea from Egypt and Syria.'[40] Gillies, considering eastern influence as beneficial and culturally enriching, interprets the state of Greece as 'happy'. But William Mitford, writing in 1814, gave a very different description of the situation between east and west in Greece. Writing about the Persian war in the early fifth century BC, Mitford argues that it was 'during those great transactions in Greece and its eastern colonies, which decided, for the time, the fate of Europe and Asia, and then first displayed that superiority of the former over the rest of the world which it still maintains', that the relationship between west and east, based upon war, conquest and dominance, was established.[41]

Conquest certainly dictated the early-nineteenth century identity of Greece. It cannot be ignored, when the literary associations of Greece with the east are considered, that Greece was part of the formidable Ottoman Empire at this time. Travellers to Greece encountered Turkish customs there as much as European.[42] William Gell wrote enthusiastically of his experiences, in the typical glossy style of a guide-book:

> There is [no country] which offers an opportunity of witnessing and comparing with so much ease the opposite customs of Europe and Asia: or of changing the scene with such rapidity: for when the classic traveller is satisfied with the simplicity of the heroic ages in the mountains of Arcadia, he may descend in the course of one hour into the plain, and, drinking coffee in

a cup set with rubies, realise the splendid visions of the Arabian Nights in the court of the Pacha of Tripolizza.[43]

Other travellers were less enthusiastic, feeling that the European way of life had been virtually eradicated by the dominance of the Turks. 'It is certain that the Christians . . . are scarcely, if at all, to be distinguished from the Mahometans', John Cam Hobhouse declared in the account of his travels with Byron.[44] Shelley displayed a similar disregard of the distinction between Greek and Turk. In his letter to Peacock, he referred to the Greek prince, Mavrocordato, as 'our turbaned friend'.[45] The difficulty of distinction was due to the complete submergence of Greece in Turkey. At the beginning of his guide to the Peloponnese, William Leake admits: 'Greece, in fact, abstracted from its ancient history, has, until very recently, been no more than the thinly peopled province of a semi-barbarous empire, presenting the usual results of Ottoman bigotry and despotism.'[46] Reflecting this lack of distinction between the two nations, Turkey and Greece appear to have been interchangeable names for the country. Greece was frequently called Turkey, or the Levant, or the Ottoman Empire. Dr Henry Holland's contemporary travels in Albania, Thessaly, Macedonia and the Ionian islands are advertised in the *Monthly Magazine*:

> Dr. Holland is preparing for publication a Narrative of his Travels in the South of Turkey, during the latter part of 1812, and the spring of the following year. It will be the principal object of this work to afford sketches of the scenery, population, natural history, and antiquities of those parts of Greece which hitherto have been little known or described.[47]

Holland apparently sees no difference between the terms Turkey and Greece, both terms being used here.

The observations of the eastern characteristics of Greece were made from a western perspective. Indeed, the ability to write about the country was supposed to be the privilege of the west. Just as James Mill assumed the burden of writing the authoritative history of 'British India', despite never having been to the country, so the British felt compelled to write the history of the uneducated Greeks.[48] James Dallaway justified his account:

The haughty uncommunicative Turk, undervaluing all without the pale of Islamism, and the boasting uncandid Greek, are equally incapable of liberal intercourse on subjects which would tend to ascertain the true standard of their national character.[49]

The ability to write and express knowledge of the other country gave the west a position of power over Greece. Dallaway felt able to decide the 'true standard' of the Greek character better than the indigenous people. Said argues that this wielding of knowledge of the other culture is a feature of the west's control of the east: 'Knowledge of subject races or Orientals is what makes their management easy and profitable; knowledge gives power, more power requires more knowledge, and so on in an increasingly profitable dialectic of information and control.'[50] But Javed Majeed challenges Said's 'monolithic' approach, arguing that the individual political motives behind different writers' exploration of the eastern world – and especially those of Sir William Jones, Thomas Moore and James Mill – affected the type of power wielded.[51] Majeed is right to question the sweeping nature of Said's argument. Indeed, my extension of the theories of orientalism to cover Greece follows the same desire to question and explore Said's arguments more specifically. However, Majeed's exemption of Jones's scholarly historical research from the dominating programme of orientalism seems to risk underestimating the complexity of Said's theory of knowledge and power. While writers like Jones and indeed Moore might have shown more interest in the native culture of India, they were still concerned with what message India could convey about their own country, whether that was Christian mythology in Jones's case or Anglo-Irish relations in Moore's. Moreover, as Majeed himself admits, knowledge and description of another country does inevitably involve the writer in a network of power and dominance.[52]

Quite what the Greeks themselves thought of their 'national character' and western control of their identity is difficult to assess. This is partly because of the continuing western bias of studies of Greece in Britain and because of the European influence upon Greece. In many ways the Greek people fitted the stereotype of the east imposed upon them by European culture. Theodorus Kolokotrones, one of the leaders in the Greek War of Independence, needed the aid of an amanuensis when composing his autobiography because he was illiterate.[53] The mute eastern voice reminds us of the classic feminist analysis of the inexpressive female presence, struck dumb by the overwhelming demands of patriarchal discourse. Admittedly the literate Greeks attempted to assume some degree of control over their identity. Georgios Konstantinides began the history of his people: 'τὸ γνῶθι σαυτὸν δικαίως ἀνεκηρύχθη ὑπὸ τῶν ἡμετνρωε προγόνων ὡς ἡ τελειοτάτη καὶ ὑφίστη ἀνθωπίνη σοφία.[54] But the histories are heavily influenced by the western construction of Greece as the origin of European civilisation. 'Les Grecs, vains de leur origine, loin de fermer les yeux aux lumières de l'Europe, n'ont regardé les Européens que comme les debiteurs, qui leur remboursoient avec de trés-gros interêts, un capital qu'ils avoient reçu de leurs ancêtres', wrote Adamantios Korais, significantly in the western environment of France.[55] Korais's account takes on the opinions of the west in a way that masks any independent, different Greek opinion. Said has observed that 'knowledge of the Orient, because generated out of strength, in a sense creates the Orient, the Oriental and his world'.[56] Like the woman who remains unknowable behind the never-ending layers of male speculation in Luce Irigaray's writing, the 'real' identity of Greece is overwhelmed by the feverish escalation of western interpretation and imagination.[57]

LOVE

The ambiguous orientation of Greece affects the western writer's relationship with it. The relationship is not a simple one of cultural influence – as the non-political critics of Hellenism argued in the past – nor is it simply one of power and control, upon which Said maintains that the relationship with the Orient is based. Rather it is informed by a mixture of power and love, seduction and attraction. Shelley's theory of love proves useful in understanding the relationship. In his 'Essay on Love', Shelley argues that the lover projects his own qualities on to an imagined prototype and then looks for its replica in the real world. 'We are born into the world and there is something within us which from the instant that we live and move thirsts after its likeness', he writes. Later, he observes: 'We dimly see within our intellectual nature a miniature as it were of our entire self . . . the ideal prototype of everything excellent and lovely that we are capable of conceiving as belonging to the nature of man.'[58] This view of love is similar to the western idealisation of Greece, which uses Greece as a focus for all the qualities and values which European culture most admires as its own. Yet Shelley apparently contradicts himself by arguing that love is also 'that powerful attraction towards all that we conceive or fear or hope beyond ourselves when we find within our own thoughts the chasm of an insufficient void.'[59] Whereas before the lover was driven by a desire for sameness, now, according to this argument, he is driven by a desire for difference. He is conscious of a deficiency within himself, and wants completion through union with the Other, with all that he is not. This is parallel to the western attraction towards the eastern alterity which Greece is assumed to offer.

The seductive relationship between Greece and the west is ambiguous. It could be argued that the fact that the poet is attracted to what he lacks undermines his power and dominance. Hence many Romantic tales recount the suffering of the hero led astray by the seductive woman. The knight in Keats's 'La Belle Dame Sans Merci' is discovered 'alone and palely loitering', after he has been abandoned by his exotic seductress. Some feminist critics have argued that male representations of highly desirable women actually empower the feminine. Nina Auerbach, in *Woman and the Demon*, maintains that the mythologising of women in tales of relationships with men gives the feminine a transcendent status which is ultimately more powerful and lasting than that of the status of the masculine.[60] According to this argument, it is possible to understand the literary tradition of western seduction by the timeless, exotic atmosphere of the east, a tradition which stretches from Byron to E.M. Forster, as an acknowledgement of the power of the east. However, these representations of the feminine or of the east are themselves dependent upon the masculine or western consciousness. The very characteristics of the object of desire are dependent upon the masculine or western construction and defined in opposition. Literary critics and historians continue to write of Greece in female terms, suggesting that writers such as Byron were captivated by the country. 'Byron and Greece waited for each other, like Jacob and Rachel, for seven years', Elizabeth Longford writes; and Harold Spender draws the analogy with female seduction even more strongly: 'Greece proved stronger than even the Countess Guiccoli, always hitherto the most potent of his charmers.'[61] 'Potent' the feminised Greece might be thought to be, but it is still brought into being through language for the benefit of the poet. Byron enjoys the representation of a charming Greece for his own poetical purpose, for his own understanding of his poetic identity.[62]

Indeed, Byron's and Keats's treatment of women serve as metaphors for their views upon the seductive allure of Greece. Byron's general opinion and treatment of women in Italy shocked Shelley. Shelley wrote to Byron on Claire Clairmont's behalf, stressing the natural ties which exist between a mother and her child in the hope that Byron might relent and allow Claire free access to her daughter, but Byron was unmoved.[63] Indeed, Byron never seemed to allow for the feelings of women, considering them as sexual objects to be gained through negotiation. Shelley wrote to Thomas Love Peacock after meeting Byron in Venice:

> Lord Byron is familiar with the lowest sort of these women, the people his gondolieri pick up in the streets. He allows fathers and mothers to bargain with him for their daughters, and although this is common enough in Italy, yet for an Englishman to encourage such sickening vice is a melancholy thing.[64]

In keeping with these views, Byron was happy to depict a seduced and abandoned Greece again and again in his poetry. It is true that he criticised the invasion of the Athenian acropolis by the British and the seizure of the Elgin Marbles.[65] In this and in his translations of various Greek songs, he does seem to have given voice to the conquered country. But his *Oriental Tales* depict women as victims in the love affairs between western men and eastern women and the stories end in tragedy. In the *Bride of Abydos*, love for the western, admittedly Greek, Selim drives the Turkish Zuleika to death. Similarly, *The Giaour* depicts the rivalry between an eastern husband and a western lover over a silent, unrepresented woman who dies in the struggle. Any power the woman might have, and her ability to use this to resist, is repressed by Byron in his pursuit of the male heroic identity. Even in *The Corsair*, when Gulnare threatens to take over Conrad's role and become strong and independent, Byron retracts and fades Gulnare inexplicably out of the poem's action.[66]

Keats was worried by the potential intellectualism of women, preferring, like a typical adolescent, their beauty and physical attractions. 'I never intend hereafter to spend any time with women unless they are handsome', he avowed to his brother, and even went as far as admitting to his fiancée Fanny Brawne: 'Why may I not speak of your Beauty, since without that I would never have loved you?'[67] In his preference for sensual beauty, Keats endorsed the existing assumptions about the representation of Greek or eastern women. His poetry abounds with tales of the meeting of hero and heroine, and the final demise or disappearance of the woman. To some extent, the female figures could be thought to betoken a different world of the imagination, an envied alternative to the male world of reality. But that they are also associated with the east, and that the east was understood as constructed according to western desire, may be illustrated by one of Keats's letters to Fanny Brawne. Recounting his idea of a typical oriental tale, Keats wrote:

> I have been reading lately an oriental tale of a very beautiful colour – it is a city of melancholy men, all made so by this circumstance. Through a series of adventures each one of them by turns reaches some gardens of Paradise where they meet with a most enchanting lady; and just as they are going to embrace her, she bids them shut their eyes – they shut them – and on opening their eyes again find themselves descending to the earth in a magic basket. The remembrance of this Lady and their delights lost beyond all recovery renders them melancholy ever after.[68]

The woman here represents the inaccessible point of unity for the poet, the memory of which will remind him continually of his loss. The realisation of the incompleteness of the hero's soul, because he cannot possess the woman, drives him to despair for ever after. The woman, it is clear, serves only to reflect upon the state of the man's soul, and thus can appear or disappear according to poetic need.

Women writers, in contrast, resisted this eroticised representation of Greece and the Orient. Lady Mary Wortley Montagu was one of the first people from the west to travel in the Levant, and is unusual for the alternative, feminine perspectives she offers of the unknown east. Her letters are directed specifically to each correspondent, carefully selecting which travel details will be of interest. Significantly, when corresponding with the Abbé Conti, Lady Mary writes only of public affairs, of the Islamic religion and then finishes: 'I have now told you all that is worth telling you ... relating to my journey.'[69] But on the same day she writes to a woman, giving a detailed account of her visit to a Turkish bath and expressing her astonishment at the fact that all the women gather completely naked and unashamed. In a conventional travel piece written by a man, these women would be treated as symbols of the exotic, feminised east – the typical eastern harem – and portrayed seductively. But Lady Mary converses with them on an equal basis, and is amused to imagine the contrast between what she sees and the conventional objects of male art:

> To tell you the truth, I had wickedness enough to wish secretly that Mr Jervas could have been there invisible. I fancy it would have very much improved his art to see so many fine women naked in different postures, some in conversation, some working, others drinking coffee or sherbet. . . .[70]

Lady Mary empowers the women, making them active – talking, working, drinking – instead of objects for the male gaze. This is possible because she is writing woman to woman, and thus she is resisting the usual discourse of travel books about the east. As she finishes in her letter:

> I am sure I have now entertained you with an account of such a sight as you never saw in your life and what no book of travels could inform you of. 'Tis no less than death for a man to be found in one of these places.[71]

Her account amounts to a private female communication, not suitable for the Abbé Conti and not suitable for the standard official travel book. In this way, it manages to avoid the problems of power and difference prevalent in conventional orientalist discourse.

Even more influential for Shelley was the writing of Sydney Owenson, the later Lady Morgan. Her novel *Ida of Athens* adopts a similar format to Madame de Staël's *Corinna* or many of Byron's poems. A man from the west travels to the east and falls in love with a beautiful woman who in some way represents her native country. Owenson is quite explicit in her use of Ida to symbolise the conquered state of Greece. The hero, Lord B, links the woman and the country in his mind as he falls in love with them:

> Your climate, like some of the creatures it forms, is but too delightful, but too dangerous; it deprives the mind of energy, it deprives the faculties of power; but we breathe a new existence in its delicious temperature.[72]

However, Owenson offers a twist to the classic oriental tale. Her heroines do not capitulate, do not die. Having aroused expectations as to the outcome, she goes on to flout them. Just as Greece according to Owenson remained free even when under the empire of the Romans, so Ida speaks out against Lord B's marriage proposals, both in Athens and London, and marries a Greek resistance fighter to form an all-Greek partnership. Greece is not appropriated and the female remains elusive and powerful.

These two writers, Lady Mary Wortley Montague and Sydney Owenson, offer very strong images of Greece and women. The fact that they are women apparently allows them a sympathy with the conquered country and the capacity to give it an independent and powerful voice and identity. It seems that Shelley was drawn to this depiction of the other country. Although there is no evidence that he read *Ida of Athens*, he certainly praised Owenson's next novel, *The Missionary*. This also deals with east–west confrontation, although this time in India, and again centres on the encounter of a western missionary and an eastern priestess. Shelley wrote several letters to friends, admiring the principal female figure: 'It is really a divine thing. Luxima the Indian is an Angel. What pity that we cannot incorporate these creations of Fancy; the very thought of them thrills the soul.' Yet while he admired the liberated character of Luxima, he still perceived her from a male perspective. She is understood in terms of love and possession: 'the very thought of them thrills the soul'. Just as Lady Wortley Montagu's Mr Jervas is supposed to transform the independent Turkish-bath users into a seductive harem, so Shelley is in danger of converting the independent spirit of Luxima into an object for his own desire.

Shelley had the inclination and the beliefs to write of Greece in a new, liberated way, resisting the established power structures involved in its depiction. But he had a more difficult task than Lady Mary Wortley Montagu or Sydney Owenson. He was a man and he was a poet. The poetic tradition was based around the concept of the male poet and the female muse. In *Women Writers and Poetic Identity*, Margaret Homans discusses the consequence of this belief for the subjectivity of both male and female poets in the early nineteenth century. The poet needed to construct his own identity in opposition to the external world, or to the Other, as she terms it, which was 'frequently identified as feminine, whether she is nature, the representation of human woman, or some phantom of desire'.[73] Although this assumption about the poet is a perennial one, still influential today, it seems to have carried even more weight in the Romantic period. In an age when one of the dominating concerns was the loss and recovery of the creative powers of the imagination, the relationship between the sexes had a particular potency as a metaphor for this desire for wholeness in poetry. The feminist critic Barbara Charlesworth Gelpi considers the gender metaphors for poetic identity when writing about the aspiration of Blake and Shelley in her article 'The Politics of Androgyny':

> Both men are working with a knowledge of the hermetic tradition, both are troubled by modern divisions, which they see as a division between the masculine and feminine aspects of the psyche, and both rejoice in imagining a reintegration and return to primal unity.... But in his long prophetic poem *Jerusalem*, Blake sees that unity as the awakening in Albion's bosom of his emanation Jerusalem, and Shelley in *Prometheus Unbound* sees it as the reunion of Prometheus with his beloved, Asia. Albion and Prometheus are the whole beings in whom all creation finally rejoices. These poems do not describe a similar process of integration in the feminine psyche. One need not quarrel with that: the poet-visionaries were men.[74]

A desire for unity could result in the inevitable appropriation of the feminine and its loss of subjectivity.[75]

The creation of poetry, the constitution of the poetic voice, is thus perceived as an act of appropriation and domination. Indeed, the very act of writing poetry was seen by some of Shelley's contemporaries as an act of power. In an essay on Shakespeare's *Coriolanus*, Hazlitt made the well-known observation that 'the language of poetry naturally falls in with the language of power'. He goes on to explain: 'The imagination is an exaggerating and exclusive faculty: it takes from one thing to add to another: it accumulates circumstances together to give the greatest possible effect to a favourite object.'[76] While it was the political apostasy of the Older Romantics which was the specific motivating factor behind this essay, Hazlitt seems also to be alluding to the effect of the unifying purpose of Romantic poetry. In his 'Defence of Poetry', Shelley, like Hazlitt, contrasts the imagination with the understanding. For him too the imagination is a synthesising faculty, and the terms he uses to describe it do suggest the language of power. The imagination is described as 'that imperial faculty', and poetry is 'something

divine' and 'the centre and circumference of knowledge'.[77] The
idealisation of poetry, which is termed 'eternal truth' and boasts
complete knowledge, is disconcerting, especially for us now in the
post-Foucault age. Moreover, poetry is apparently entirely the
province of the male. Poets are the 'legislators and the prophets',
the 'trumpets which sing to battle, and feel not what they inspire'.
The rallying-call of poetry is expressed in male terms, in the exclusive metaphors of war and religion. These assumptions about
poetry, about its masculine perspective and position of authoritative power, made the task of expressing a liberated, independent
Greece much more difficult. The difficulty of adequately representing Greece from a distant male perspective, which yearns both
for closeness and mystery, is explored particularly in Shelley's
masterpiece in self-conscious poetry, *Epipsychidion*.

EPIPSYCHIDION

Epipsychidion was written in 1821, at the height of Shelley's strange
but overwhelming passion for Emilia Viviani, the young woman
held prisoner by her father until a suitable husband could be found
for her. All the Shelley circle adopted Emilia as their friend, but
Shelley, attracted by her state as victim of oppression, seems to
have fallen in love. Critics have read the resulting poem – addressed to an 'Emily' rather than 'Emilia' – as a coded biography of
his love-life and ransacked it for biographical details.[78] Shelley
bizarrely portrays himself as the world, the centre of the universe,
around whom various planets roll. The poem can also be read as a
poem about captivity, about the imprisoned woman and the delight in liberation. Emily is as imprisoned by her society as Byron's
Leila is in *The Giaour*, and gender and cultural origins in both
poems become linked by the common bond of dependence and
subservience. Increasingly critics have concentrated upon the self-
conscious, self-referential nature of the poem, observing that
'Emily', the subject, exists because she highlights the difficulty in
adequately representing her alterity, her otherness. She is the unknown Other, which challenges the omniscient power of the poet,
and questions the boundaries and limits of his world. But critics
have not noticed the degree to which the exploration of poetic
expression in the work is articulated in terms of cultural orientation. The course of the poem moves from one attempt after another

to define Emily, but two main strategies for representation dominate the work: first, a western assumption of 'sameness' and accessibility is used to constitute the subject; and second, the mood
switches to an eastern exotic representation, where the subject is
constructed as different, seductive, pleasure-giving.

Shelley expresses his ideal concept of relationship early in *Epipsychidion*:

> . . . are we not formed, as notes of music are,
> For one another, though dissimilar;
> Such difference without discord . . .
>
> (142–4)

The phrase 'difference without discord' describes a relationship
which is not dependent upon dominance and imaginary construction; but this ideal cannot be sustained. A choice must be taken
between a western Emily or an eastern. The western definition of
Emily concentrates upon her similarity to the poet, her continuous
link with his world. The very first line of the poem describes her as
the poet's sister, with the alliterative 's' stressing the connection
between her nurturing qualities and her closeness: 'Sweet Spirit!
Sister of that orphan one'. The word 'sweet' has been used three
lines earlier to describe the poem. Its repetition here to describe
Emily points out the connection between the woman and the poem,
highlighting the metaphorical level of the work. Emily is 'this soul
out of my soul', the ideal prototype of Shelley's 'Essay on Love',
and 'not mine but me'. Later the assertion of sisterhood is muted to
the optative: 'Would we two had been twins of the same mother!'[79]
While the heroines in some of Shelley's other poems – Cythna or
Asia – assert their connection to the heroes by drawing upon sib-
ling status as well as lover, Emily's exact relationship must remain
less defined. Is she sister, not twin? Is the connection through
father, not mother? Or is sisterhood only wish-fulfilment, only
fictionalising? The meaning of the title, *Epipsychidion*, is similarly
tantalising in its simultaneous suggestion and withholding of
sameness. While it could mean simply 'on the soul', it could also
draw upon the alternative connotation of the prefix 'ἐπί – 'in addition to' – in order to convey the sense of 'a being who is part of and
addition to the soul'. As part of the poet's soul, Emily is enshrined
internally, as Psyche is welcomed into the temple of Keats's mind
in his Ode: 'In my heart's temple I suspend to thee / These votive

wreaths of withered memory' (3–4). But there are hints that this internalisation imprisons Emily as painfully as the locked doors of her father's oppressive house, since the following lines – 'Poor captive bird! who, from thy narrow cage, / Pourest such music' (5–6) – could refer either to the poet's imagining of Emily's position in his heart or to her literal condition. The clarity demanded by a relationship based upon closeness is thus compromised by Shelley's strange resistance to directly referential language, understood by all:

> 'The present Poem, like the *Vita Nuova* of Dante, is sufficiently intelligible to a certain class of readers without a matter-of-fact history of the circumstances to which it relates; and to a certain other class it must remain incomprehensible, from a defect of a common organ of perception for the ideas of which it treats.'[80]

Shelley appeals to clarity again in his search for suitable adjectives for Emily and appropriate qualities with which to endow her. She is defined with stereotypically western characteristics. Primarily she is light and pure. This is conveyed in numerous images of lamps and suns. Her lightness also suggests divinity, and she is described as a 'Benediction', a 'Glory', a 'Seraph'. Her divine nature is generously bestowed: 'A lovely soul forever to be blest and bless . . . Vanquishing dissonance and gloom' (57, 60). She crucially appears to provide fulfilment, in contrast to the deceiving woman in *Alastor*, proving 'Youth's vision thus made perfect'. Her perfection extends to music – she is described as the 'Harmony of Nature's art' (30) – and to intellectual endeavour – the poet briefly mentions her 'wisdom' (147), although it is a 'wisdom' which accords with his desire. Each of these images, as Michael O'Neill has said, 'represents a new attempt to define completely'.[81] The impulse to 'define completely' derives from a Dantean view of literature, or in Ralph Pite's terms, 'an effort to be precise and minute where their predecessors had been Miltonic and grand, to bring inspired vision into the light of common day'.[82] Henry Cary, Dante's translator, had written of Dante's 'solicitude' to 'define all his images in such a manner as to bring them distinctly within the circle of our vision and to subject them to the power of the pencil'.[83] Emily's epithets also attempt to contain her within the poet's 'circle of vision'.

The image which draws Emily 'within' the poet's 'vision' most obviously is Dante's Beatrice. Beatrice assures Dante of their eventual union in heaven, and her physically strong presence fills the

Vita Nuova, which Shelley studied during his composition of *Epipsychidion*.[84] Unlike the oriental vision, she does not disappear but remains reassuringly present continuously:

> She seemed like a daughter not of a mortal, but of a god: And though her image which remained constantly with me, was Love's assurance of holding me, it was of such a pure quality that it never allowed me to be ruled by Love without the faithful counsel of reason.[85]

Like Beatrice, Emily is thought to be dependable – 'art thou not void of guile?' – although the impact of dependability is rather undermined by Shelley's question mark. The strong image of Beatrice is combined also with that of Diotima, who appears in Plato's *Symposium* as the woman who explains to Socrates the soul's progression to the Form of the Good.[86] Since Shelley was influenced by the Neoplatonic emphasis on spiritual and emotional motivation towards transcendence rather than Platonic rationalism, he privileged the role of Diotima far more than in the original Greek version. For him, she came to represent the Form of Goodness itself, not just the means towards it, and like Beatrice developed divine significance, 'distant Plenty'.[87] In the draft version of the fragment 'The Colosseum' in Shelley's notebook, Diotima is pencilled in as the title of the piece; and the fragment ends, after allowing the old man to speak about love and the power of nature to inspire, with the question: 'Is not this what Diotima calls love?'[88] So Diotima and Beatrice both represent an independent source of inspiration which derives its existence not from the representing mind of the egotistic poet, but from elsewhere, from the divine. The earthly appearance of Emily is used as a form of mediation towards this higher existence.

But while Beatrice and Diotima encourage and inspire their worshippers by their dependability, Emily appears to entice only to resist definition. The images are intended to suggest plenitude but come across as empty and inadequate.[89] Each phrase is immediately replaced by another, in the attempt to express Emily more fully. The effect of such a disjointed, list-making structure for the poem is to make any phrase easily replaceable by another or even dispensable from the poem altogether. When the poet calls desperately to his subject, 'Spouse! Sister! Angel! Pilot of the Fate!', it seems that any of these words could be omitted from the poem and not be missed. Even the attempt to express the relationship in narrative in the middle, 'autobiographical', section of the poem is flawed and insubstantial, drawing attention to the opacity of language rather than the narrative. The power of Emily becomes destructive to the poet's interests, so that the 'honey-dew' from her lips which earlier instilled passion is discovered, in her different incarnation in the middle section, to be poison:

> And from her living cheeks and bosom flew
> A killing air, which pierced like honey-dew.
>   (261–2)

The light of the Beatrice-like Emily becomes burning and dangerous: 'Sweet Lamp! my moth-like muse has burnt its wings' (153). And the writing, asserting unity by confidently making connections between the poet and the vision, cannot be sustained:

> Ah, woe is me!
> What have I dared? where am I lifted? how
> Shall I descend, and perish not?
>   (123–5)

In the failure of confidence, Shelley admits that the vision has been a product of his own creative, colonising imagination:

>   . . . I measure
> The world of fancies, seeking one like thee,
> And find – alas! mine own infirmity.
>   (69–71)

His effort to imagine and express Emily has conformed to his theory of love, which desires sameness, an aspect of the man's soul. He has projected on to Emily his own identity, attempting to create her as western so that he can reach her as his own. The references to Dante's Beatrice leads the reader to assume a similar accessibility in Emily but the colonising strategy, which such western imagining involves, has been shown to be unsustainable.

In the realisation of the failure of the western presentation of Emily, the poem moves to a contrasting eastern presentation. The poet abandons the western clarity of 'defining completely', and opts instead for what Nigel Leask has identified as the style of 'Oriental obscurity'.[90] Static epithets are replaced by fluid ones –

'kissing', 'undulating' – and definition gives way to narrative: 'The
day is come and thou wilt fly with me'. The change is exemplified
by the imagined hasty elopement to the east, to an Ionian island.
Emily is compared to the island, both becoming equally distant and
attractive, provoking desire. The paradisal distance of the island,
with its connotations of an unattainable life beyond the grave, is
suggested in the preface to the poem:

> The Writer of the following lines died at Florence, as he was
> preparing for a voyage to one of the wildest of the Sporades,
> which he had bought, and where he had fitted up the ruins of an
> old building, and where it was his hope to have realised a scheme
> of life, suited perhaps to that happier and better world of which
> he is now an inhabitant.

Paradise here represents simultaneous fulfilment and death. In
the same way, the eastern landscape mingles sensual abundance
and elusive obscurity. The depiction of the eastern landscape and
Emily in the poem is as idyllic as Byron's Greek island of Haidee,
and as fleeting as Keats's oriental enchantress described in his
letter. The sensuality of the island is emphasised:

> The blue Aegean girds this chosen home,
> With ever-changing sound and light and foam,
> Kissing the sifted sands, and caverns hoar;
> And all the winds wandering along the shore
> Undulate with the undulating tide
>
> (430–4)

The island and the woman are represented as voluptuous and
seductive, awaiting the embrace of the poet. Emily is addressed
'even as a bride, delighting and delighted', and the description of
the island echoes these lines:

> Till the isle's beauty, like a naked bride
> Glowing at once with love and loveliness,
> Blushes and trembles at its own excess.
>
> (474–6)

But alongside this emphasis on bodily pleasure is the concurrent
elusiveness which lies beyond ornamental 'excess'. The elusiveness

can be detected in the degree of narcissism haunting this description, a narcissism which recalls the mood of *Alastor*. The island and the house belong to the poet – 'This isle and house are mine, and I have vowed / Thee to be lady of the solitude' (513–14) – and the possession of the woman will just complete his empire. She exists to delight him, as does the island. The seductive language renders the whole place a construct for his pleasure.

The climax of the poem is the imagined sexual union of the poet with the woman. As in *Alastor*, the description of the lovemaking tantalises with its dual depiction of fulfilment and disappointment:

> Like flames too pure and light and unimbued
> To nourish their bright lives with baser prey,
> Which point to Heaven and cannot pass away;
> One hope within two wills, one will beneath
> Two overshadowing minds, one life, one death,
> One Heaven, one Hell, one immortality,
> And one annihilation. Woe is me!
> The winged words on which my soul would pierce
> Into the height of love's rare Universe,
> Are chains of lead around its flight of fire –
> I pant, I sink, I tremble, I expire!
>
> (581–91)

This description of sexual union is more abstract than the one in *Alastor*. It is even clearer that the passage is concerned with the problem of expression and the construction of poetic identity rather than with any literal representation of lovemaking. The passage charts the process of coming to terms with the alien, inexpressible world and the discovery of the limitations of the poetic imagination. While phrases like 'one immortality' suggest the possibility of a transcendent world, where the two beings can unite beautifully and which language is inadequate to describe, the descent presaged by 'one annihilation' implies failure. Words that should be Homerically 'winged' are discovered to be 'chains of lead', earth-bound and heavy, unable to convey anything beside the referent. The repeated 'I' of the final line emphasises the narcissism of Shelley's project. Despite attempts to 'pierce' – itself a masculine image – to the independent realm of 'Love's rare Universe', Shelley's writing can never move beyond his own world and his own condition. The imagined union is no more than an excited projection of 'I'.

Neither construction of Greece, of Emily, succeeds in *Epipsychidion*. The effort to impose kinship and to contain through language proves ineffective and domineering while the alternative option of allowing for and even deliberately constituting difference in order to generate desire proves equally flawed.[91] The result is elusive, a mocking reflection of poetical egotism. The Greece which is constituted by the western–eastern construction, in fact questions and thwarts such assumptions. Only possibly in his interest in androgyny could Shelley hope to transcend the convention of self-constitution through difference, through relationships of power. He was fascinated by the sculpture of the hermaphrodite in the Uffizi in Florence, gazing upon its plenitude, its depiction of the characteristics of both sexes.[92] But his own representation of a hermaphrodite in *The Witch of Atlas* is not so much doubly sexed as sexless. It is a cold machine-like figure, the creation of its Frankenstein-like mistress, the witch. And she, herself unattached and autonomously creating without love – 'a sexless bee' – is a similarly peculiarly unsatisfied figure, longing, like Shelley's 'Sensitive Plant', for love:

> Tis said in after times her spirit free
> Knew what love was, and felt itself alone.[93]

The inertia of the hermaphrodite, its sexlessness, does not seem to have been a satisfactory way of representing the alterity of Greece to Shelley. The hermaphrodite was too disengaged, too lacking in vitality and motivation, too self-absorbed. *Epipsychidion*, on the other hand, written after *The Witch of Atlas*, yearns for the world beyond the self. A quotation from Emilia Viviani herself prefaces the poem, emphasising the aspirations of imaginary conception to follow: 'The loving soul launches itself beyond creation, and creates for itself in the infinite a world all its own, far different from this dark and terrifying gulf.'[94] The significance of the poem seems to rest more in its attempt to express a union with Emily than in any union itself. The meaning, in other words, lies in the process rather than the attainment. Although the poet fails and sighs 'woe is me', the power and beauty of his language have created a highly charged poem:

> . . . towards the loadstar of my one desire,
> I flitted, like a dizzy moth, whose flight

> Is as a dead leaf's in the owlet light,
> When it would seek in Hesper's setting sphere
> A radiant death, a fiery sepulchre.
>
> (219–23)

It seems that Shelley preferred the process of loving to the attainment of his love. It was from the search for the woman rather than from the union and consummation that he derived meaning. This view is confirmed by his remarks in his 'Essay on Love':

> ... this is the invisible and unattainable point to which Love tends; and to attain which, it urges forth the powers of man to arrest the faintest shadow of that, without the possession of which there is no rest or respite to the heart over which it rules. Hence in solitude, or in that deserted state when we are surrounded by human beings and yet they sympathise not with us, we love the flowers, the grass. . . . So soon as this want or power is dead, man becomes the living sepulchre of himself. . . .

What is important is that the man continues the process of loving and desiring, because otherwise he is in danger of stagnating and becoming a 'living sepulchre'. The object of the love is unimportant. Shelley confessed to a friend when explaining his composition of *Epipsychidion*, 'I think one is always in love with something or other.'[95] The attempt towards establishing a bond with the objective world or the gendered Other is more important for energetic, creative poetry than the comfortable attainment and satisfaction of unity.

Perhaps it was the wish to keep the relationship fresh and alive, and to write beautifully, that influenced Shelley in his decision not to travel to Greece and not to experience it at first hand. With the consequences of unity so damaging to the independence of the Other, he was compelled to pin his poetic theories on the importance of continually striving, never reaching. Unlike Byron, who could counter Wordsworth's fanciful description of Greece with real knowledge, Shelley did not have, and did not wish for, first-hand experience of Greece. He preferred the imaginative possibilities of orientalising Greece, of negotiating the different ways of representing Greece according to the nature of the relationship assumed each time. These possibilities could be narrowed down if forced to define too clearly or to describe too closely. As he said to

Trelawny when the possibility of travelling to Greece arose: 'I had rather not have any more of my hopes and illusions mocked by sad realities'; and he went on hoping for and imagining a journey to Greece instead.[96]

5

'Grecian Grandeur': Authority, Tyranny and Fragmentation

> The human form and the human mind attained to a perfection in Greece which has impressed its image on those faultless productions, whose very fragments are the despair of modern art.
>
> Shelley: Preface to *Hellas*

> Such dim-conceived glories of the brain
>   Bring round the heart an undescribable feud;
> So do these wonders a most dizzy pain,
>   That mingles Grecian grandeur with the rude
> Wasting of old Time – with a billowy main –
> A sun – a shadow of a magnitude.
>
> Keats, 'On Seeing the Elgin Marbles'

Henry Fuseli's sketch, drawn in the 1770s, entitled 'An artist in despair over the magnitude of ancient fragments', is one of the most moving images of Romantic hellenism.[1] The drawing depicts a man huddled over and clutching his head in bewilderment and despondency. Beside him are an enormous marble foot and a huge hand, with index finger raised as if issuing a command. The fragmented state of the marble remains is powerful. If this is only the foot, the question raises itself, what must the rest of the sculptured body have looked like? It is little wonder that the artist, attempting to contemplate what is only suggested by the few remaining fragments, experiences what Keats calls a 'most dizzy pain'. In the previous chapters, I have dwelt on the imaginative possibilities of Greece to liberate and to challenge with its difference. In this chapter, I deal rather with the notion of Greece as authority, as the classical ideal of western culture. Although the imaginary space of Greece at times allowed an erotic construction of difference, it also

148

could imply, as here for Fuseli's artist, an exemplary magnificence beyond human expression.

The authority of Greece stemmed in part from its perceived aesthetic perfection. Writers developed theories of beauty from their experience of Greek sculpture which were then adopted as a standard of orthodox taste, influencing education, literature, art and museums. The organisation of taste led to an interest in definitions and categorisations, as new methods of approaching ancient Greek art and literature became institutionalised in scholarship. In part also the authority of Greece was linked to the widespread debate during the Romantic period about the importance of the past. Ideas about the past were articulated through the rhetoric of the sublime, which celebrated immensity and obscurity in nature and expressed the consequent feelings of inadequacy in the observer. The discourse of the sublime could be used to describe aesthetic, literary and political responses to the past. Questions about the perfect origins of a past culture were linked to questions about literary originality and political freedom. As a result, admiration for the past was mingled with anxiety about the present, anxiety about the contemporary artist's ability to rival former works and anxiety about the literary and political consequences of the authority perceived to rest in the ancient literary heritage. Faced with the awe-inspiring products of the past, writers either fell into despondency and failed to create at all or they were provoked into an energetic imaginative response, fired by the aggressive struggle of what Harold Bloom terms 'misreading'. Neither response was satisfactory, since the authority of Greece remained unconfronted and as 'dizzying' as ever.

Shelley's relationship with an oppressive, authoritative Greece was particularly problematic for him because of his hatred of tyranny of any kind. His admiration for the Greeks placed him in the vulnerable position of disciple and follower. 'Their sculptures are such as we in our presumption assume to be the models of ideal truth and beauty', he wrote in 'Discourse on the Manners of the Ancients', and Greek literature was 'the finest the world has ever produced'.[2] These sentiments about the perfection of the Greeks echo much of the contemporary and later thinking which sought to situate Greece at the heart of British culture, dominating aesthetics and ethics. Yet Shelley instinctively rebelled against such thinking and thinkers, denouncing any culture which could be thought to be exploited by authority to inculcate codes of opinion or behaviour.

The sense of the oppressive past bearing down upon contemporary freedom of thought and expression found an echo in Shelley's attacks upon hereditary power and narrow traditions. Edmund Burke articulated established sentiments in *Reflections on the Revolution in France*, when he famously argued that past traditions should influence contemporary political decision-making and confirm the *status quo*: '[Society is] a partnership not only between those who are living, but between those who are living, those who are dead, and those who are to be born.'[3] Shelley apparently admits a similar degree of influence from the past, when he argues in his note to the line 'Necessity! Thou Mother of the World', in *Queen Mab*, that

> every human being is irresistibly impelled to act precisely as he does act: in the eternity which preceded his birth a chain of causes was generated which, operating under the name of motives, make it impossible that any thought of his mind, or any action of his life, should be otherwise than it is.[4]

However, as Chapter 1 illustrated, the underlying patterns of *Queen Mab* belie this belief, suggesting rather the importance of the freedom of the will and the power of each generation to make a difference in the world. Like Paine, Shelley turned to the model of the free, non-hereditary system of America, arguing, in 'A Philosophical View of Reform', that '[America] has no hereditary oligarchy; that is, it acknowledges no order of men privileged to cheat and insult the rest of the members of the state and who inherit a right of legislating and judging which the principles of human nature compel them to exercise to their own profit'.[5]

Shelley's complicated response to the notion of exemplary Greece, a mixed reaction of admiration and rebellious rejection, is explored most fully in *Prometheus Unbound*. Not only does the poem re-write and re-define Aeschylus's *Prometheus Bound* but it is also concerned with the process of such a transformation. Prometheus's rebellion against Jupiter becomes a metaphor through which Shelley can consider his own relationship with Aeschylus and with the Greek literary heritage in general. Before discussing Prometheus's dissent from Jupiter's authority, however, this chapter will examine the gradual acceptance and institutionalising of Greece, and the type of rhetoric adopted to describe it, in order to gain an understanding of the growing authority which Shelley felt had to be approached so cautiously. The acceptance of Greece is illustrated most clearly in the changing attitudes towards Greek statues and in the development of an aesthetic vocabulary to describe Greek beauty.

SUBLIME SCULPTURE

When Winckelmann first wrote his theories about Greek art in the mid-eighteenth century, the dominant aesthetic culture was Roman. The reaction to his advocacy of raw, Greek simplicity was mixed.[6] The French brought out translations of his work almost immediately, publishing a translation of his *On the Imitation of the Painting and Sculpture of the Greeks* in 1755, the same year as the original work, and a translation of *History of Ancient Art* in 1766, two years after the German edition. But the British paid hardly any attention to the new theories at all. Winckelmann's *History of Ancient Art* was not translated into English until 1880, and *On the Imitation of Painting* did not appear in Britain until ten years after its original publication. Indeed when Shelley read Winckelmann, he used the French translation, *Histoire de l'Art chez les Anciens* (1798–1803).[7] Perhaps as a consequence of this lack of mainstream, establishment recognition, Winckelmann's theories were adopted as a major influence for the young, radical artists gathering in Rome in 1770s, who were to initiate what became termed the Greek Revival.[8] Chief among these was Henry Fuseli, who in fact was the translator of the 1765 English edition of *On the Imitation of the Painting*. Through Fuseli, the ideas of Winckelmann, and in particular the preference they show for the naked male body in art reduced to the classic simplicity of form and line, were transmitted to radical artists in Britain like William Blake. Blake came to associate male nakedness in his art with heroic, individual resistance to oppression. Similarly, inspired by Winckelmann-led neoclassicism, the French revolutionaries cultivated simple classical fashions in clothes and general iconography. These new artistic movements revealed that Winckelmann's theories could be used, when not tainted by establishment approval, to promote a radical message.

Over the next few decades, however, Winckelmann's theories became central to an orthodox idealisation of Greece, and thus he was abandoned by the very artists who earlier had revered him. Henry Fuseli for one accused him of indulging in 'frigid reveries',

of admiring order at the expense of passion.[9] Lessing disagreed
with Winckelmann's policy of applying observations about sculpture to his account of Greek literature and Greek culture in
general.[10] For Winckelmann's emphasis upon the naked beauty
and harmony of Greek sculpture was used to shape all standards of
artistic criticism, both material and literary. In 1816, for example,
the amateur art historian and writer James Dallaway repeated
many of Winckelmann's descriptions of Greek sculpture in his
guide to Greek art. 'The Greek statuaries', he wrote, 'proposing to
themselves objects of worship superior to nature, always represented them in the springtide of life and eternal youth.'[11] For Dallaway, as for Winckelmann, the epitome of Greek beauty was evident
in the Spartan tradition of naked exercise and competition, where
the beauty of the male bodies matched the perfection of the climate
and inspired artists. 'The forms of the Greeks, prepared to beauty
by the influence of the mildest and purest sky, became perfectly
elegant by their early exercises' Winckelmann had written, contri-
buting to the growing tradition of Spartan admirers in Germany,
and Dallaway echoed him:

> As the individual model could not be found, [the artists] applied
> themselves to the study of select parts of various bodies, and
> composed from them a more perfect form. The gymnastic exer-
> cises, especially those in Sparta . . . exhibited the most symmetri-
> cal human figures unencumbered by drapery, from whence the
> best examples might be selected.[12]

Winckelmann's categorisation of Greek art into three periods –
development, peak, and decline – was also greatly influential in
moulding dominant aesthetic judgement. August Wilhelm Schlegel
adopted this programmatic model for his lectures on Greek literature in 1808. Indeed he openly compared Greek literature to
sculpture: 'We have no better means of feeling the whole dignity of
the ideas of the tragic, and of giving it a sort of theatrical anima-
tion, than to have always present to our fancy the forms of the gods
and heroes.'[13] According to the sculpture analogy, Homer and
Hesiod marked the development stage, the tragedians constituted
the peak, and the urbane Alexandrian poets were evidence of decline. More specifically, Aeschylus was the Pheidias of literature,
Sophocles the Polycleitus – the Romantics preferred fourth century
to fifth century sculpture – and Euripides Lysippus.[14] Tragedy

constituted the most perfect aspect of the Greek heritage. Schlegel described it as a 'harmonious unity', the 'blending of the sensual man in the mental', and for him *Prometheus Bound* was the tragedy which most effectively represented this ideal, and thus the essence of the Greek heritage:

[Prometheus] atones for his disobedience, and that disobedience consists in nothing but the attempt to give perfection to the human race. It is thus an image of human nature itself: endowed with a miserable foresight and bound down to a narrow exist-ence, without an ally, and with nothing to oppose to the com-bined and inexorable powers of nature, but an unshaken will and the consciousness of elevated claims. The other poems of the Greek tragedians are single tragedies; but this may be called tragedy itself: its purest spirit is revealed with all the annihilating and overpowering influence of its first unmitigated austerity.[15]

Schlegel describes Prometheus in terms heavily indebted to sculp-ture. The static notion of tragedy, which relied upon 'an unshaken will and the consciousness of elevated claims', and which became after Schlegel the dominant interpretation of the genre, was in-fluenced by the marble statues which now were thought to epi-tomise Greek perfection.

One of the events which most clearly illustrated the formation and education of correct taste in Britain was the arrival of the Elgin Marbles. As was noted earlier, when Lord Elgin first bought the statues in 1808, they were rejected because they were thought to be not genuine and not specimens of exemplary beauty. Over the next few years, while Elgin, unrecompensed for his patriotic purchase, grew increasingly burdened by debt, the statues were left to decay in a garden-shed in Park Lane. But once various artists, most vocife-rously Benjamin Haydon, had convinved the House of Commons of their value, they were re-housed in a purpose-built room in the British Museum, and accorded all the publicity and admiration of a major national asset. Benjamin Haydon expressed pride in his diary that he was responsible for recognising the statues' worth and salvaging them for the nation:

Those divine things which I and I alone studied in a damp outhouse, when they were covered with dust and filth, and a gloom hung over their fate, which pressed with malignant hue upon their glory. I have lived to see them felt with enthusiasm by the whole of civilised Europe . . . To have lived in such times of Art is glory, but to be a prime mover and agent of them is immortality.[16]

Keats referred to this achievement in his sonnet, 'To Haydon with a Sonnet Written on Seeing the Elgin Marbles', giving it almost as much space as the description of the statues themselves:

> For when men stared at what was most divine
>   With browless idiotism – o'erweening phlegm –
> Thou hadst beheld the Hesperean shine
>   Of their star in the east and gone to worship them.[17]

Just as Elgin had insisted that his name should be given to the statues, Haydon felt that he had some sort of personal hold over them: 'The Elgin Marbles are an Aera in the Art and the World, and I hope in God I have connected my name with this Aera.'[18] Personal pride was mingled with a national pride in the acquisition of such artefacts, a feeling that the possession of the Greek sculpture elevated the status of Britain and reflected upon its cultural values: 'Italians and Spaniards coming to study the art in England! This is as it should be, and but the commencement of part of the glory that will accrue to the country from their purchase.'[19] The cultural mastery for Britain was gained through conquest and commercial power, and used to maintain that national dominance. Greece was something to be seized and owned.

As Winckelmann's theories of Greek beauty and the Elgin marbles were being instituted as exemplary models of taste, a need arose to develop a way of approaching such perfection, to develop an appropriate response which would in turn become canonical. Haydon's comments in his diary echo some of the responses suggested by Winckelmann, by then of course common currency: 'it is this union of the truths and probabilities of common life, joined to elevated and ideal nature, that goes at once to our hearts and sympathies in the Elgin Marbles, and makes them superior to all the works of art hitherto known in the world'.[20] Greek art, for Haydon, was both the stuff of 'common life' and yet also 'elevated and ideal'. Similarly Hazlitt admired the Parthenon statues, which he described as 'the paragons of sculpture and the moulds of form', because they mingled the real with the ideal.[21] He remarked on the trueness of the statues to the human body, even noticing the lifelike depiction of muscles on the bodies:

> Let anyone, for instance, look at the leg of the Illissus or River-God, which is bent under him – let him observe the swell and undulation of the calf, the intertexture of the muscles . . . and the effect of action everywhere impressed on the external form, as if the very marble were a flexible substance, and contained the various springs of life and motion within itself.[22]

In this admiration for the physical nature of the statues, Hazlitt was participating in the school of thought, led by Schiller's polarisation of the classical and the romantic in 'On Naive and Sentimental Poetry', which regarded the Greeks as primarily interested in the external world and in the human body. Hazlitt himself described the classical style as 'conversant with objects that are grand and beautiful in themselves' in his review of Schlegel's lectures.[23] The Elgin Marbles, with their open celebration of the human body, appeared to endorse the new German interpretation of the classical aesthetic as one of contentment and self-sufficiency.

Yet coupled with the admiration for the statues' 'truths and possi-bilities of common life', was the aesthetic of the sublime. While the gaze focused upon the muscle-bound bodies of the statues, the mind was lifted in wonder at the ideal nature of the ancient Greeks and at the grandeur of the past. Edmund Burke's sublime, the quality in nature which causes terror and awe in the observer, was becoming even more internalised so that the emphasis was no longer upon the sublime qualities in nature which would produce certain psychological effects but upon the sublime elevation of the mind which could rise beyond the senses altogether.[24] Schiller, for example, argued that the sublime entailed the liberation of the mind: 'that mental temperament which is indifferent whether the beautiful and the good and the perfect exists, is above all called great and sublime'.[25] While the classical appeared earth-bound and unromantic, the sense of the past which it evoked conveyed a sublime sensation in the mind. Edward Clarke used the term 'sub-lime' in his reflections upon the past when wandering around the ruins of Athens:

> in any part of Greece [can there] be found a nobler association of sublime and dignified objects than was here collected into one

view . . . overwhelming the mind with every recollection that
has been made powerful by genius and consecrated by inspiration.[26]

The past 'overwhelms' the mind, creating an imbalance of power in
which the past assumes indisputable authority while the passive
mind imbibes and struggles to comprehend. Tom Furniss has
argued recently that Burke's sublime was an artificial rhetoric,
calculated to give the observer a frisson of danger within a framework of safety in which he knew there was no real threat.[27] But the
relationship between sublime object and observer seems to have
been more complicated than this description suggests, leaving it
ambiguous how genuinely threatened the observer was by the
'overwhelming' power of the past, by huge objects, by terrifying
landscapes.

This ambiguity is particularly evident in the responses to the
sublime state of fragmentation. It was the ruination of the objects
which Edward Clarke saw in Greece that conveyed their immense
importance and it was the fact that the Elgin Marbles were fragmented, and that only the trunks of the bodies remained, which
paradoxically thrilled visitors. But the interpretation of this fragmentation was equivocal. Ruins could prompt either the awesome
sense of the grand obscurity of the past or a Gothic pleasure in
decay and decline.[28] Fragments could stimulate the imagination to
create in the mind a greater, inexpressible whole, as some have
suggested Coleridge intended in 'Kubla Khan'.[29] Shelley adopted
this interpretation in 'A Discourse on the Manners of the Ancients':
'The wrecks and fragments of those subtle and profound minds,
like the ruins of a fine statue, obscurely suggest to us the grandeur
and perfection of the whole.'[30] Byron's pleasure in the sublime ruin
of the Colosseum in *Childe Harold* IV – 'A noble wreck in ruinous
perfection' – proved influential in articulating the feelings of Charlotte Eaton, among others. In *Rome in the Nineteenth Century*, she
drew upon Byron's vocabulary in describing the power of the
broken arena: 'Would that I could describe it to you as it stood in its
ruined loneliness amidst the deserted hills of ancient Rome, surrounded with the remains of overthrown temples, imperial palaces,
triumphal arches, and buried thermae, – mighty even in decay!'[31]

However, Byron's description of the Colosseum was more ambiguous than Eaton allows, mixing the genres of Romantic sublime
and Gothic:

There is given
Unto the things of earth, which Time hath bent,
A spirit's feeling, and where he hath leant
His hand, but broke his scythe, there is a power
And magic in the ruined battlement
For which the palace of the present hour
Must yield its pomp, and wait till ages are its dower.[32]

Byron's gloomy pleasure in the ruins themselves – the 'magic in the ruined battlement' – recalls the poems of such writers as Edward Young, Robert Blair and Thomas Warton who revel in the melancholy of disintegration. 'Beneath yon ruined abbey's moss-grown piles / Oft let me sit, at twilight hour of eve', Thomas Warton demanded in 'Pleasures of Melancholy'.[33] The fragmentation of order constitutes a source of imaginative power, allowing a fellow sense of imperfection in the author. But the Gothic delight in destruction could also have a covert political motivation, since the objects of ruin were most usually central institutions of government – the church, the castle – and the villains, whose moral integrity had fragmented into deception and corruption were frequently the established pillars of society. Matthew Lewis, for example, was vigorously attacked for his depiction of church corruption in *The Monk*.[34] By destroying the past or revealing the decay in the symbols of power, the Gothic mode could be used as a liberating style, revolutionary.

The ruined state of the Elgin marbles provoked a variety of responses. Keats responded to the sublime power created by the statues in his sonnet 'On Seeing the Elgin Marbles':

My spirit is too weak – mortality
    Weighs heavily on me like unwilling sleep,
And each imagin'd pinnacle and steep
    Of godlike hardship, tells me I must die . . .
Such dim-conceived glories of the brain
    Bring round the heart an undescribable feud;
So do these wonders a most dizzy pain,
    That mingles Grecian grandeur with the rude
Wasting of old time – with a billowy main –
    A sun – a shadow of a magnitude.
                                                    (1–4, 9–14)

The inadequacy of language to contain the intensity and magnificence of the statues is revealed here in the piling up of paraphrases: 'a billowy main', 'a sun', 'a shadow of a magnitude'. Indeed so ineffectual was one sonnet to do justice to the perfection of the sculpture that a second, through the mediation of Haydon, was required:

> Forgive me, Haydon, that I cannot speak
> Definitively on these mighty things;
> Forgive me that I have not eagle's wings.[35]

The sublime is suggested through the dislocation of articulation into silence, just as Cortez and his men are silenced when they first perceive the immensity of the Pacific ocean in Keats's 'On first looking into Chapman's Homer'. The fragmentation of Keats's verse, carefully contained as it is within the formal sonnet form, reciprocates the fragmentation of the material objects described, so that it comes to share in the greatness and monumentality of the statues described.

But the recognition of the sublime in the past did not always evoke such a reciprocal, measured response. Henry Fuseli's reaction to the statues was very different from that of Keats. When Haydon took him to see the Elgin Marbles in London, he 'strode about saying "De Greeks were godes! de Greeks were godes!" '[36] The new political, national authority gained through the possession of such statues was matched by – and indeed went some way to create – the sense of power residing in ancient art and this frustrated the independent artist or writer. It called for a Gothic or destructive response. Keats's sonnet about the sublime, broken Parthenon sculptures was answered by Shelley's 'Ozymandias', in which the headless Egyptian statue illustrates the ravaging of time and the temporal nature of past greatness:

> Look on my Works, ye Mighty, and despair!
> Nothing beside remains. Round the decay
> Of that colossal Wreck, boundless and bare
> The lone and level sands stretch far away.
>   (11–14)

Similarly, in Shelley's fragmentary prose piece, 'The Colosseum', the old, blind man enjoys the ruined nature of the building, now disintegrating and reclaimed by the natural landscape, because it reveals the vanity of human pride and self-centredness: 'It is because we enter into the meditations, designs, and destinies of something beyond ourselves that the contemplation of the ruins of human power excites an elevating sense of awfulness and beauty.' Shelley's apparent glee over the ruination of the past was influenced by Volney's *The Ruins, or A Survey of the Revolutions of Empires*, in which a parallel was drawn between the destruction of the mighty city of Palmyra and the overthrow of the French *ancien régime*.[37] Ruin was to be associated with revolution. As Volney – who had been one of the deputies to the National Assembly – declaimed to the ruins, 'Mixing the dust of the proudest kings with that of the meanest slaves, you called upon us to contemplate this example of EQUALITY'.[38] So for Shelley, the fragmentary Colosseum or the Baths of Caracalla, where he composed most of *Prometheus Unbound*, were the visible signs of the power of revolutionary change.

But the enjoyment of the fragmentation of the past could rebound. Just as the concept of the sublime was now internalised, so the understanding of ruination could apply as much to the onlooker as the object being contemplated. Byron describes his reflections when visiting the Colosseum, in *Childe Harold* IV:

> To meditate amongst decay, and stand
> A ruin amidst ruins; there to track
> Fall'n states and buried greatness.
>
> (xxv. 2–4)

The fragmentary state of the past, its 'decay', could indicate a waning of its power and therefore the modern spectator need not therefore feel threatened by it. And yet Byron stands a 'ruin amidst ruins', awed before such 'buried greatness'. The past creates a fragment of the poet, an acknowledgement of failure. Hazlitt wrote about the power of the past, prompted by the example of Coleridge:

> We are so far advanced in the Arts and Sciences, that we live in retrospect, and doat on past achievements. The accumulation of knowledge has been so great, that we are lost in wonder at the height it has reached, instead of attempting to climb or add to it.[39]

Coleridge, 'overwhelmed' like Clarke by 'past achievements', had written only a few fragmentary poems and the disjointed *Biographia Literaria*, and produced much enthusiastic but confused conversation. In discussing Coleridge's case in *Romanticism and the Forms of Ruin*, Tom McFarland charts the very narrow distinction between success and failure which fragmentation signified.[40] The avowal of weakness and fragmentation could serve as a mask for the aspiration towards unity and synthesis. For only by the inclusion of apparently disparate parts could complete synthesis be achieved. But there was a great danger that this imaginative tactic would fail and that the writer would be left with only a collection of insubstantial parts, a 'ruin amidst ruins'. Thus, through fragmentation, the poet could either liberate himself from the past or alternatively himself suffer disintegration and weakness.

Shelley's response to the fragmentary Elgin marbles is not recorded, although it is known that he visited them in the British Museum just before travelling out to Italy in 1818.[41] What is recorded, in his notebook, is his detailed reaction to the sculpture in the museums of Rome and Florence. His appreciation of the statues' quality is articulated in terms similar to those used by Haydon and Hazlitt and indeed the growing orthodoxy of art criticism. He admires in Greek art the juxtaposition of realism and idealism. He described the statues as if they had been caught in a lifelike act with which he could sympathise – Venus 'seems to have just issued from a bath'. Yet he also welcomed the artistic idealising of their bodies. The athlete, for example, has perfect muscles which are 'represented how differently from a statue since anatomy has corrupted it', while a statue of Cupid earns his disapproval because 'it seeks to express what cannot be expressed in sculpture – the coarser and more violent effects of comic feeling'. But about the Laocoön he disagrees with Byron who thinks that the statue shows 'a mortal's agony . . . blending with an immortal patience', as Winckelmann did, and argues instead that the statue depicts real physical suffering as an 'overwhelming emotion'.[42] At times, indeed, he lapses into the language of the sublime, rendered inarticulate by the power of a particular statue's beauty. The statue of Niobe, for example, the 'consummation of feminine majesty and loveliness', defeats his powers of expression: 'it is difficult to speak of the beauty of her countenance, or to make intelligible in words the forms from which such astonishing loveliness results'.

Yet it is evident that he is eager to avoid the passive admiration of fellow writers responsible for investing Greece with such indisputable priority. He is not afraid, albeit only in his notebook, to admit if a statue is less than perfect. The body of one Venus is 'correctly but weakly expressed', while another Leda is dismissed simply as 'a dull thing'. Crucially, moreover, he acknowledges the transmission of the ancient art, the effect the contemporary observer has upon the perception of the statues and the way that they are displayed. Sometimes this involves discussing the restoration of particular statues, recognising the juxtaposition of old and new. A statue of Hercules carries the note: 'The arms probably restored, for the right hand especially is in villainous proportion'. At other times he interjects witty anachronistic comments about ancient scenes and their relevance to contemporary life. He writes a lengthy narrative of a bas-relief scene, depicting women in distress and fathers seeing babies for the first time, and drawing upon contemporary experience when interpretation becomes problematic: 'What they are all wailing at, I don't know; whether the lady is dying, or the father has ordered the child to be exposed: but if the mother be not dead, such a tumult would kill a woman in the straw in these days.' His comments become even more earth-bound when describing a statue of Leda: 'Leda with a very ugly face. I should be a long time before I should make love with her.' By this witty irreverence and acknowledgement of historical differences, Shelley manages to circumvent feelings of inadequacy in the face of awesome perfection.

The main burden of the past for Shelley, however, was not primarily aesthetic but literary. As a writer interested primarily in a textual Greece, his main ambiguous influence derived not from the statues but from the poems of the ancient world. Byron and Keats, who were interested less in specific Greek works and more in a general Greek image or landscape, were not so concerned about acknowledging their poetic debt to Greece. Byron freely admitted that Greece had inspired his poetry and, when Francis Jeffrey commented in the *Edinburgh Review* on the Promethean elements in *Manfred*, he acknowledged a more specific debt: 'The Prometheus – if not exactly in my plan – has always been so much in my head – that I can easily conceive its influence over all or anything that I have written.'[43] Keats was more self-consciously aware of his belatedness, writing in the preface to *Endymion* that 'I hope I have not in too late a day touched the beautiful mythology of Greece and dulled its brightness.' This nicely poised statement expresses concern about the superiority of the ancient Greek world as well as implying the possibility that Keats is the more powerful, able now to affect the ancient mythology and to 'dull its brightness', with his belated misreading. Keats's relationship with Greece is a personal tie, with implications for his creative self, his integrity and ident-ity.[44] But Shelley's relationship with the revered, sublime Greece of the past was less psychological and more implicated in his political ideology, in his hatred of tyranny and oppression. And it was not so much a general feeling of belatedness as a struggle with specific authors over the notion of authority. Schlegel had written that Aeschylus's *Prometheus Bound* should be considered the essential Greek tragedy, itself the highest genre produced in Greece. Thus it was *Prometheus Bound*, the newly designated emblem of the Greek literary heritage, which demanded an appropriate response, an unbinding which could fruitfully mingle admiration with inde-pendence.

PROMETHEUS UNBOUND

The myth of Prometheus essentially tells of a battle over who is to be considered the original god, Prometheus the Titan or Zeus the Olympian. Shelley's view of literary originality was similarly com-petitive. In his preface to *The Revolt of Islam*, he asserted defiantly that 'I am unwilling to tread in the footsteps of any who have preceded me . . . designing that, even if what I have produced be worthless, it should still be properly my own.'[45] He used the lan-guage of defiance to respond both to literary influence and to political oppression, which were linked in his mind. In the preface to *The Revolt of Islam*, he describes the 'submission' into which the people of France were deluded before the revolution, the 'fetters' from which they were loosened in 1789, and the need for his poem, and 'its influence in refining and making pure the most daring and uncommon impulses of the imagination', to continue the work of the revolution. This vocabulary is then continued in his discussion of poetic influence where the word 'subjection' must recall the earlier 'submission': '[writers] cannot escape from subjection to a common influence'. The preface to *Prometheus Unbound* echoes these words: 'Poets . . . are, in one sense, the creators, and in an-other, the creations, of their age. From this subjection the loftiest do not escape.'[46] While Shelley acknowledges in *Prometheus Unbound* that to write without contemplating the work of others would 'be a presumption in any but the greatest', nevertheless he places himself in just that 'greatest' category: he has 'presumed to employ a licence', similar to that of the Greek tragic writers and Milton. Milton's 'presumption' was also crucially linked to his political views according to Shelley. 'The sacred Milton', he wrote, 'was, let it ever be remembered, a Republican, and a bold enquirer into morals and religion.'[47] The active and independent mind, which is able to 'escape subjection' both poetical and political, can set about instigating 'some unimagined change in our social conditions and opinions'.

To describe the process of that change, Shelley drew in the preface to *Prometheus Unbound* upon the imagery of the tragedy competition held at the Greek dramatic festival, an event that must have appealed to his competitive imagination. He writes that the ancient Greek dramatists 'by no means conceived themselves bound to adhere to the common interpretation or to imitate in story . . . their rivals and predecessors', thereby hinting at the alternative, metaphorical significance of the binding and unbinding of the title of his own poem, *Prometheus Unbound*. Instead of being 'bound' to a story, he writes of 'framing' his story upon a particular model, of having his thought 'modified by the study of the productions of those extraordinary intellects'. The active verb 'framing' asserts independence – Shelley uses it to describe the writing of the American constitution in 'A Philosophical View of Reform' – while the passive 'modified' suggests a degree of contingency, the shared discourse of any writing. The ambiguous image of lightning illustrates the careful line to be taken between complete independence from other writers and complete dependence upon the past. First, the spirit of poetic composition, produced by the original mind, is compared to 'uncommunicated lightning'; but later the lightning image is picked up in the phrase the 'collected lightning' of the spirit of the age. Once the energy was shared it could be more effective in restoring the 'equilibrium between institutions and opinions', but it might not be as electrifying, if not original.

The process, then, of translating or 'modifying' Aeschylus in *Prometheus Unbound* was complex. It demanded both a freedom from binding influence, and a degree of authority which derives from the 'familiarisation' of the mind with the best productions of the past; and it was intimately connected with the equivocal, difficult nature of radical political activity. Shelley drew upon Milton's

Satan to 'misread' Prometheus: 'the only imaginary being resem-
bling in any degree Prometheus, is Satan'.[48] Indeed, he believed
that by depicting Satan's irreconcilable opposition to God, Milton
had improved upon Aeschylus's 'feeble catastrophe' of 'reconciling
the Champion with the Oppressor of mankind'. Satan offered a
general icon of resistance at this time, particularly after Fuseli had
illustrated scenes from *Paradise Lost* for display in a Milton Gallery,
planned to counter the establishment's Boydell gallery.[49]

    Further resistance, which enabled Shelley to define his own inde-
pendence from Aeschylus's authority, derived from other versions
of Prometheus. Byron and Mary Shelley wrote loose versions of the
Prometheus myth after Shelley had translated Aeschylus's play
orally for them in 1816.[50] Goethe's 'Prometheus', probably inspired
by Georg Christoph Tobler's translation of Aeschylus into German
in 1782, poured defiant scorn upon an Olympian heaven which
represented Christoph Wieland's placid depiction of the Greek
gods:[51]

> I know of nothing more wretched
> Under the sun than you gods!
> Meagerly you nourish
> Your majesty
> On dues of sacrifice
> And breath of prayer.[52]

Richard Potter's translation of *Prometheus Bound*, the only one existing in English at the time, rendered the play political by drawing
upon the rhythms of Shakespeare's blank verse and endowing the
poetry with his belief that Aeschylus's dramas revealed the manly
spirit and love of liberty which Aeschylus had showed at the battle
of Marathon.[53] After fighting to defend his country at Marathon,
Aeschylus was later forced into exile, possibly for political reasons.
Thus marginalised for his integrity, the 'wildness' of Aeschylus's
work – like the unruliness of Shakespeare who broke French neo-
classical rules – testified for Potter to his heroic, political spirit.
Besides Potter's political version, there was also Schlegel's account
of a hero who resisted oppression with his 'unshaken will and the
consciousness of elevated claims'.

    These defiant and political versions of Prometheus offered Shel-
ley a focus for and a means of asserting his creative independence,
wresting the priority, in Bloom's terms, from Aeschylus.[54] But it

was a delicate task, requiring the use of Prometheus to assert independence not from any writer but from Aeschylus, the creator of Prometheus. Aeschylus was thus both source of literary oppression, and Shelley's bulwark against it. Critics, such as Earl Wasserman, have noted the echoes of Aeschylus's play throughout the first act of *Prometheus Unbound*, although they have not emphasised the defiant and competitive tone with which the echoes are expressed.[55] Shelley's Prometheus is 'sleepless'(4) while Aeschylus's is ἔυπνος (*PV* 32). His curse of Jupiter has a similar bravado: 'Rain then thy plagues upon me here, / Ghastly disease, and frenzying fear; / . . . Aye do thy worst' (266–7, 272). But the Promethean bravado extends to the subtle inversion of the original Greek. Where the Greek Hephaistus mockingly foresees Prometheus's torture between the extremes of midday heat and midnight cold (*PV* 22–5), Shelley's Prometheus speaks from a position of survival, indicating his acceptance of this aspect of his condition by subtly altering the mood and context of the Greek 'ἀσμένωι' (glad):

> And yet to me welcome is Day and Night,
> Whether one breaks the hoar frost of the morn,
> Or starry, dim, and slow, the other climbs
> The leaden-coloured East.
>
> (I.44–7)

The cyclical movement of Aeschylus, where day replaces night and each panacea is longed for 'gladly', becomes the continual torture of day *and* night borne stoically. Moreover, where Aeschylus's Prometheus begins his first speech with the dramatic invocation to the elements to witness his torture, 'O divine air and swift-winged breezes and river springs and the numberless joys of wavy seas and all-mother earth and all-seeing sun – I call you' (*PV*, 88–91), Shelley's Prometheus asserts his greater solitude, his greater endurance, without even the consolation of the sympathetic elements: 'No change, no pause, no hope! – Yet I endure' (I. 26). He has not only more 'elevated claims' than Aeschylus's Prometheus, but more 'elevated' powers of endurance.

But defiance of Aeschylus using Aeschylus's hero proves problematic. Critics have noticed how Prometheus and Jupiter are in fact very alike in the first act. Prometheus's language, which he uses to assert his independence from Jupiter, paradoxically adopts imperial words. 'Scorn and despair – these are my empire' (15) he

asserts, and later, 'Yet am I King over myself, and rule / The tortur-
ing and conflicting throngs within' (I. 492–3). Indeed Prometheus's
imperial status has been granted him by Jupiter:

> . . . me, who am thy foe, eyeless in hate,
> Hast thou made reign and triumph, to thy scorn,
> O'er mine own misery and thy vain revenge.
>
> (I.9–11)

'Reign', 'scorn', 'misery' and 'revenge' are part of a shared vocabulary, which is applied to or used by either opponent in this deadlock of hatred. The similarity between the two reaches a climax, as
commentators have frequently pointed out, in the scene in which
Prometheus hears a repetition of the curse which he had originally
uttered against Jupiter. The curse is repeated not by an emanation
of Prometheus as expected, but by a phantasm of Jupiter, mouthing
Prometheus's defiant words.

As revealed in the discussion of Shelley's *Cyclops*, there was wide
acceptance of the view since the French Revolutionary Terror of the
1790s that in times of oppression tyrant and victim alike become
brutalised and cruel. Yet Shelley is conveying more than this observation through the similarity between Jupiter and Prometheus. In
general terms, using an Aeschylean figure to oppose Aeschylus
himself leads to an ambiguity in the confrontation. More specifically, Shelley was troubled by the changing political significance of
Schlegel. Schlegel, as already shown, was becoming the accepted
authority on tragedy and indeed on the ancient Greek world, with
his appropriation of Winckelmann's theories of sculptural beauty
for the discussion of Greek culture in general. Hazlitt admitted
certain qualms about the German's emphasis upon the unity of the
tragic hero:

> The tragedies of Sophocles . . . are hardly tragedies in our sense
> of the word. They do not exhibit the extremity of human passion
> and suffering. The object of modern tragedy is to represent the
> soul utterly subdued as it were, or at least convulsed and over-
> thrown by passion or misfortune. That of the ancients was to
> show how the greatest crimes could be perpetrated with the least
> remorse, and the greatest calamities borne with the least emotion.
> Firmness of purpose and calmness of sentiment are their leading
> characteristics.[56]

In keeping with Schlegel's growing orthodoxy, Shelley's Schleg-
elian Prometheus becomes less interested in external freedom, as
Potter's was, more in the internal spirit and personal serenity. It is
significant, for example, that whereas Jupiter holds sway in the
outside world, Shelley's Prometheus expresses the power within
his own mind: 'within [my] mind sits peace serene / As light in the
sun, throned'. In drawing upon Schlegel's interpretation of Prometheus, Shelley was in danger of becoming a Jupiter of culture,
part of the very establishment he opposed.[57] His Prometheus resists
Jupiter 'with a calm, fixed mind', but later it is Jupiter who is
described as 'calm': 'thou and thy self-torturing solitude, / An
awful image of calm power' (I.295–6).

Shelley had to alter the narrative of individual rebellion. He
endeavoured to circumvent the intransigence which was the result
of his attempt to outwit Aeschylus, and to fragment the kind
of calm, monolithic Greece which had become associated with
Schlegel's tragedy. He did this by exploding Aeschylus as the
single source for his work and thus revolutionising his idea of
the 'modifying' of past texts. Just as the monologue initially
directed to Jupiter in the first act is widened to include Ione,
Panthea, Asia and the chorus, so the single voice of Aeschylus
is diffused through many voices from the classical Greek inheritance. The multiple Greek sources transmit alternative stories
and alternative 'energies', dissolving fixed boundaries of genre and
language through their own narratives of transformation and
translation.

In her comments on *Prometheus Unbound*, Mary Shelley mentioned the influence of Sophocles upon Shelley as well as the influence of Aeschylus.[58] Indeed the voices of all the Greek
tragedians appear in the poem, besides the single voice of Aeschylus. The isolation of Prometheus, which he welcomes in a spirit of
martyrdom, recalls the determination of Sophocles' Antigone to die
alone. The madness and forgetfulness which had swept over Prometheus when he originally uttered the curse, of which he later has
no memory and repents, recalls the sudden visitation and disappearance of Ate in Sophocles' *Ajax* or Euripides' *Hercules Furens*: 'It
doth repent me: words are quick and vain; / Grief for awhile is
blind, and so was mine' (I.303–4). Lines in the curse directed at
Jupiter recall both the fate of Heracles, tortured by Deianira's mis-
taken gift in Sophocles' *Trachiniae*, and also that of Jason's bride,
burnt by the poisoned robe sent by Medea:

> I curse thee! let a sufferer's curse
> Clasp thee, his torturer, like remorse,
> Till thine Infinity shall be
> A robe of envenomed agony;
> And thine Omnipotence a crown of pain
> To cling like burning gold round thy dissolving brain.
>
> (I.286–91)

The references to these plays open up a new interpretation of the relationship between Prometheus and Jupiter. Heracles suffers because of Deianira's excessive but deluded love, and is reduced to a most unheroic and, as he sees it, embarassingly emasculated death. Creusa burns because of Medea's misery. As a result, the relationship between Prometheus and Jupiter becomes one of misplaced love or mutual feminine suffering rather than masculine bravado, and thus the deadlock of hatred is displaced.

These allusions to Greek tragedies widen the former single connection with *Prometheus Bound*, but are also themselves widened, accepting influences from other poetry and from mythology, as distinctions between genres are broken down. For example, all choruses of furies and spirits are based not only upon Greek tragedy but also upon the common conception of the Greek mythological world, as articulated by William Godwin in his mythology for schools, *The Pantheon*: 'The language of the Greeks was the language of poetry: everything with them was alive; a man could not walk out in the fields, without being in the presence of fauns.'[59] The Greek archaic poets also offer alternative perceptions of Jupiter from that of Aeschylus. In Act III, scene i, Jupiter's decadent celebrations in heaven are based upon the drinking songs of Anacreon:

> Pour forth Heaven's wine, Idaean Ganymede,
> And let it fill the daedal cup with fire.
>
> (III.i.25–6)

Anacreon is of course associated with the 'make-love-not-war' school of poetry. In contrast, this couplet comes after lines describing Jupiter's determination to 'trample out the spark' of human resistance. Anacreon is darkened; Ganymede reminds us of Jupiter's rapaciousness rather than the Bacchic idyll of heaven. But on the other hand, the possibility that Jupiter could become a peaceful hedonist like Anacreon remains, and helps to replace the tyrannical image of Jupiter with a more passive one.

The single Aeschylean account of the Prometheus story is mediated by other sources and stories, indicating alternative ways of delivering the same narrative. In Act II, as Asia and Panthea are travelling to Demogorgon, they move into the Arcadian world of Theocritus's *Idylls* or Virgil's *Eclogues*. Silenus, the typical Arcadian figure, sits in the shade of a tree, playing his flute and telling stories. A faun speaks:

> . . . should we stay to speak, noontide would come,
> And thwart Silenus find his goats undrawn
> And grudge to sing those wise and lovely songs
> Of fate, and chance and God, and Chaos old,
> And love and the chained Titan's woful doom
> And how he shall be loosed, and make the Earth
> One brotherhood.
>
> (II.ii.89–95).

The familiar Arcadian topic, the temptation of laziness and narrative at the expense of work, is alluded to here: 'if we stay to speak, noontide would come'. But laziness, paradoxically, would prevent the narration of Prometheus – 'the chained Titan's woful doom'. The re-telling of Prometheus, with its utopian ending, thus relies upon the eclogue mode while inverting its ethos. Likewise, the framing device of the 'Homeric Hymn to Athene' is used to re-tell the transfiguration of Asia. As she glows with electrifying light, Panthea says that Apollo 'is held in Heaven by wonder' (II.v.11), just as when Athene was born, 'Hyperion's son long time / Checked his swift steeds.'[60] The 'Hymn to Aphrodite' is next recalled: 'on the day when the clear hyaline / Was cloven at thine uprise, and thou didst stand / Within a veined shell' (II.v.21–3). Yet Shelley's version is more dramatic than the Homeric one – Asia leaps from the sea more as Athene leapt from the brow of Zeus than Aphrodite gently wafted over the foam – and, with its 'veined shell', must have been modified also by Botticelli's *Birth of Venus*, which Shelley had seen in the Uffizi.

The exciting potential for alternative stories is particularly evident in the figure of Thetis and narratives associated with her myth. In Greek mythology it is the doomed marriage between Jupiter and

Thetis which Prometheus retains as his secret foreknowledge and which he finally reveals to Jupiter, so that it can be averted, in the spirit of reconciliation. The fruit of the marriage between Jupiter and Thetis was doomed to overthrow his divine father. But this potential story is diverted since Jupiter, warned by Prometheus, allows Thetis to marry Peleus instead of him, and of course they produce Achilles. Ovid describes Peleus's rape of Thetis which begins violently, with Thetis seeking escape by changing shape, but ends joyfully in mutual embrace: 'exhibita estque Thetis: confessam amplectitur heros'.[61] In contrast, Shelley's Prometheus does not warn Jupiter about the dangers of the Thetis connection, with the result that Jupiter keeps to the original Greek omen and rapes Thetis extremely violently. During the rape, Thetis is transfused not with Peleus's loving embrace, but with 'Numidian poison' (III.i.40), a reference to the fate of a soldier, dissolved by the venom of a snake's bite, in Lucan's *Civil War*. Thus the images of dissolving and penetration – the 'penetrating presence' (III.i.39) – which earlier, in the dream sequences, had suggested the sexual transmission of inspiration from Prometheus to Panthea to Asia (II.i.80), in this story's retelling are tained by overtones of sexual aggression and putrid degeneration.

There are also covert allusions to the other main role of Thetis in Greek literature, and these particularly illuminate the mysterious figure of Demogorgon. In the first book of the *Iliad*, Thetis travels up to Olympus to plead with Zeus to support the Trojans in the war so that her slighted son Achilles will be missed by his fellow Achaeans. In her effort to persuade the god, she reminds him indirectly of a time when the other gods attempted to overthrow him and she rescued him. According to Achilles, she summoned

> the hundred-handed one to high Olympus, the one whom the gods call Briareos, but all men call Aigaion – for he is greater in strength than his father – who rejoicing in his glory, sat beside the son of Khronos. And the blessed gods feared him, and ceased binding Zeus.[62]

Zeus's supremacy, and apparently the whole order of the Homeric world, is dependent upon the power of Thetis. Conversely, it is within Thetis's power to upset it all again. The mysterious hundred-handed one, for which no other literary source has been found, must lie behind the shadowy Demogorgon, whose potential for overthrowing Jupiter derives precisely because he is so apparently without precedent, unbound. His reply to Asia – 'the deep truth is imageless' – refuses to assign causes to events in a way which unbinds language as well as mythological sources. In Shelley's version, Demogorgon destroys Jupiter:

> *Jupiter*: Awful shape, what art thou? Speak!
> *Demogorgon*: Eternity. Demand no direr name.
> Descend, and follow me down the abyss.
>   (III.i.51–3)

In the *Iliad*, the story of the hundred-handed one remains just a covert allusion, a digression. But, according to Laura Slatkin, such 'oblique references, ellipses or digressions' form the texture of Homeric epic, in order to illustrate that 'the process of participating in a poetic tradition, far from being a simple matter of inflexible dependence on antecedents, has emerged, on the contrary, as a process of selection at every stage'.[63] The potential for other stories which Thetis embodies in the *Iliad* serves as a metaphor for the adaptation of poetic traditions itself. Shelley's veiled allusion to Thetis through Demogorgon and the hundred-handed one participates in this liberating tradition of evoking other stories.

These Greek sources modify the Aeschylean story, bringing in other voices to suggest the plurality of the Greek inheritance rather than the single, confrontational relationship. Other sources deal specifically with ideas of transmission and transformation, thereby illustrating the dissolving model of translation through their own fluidity. There are, for example, various references to the legends which appear in Ovid's *Metamorphoses*.[64] The inspiration which comes upon Asia in Act II to travel West, nearer to Prometheus and Demogorgon, in order to learn about the world and release the process of revolution, is modelled on the Hyacinth story in the *Metamorphoses*. When Apollo was grieving for his beloved, dying Hyacinthus, he changed him into a flower and 'not content with that, he himself inscribed his own grief upon the petals, and the hyacinthus bears the mournful letters 'AI AI' marked upon it'.[65] Shelley alludes to the story, translates it to the context of Prometheus, and replaces the static grief of Apollo with the urgent, moving message of 'Follow':

> But on each leaf was stamped – as the blue bells
> Of Hyacinth tell Apollo's written grief –
> O, *follow, follow!*
>
> (II.i.139–41)

Sources of transformation are not only derived from Ovid. When Panthea describes to Asia, in Act II, her vision of the transfiguration of Prometheus, she recalls Shelley's descriptions of the Greek sculptures in the Uffizi, particularly that of Venus Anadyomene just emerged from her bath:

> . . . the overpowering light
> Of that immortal shape was shadowed o'er
> By love; which, from his soft and flowing limbs
> And passion-parted lips, and keen faint eyes
> Steam'd forth like vaporous fire; an atmosphere
> Which wrapt me in its all-dissolving power.
>
> (II.i.71–6)

Transforming Prometheus into a marble 'Praxitelean shape', as Shelley described it, might be thought to prevent the fluid process of transfusion which marks the Promethean revolution. But Shelley's descriptions of the sculptures defy materiality as living and breathing 'vaporous fire'. Indeed although initially we argued that Greek authority was synonymous with sculpture, Prometheus's revolution becomes less a process of brittle fragmentation and more one of fluid transformation and elision. The dreams illustrate this dissolution of distinction between the abstract and the material. The dramatic fashioning of the dreams in the *Odyssey*, created out of nothing by Pallas Athene, is evoked to form the dreams which appear to Ione and Panthea in Act II. One of Homer's dreams, which appears to Penelope, reveals its transient, semi-sentient state by its ability both to appear palpable to sight yet also to slip through keyholes and doorbolts.[66] Shelley's dreams transfuse themselves into the consciousness of their dreamers, uniting thought with sense:

> What shape is that between us? Its rude hair
> Roughens the wind that lifts it; its regard
> Is wild and quick, yet 'tis a thing of air
> For through its grey robe gleams the golden dew
> Whose stars the noon had quench'd not.
>
> (II. i.127–31)

The dream, at once a scruffy messenger and a 'thing of air', initiates the urgency to 'follow', before it dissolves into, or is elided with, the Hyacinthus.

There are possible similarities between this state of dissolution and what Paul de Man has identified as 'erasure' or 'forgetting' in *The Triumph of Life*.[67] *The Triumph of Life* is overshadowed by the past, by its sense of its powerful predecessors, symbolised by the procession of past heroes, but most forcefully represented by Rousseau who in turn recalls Virgil's Anchises. De Man argues that the dreamy quality of the poem is created by the impermanence and disintegration of all expression and figuration, a process in which images do not derive significance through a contrasting context or origin, but occur through the arbitrary positing power of language. The sun is suddenly evoked out of nothing; the chariot inexplicably arrives and is gone. The past – the origin – has no power or significance, and because of the disintegration of the subject–object polarity in language, it is uncertain whether it has ever existed. Rousseau describes the pattern of life:

> 'Figures ever new
> Rise on the bubble, paint them as you may;
> We have but thrown, as those before us threw,
>
> Our shadows on it as it passed away.'[68]

Rousseau himself emerges from 'what I thought was an old root which grew / To strange distortion out of the hill side', in this atmosphere of disintegration and insubstantiality.

But Prometheus's dissolution differs because it involves allusions, albeit fleeting and fluid, to specific myths and places. The transformation of the scene, unlike *The Triumph*'s nightmarish shadowiness, is precisely placed. Just as Aeschylus is translated in a revolutionary way, so Prometheus and Asia are literally translated to new areas of the globe. The barren Caucasus gives place to a new scene which resembles Plato's Athens and Sophocles' grove in *Oedipus at Colonus*. The grove, temple and cave into which Prometheus and Asia eventually retreat were salient features in the area where Plato's Academy met. The nightingale and clinging ivy belong to the description of the sacred grove in *Oedipus at Colonus*.[69] Indeed the translation of *Oedipus at Colonus* into *Prometheus Unbound* is significant. Oedipus, in Sophocles' drama, is undergoing a transformation. As he comes to the strange no-man's-land during his final journey and reaches the liminal stage in his life, he assumes a new transcendent identity, communicating with the gods, set apart and absolved from his former life. Something of this transformation and liminality is assumed by Prometheus; and he calls upon Oedipus as much as Satan to be his model.

Originality and communication are still at issue, even at the end of Act III, when Prometheus's final resting place is described. The Promethean ritual, the torch race, which features in *Republic*, Book I, recalls the image of the 'uncommunicated lightning' in Shelley's preface:

> [The temple] is deserted now, but once it bore
> Thy name, Prometheus; there the emulous youths
> Bore to thine honour through the divine gloom
> The lamp which was thine emblem . . . even as those
> Who bear the grave across the night of life . . .
> As thou hast borne it most triumphantly
> To this far goal of Time.
>
> (III.iii.167–74)

In contrast to the ancient race, now long since gone, where fire was passed from one runner to the next, the message of social perfectibility Shelley wanted to convey is yet 'untransmitted', uncommunicated. But Prometheus, now translated back to his sacred grove anew, has succeeded in transmitting it 'triumphantly'. Shelley has even 'presumed' to venture to the very site of ancient Promethean worship, confident now that he is not returning as a pale shadow or imitator of Aeschylus but as a successful translator, having brought about the strange revolution of dissolution and transformation.

But it is problematic whether the translation or transmission of the text is as successful as Shelley seems to be claiming here. Certainly *Prometheus Unbound* articulates the gradual dissolution of Aeschylus amidst the multiplicity of sources and models. The Promethean revolution renders the old opponents outmoded by replacing former methods of translation as confrontation with new methods involving modification, circumvention, elision. But the methods of elision are sometimes dangerously close to the insubstantial erasure of *The Triumph of Life*. 'We lose sight of persons in principles, and soon feel that all the splendid machinery around us is but the shadow of things unseen', wrote the reviewer in the *London Magazine*.[70] The unconquerable will of Prometheus, which dominates the first act, grows weaker in the second act where Asia presides, and finally dissolves with the consummation of love in the third, while his personal identity becomes suffused throughout the whole world. The name 'Prometheus' is widened in application, so that it no longer signifies the hero, but rather the activity of the whole cosmos:

> We will take our plan
> From the new world of man
> And our work shall be called Promethean.
> (IV. 156–8)

The empty monosyllabic words and simple rhyme of 'We will take our plan / From the new world of man' do not captivate or convince. 'Plan' suggests a clinical, scientific certainty which can never succeed in a flawed, real world and such efficiency and lack of opposition hardly seems 'Promethean' work. Shelley is attempting to redefine the term here, deliberately recalling the traditional connotations of 'Promethean' in order to thwart them and to connote a new beneficent, social, non-violent talent; but the redefinition is in danger of appearing insubstantial, unsatisfactory.

This insubstantiality did not suit well Shelley's efforts to recuperate a political Prometheus to counter the orthodoxy of Schlegel. The lyricism of the final acts, and the transformation of Prometheus into a 'shadow of things unseen' simply encouraged interpretations of other-worldliness. Indeed the burgeoning hegemonic interpretation of Prometheus as a stoic, passive and almost Christian hero was not prevented. Later nineteenth century translators of Aeschylus expressed views which were heavily dependent upon Schlegel and which linked their perceptions of Aeschylus and Shelley. Aeschylus, and his most famous play *Prometheus Bound*, were seen as 'sublime', associated with the grand attitude, the internal mind. Thus the drama between Prometheus and Jupiter became the 'magnificant impersonation of mind struggling against circumstance, intellect against force, providence against fate'.[71] The dissolution of conventional opposition in *Prometheus Unbound* became interpreted as passive, internal, divine acquiescence. Shelley had 'invested his Prometheus with all the placid grandeur of the deity, all

the tenderness of the good man'.[72] Placid and good, Prometheus
was a metaphor for Christ. He was 'the personification of Divine
Love, willing for the sake of man to suffer to the utmost what
divine Justice could inflict or require'.[73] Editions of the play included lengthy footnotes inventing mythological parallels between
the Olympian and Christian religions, and between the references
in Aeschylus and in the Bible.[74] For this growing Christian interpretation, Shelley bizarrely became the most appropriate translator
through whom to read Aeschylus. 'The legend of Prometheus lives
in the poetry of Aeschylus and Shelley. The power of one poet can
scarcely be measured but by the equality of the other.'[75] Even
Thomas Medwin, Shelley's cousin, appears to have made the accepted connection between Aeschylus, Shelley, sublimity and lyricism. His translation of *Prometheus Bound* is littered with the shells
of Shelleyan vocabulary, words without content or purpose: 'The
starry veil of night shall only bring / A longing after day'.[76] The
idealisation of Aeschylus in his preface is mirrored by what emerges as an idolising of Shelley. Potter is dismissed as a translator,
Sophocles as a poet. The Athenians are described as worshipping at
the shrine of Aeschylus, just as Medwin appears to be worshipping
Shelley. He is to be admired as the authority on Aeschylus, as the
'best scholar', and apparently, since Medwin religiously echoes his
words, as the arch composer of language.[77] Shelley thus becomes
the authority for the new, Victorian interpretation of Aeschylus. He
is accepted and welcomed into the tradition. Even the fierce debate
about originality and freedom are glossed over as unimportant: 'To
say that he imitates, in the modern sense, is to say nothing – to feel
that the spirit of Aeschylus has passed into the mind of Shelley, is
the fairest praise which can be awarded.'[78] The fluidity of his final
acts, which were intended precisely to regain the active political
upper hand over the static defiance of Schlegel, is used ironically to
endorse the lyrical, apolitical interpretation of both his poetry and
Aeschylus's drama.

   So is Shelley's Prometheus unbound? One contemporary wit remarked that the poem was so obscure that nobody would ever 'pay
for the binding'.[79] Its obscurity, fluidity and dissolution were actually part of a deliberate attempt to unbind Prometheus from
Aeschylus, to find a completely new method and concept of translation. It was an attempt, on Shelley's part, to confront the growing
orthodoxy and acceptance of Greece, and at the same time to explore new ways of mounting such a confrontation. But in fact the

obscurity of the poem led only to a sense of divine sublimity and mystery which bound Shelley paradoxically closer to a poetic tradition from which he so longed to escape.

6

'We are all Greeks': The Greek War of Independence

In Turkey the distinction between Mussulman and Christian is as strongly marked as at the first: it is the distinction, as Mr Eton says, of 'conqueror and conquered, oppressor and oppressed'.
Rev. T.S. Hughes: *An Appeal in Behalf of the Greeks* (1824)

They were Greeks and so are we, that's all we know. I come from Smyrna – there's an ancient Greek city for you – and I may be more Greek than the Greeks in Athens, more Greek than your Sarakatsans, for all I know. Who cares? *Greece is an idea*, that's the thing! That's what keeps us together.
Patrick Leigh Fermor, *Roumeli*

On 7 March 1821, the Phanariot Prince Alexandros Hypsilanti issued a declaration in Jassy, Moldavia, calling the Greeks to arms in order to fight for independence from the Ottoman Empire: 'The hour has struck, valiant Greeks. Let us unite with enthusiasm, our country calls us on.' Almost immediately Turks were attacked throughout Moldavia, Wallachia and Bulgaria. Two weeks later the Archbishop of Patras hoisted a blue-and-white banner and proclaimed Greek independence. Shelley described events in a letter to *The Morning Chronicle* the following month:

The Prince Ipsilanti, a Greek nobleman, who had been Aid-de camp to the Emperor of Russia, has entered the Northern boundaries of European Turkey, with a force of 10,000 men, levied from among the Greeks inhabiting the Russian Empire, and has already advanced to Bucharest. His proclamation has produced a simultaneous insurrection throughout Greece. . . . The Greeks dispersed over Europe, whether as mercenaries or students at the

178

Universities, are hastening to join the army. . . . The Turks have been completely driven from the Morea, and Revolutionary movements have taken place in several of the Islands. Every circumstance seems to combine to promise success to an enterprise, in which every enlightened mind must sympathise, not less from the hopes than the memories with which it is connected.[1]

Suddenly with Hypsilanti's declaration, images of Greece, which have been explored above, were put dramatically to the test. Shelley's letter reveals the urgency and excitement; words had to be converted into action, beliefs into creation. His 'hopes' and 'memories', which illustrate the close connection perceived between present and past which hellenism promotes, are linked now distinctly to the 'enterprise', to enactment. Like the French Revolution, when the ideas of such thinkers as Voltaire and Rousseau suddenly were converted into frightening uncontrollable action, the Greek War of Independence demanded a determination from the west to put the developing ideas about Greekness and the burgeoning notions of nationalism into dramatic effect.[2]

The concept of nationalism has elicited much debate in recent years. Commentators are divided in their analysis of the origins of national feeling, some arguing that it emerges from a groundswell of popular feeling,[3] others believing that it is cultivated by the governing groups.[4] In other words, some are keen to argue that national identity is a natural, instinctive feeling, while others wish to emphasise the constructed aspects of it, the fact that it is determined by external forces which crucially shape the prevailing mood. Homi Bhabha captures the paradoxical nature of nationalism well when he describes it as 'Janus faced', because, he argues, the nationalist at once looks back to the mythic origins of a people and looks forward to what are new ideas of progress, nationhood and independence.[5] The ambivalence which Bhabha's analysis has uncovered in nationalism generally can be discerned both within the Greek national character and in the relationship between the west and Greece. The quality of Greekness was something apparently grounded in history, to which western supporters were called to respond, and yet also something imagined and constructed by the west, which was then adopted to shape the liberation and creation of the new nation of Greece. Indeed, to some extent nationalism can be said to be a product of the imagination, a force which shapes previously unorganised collections of people into a unified group. The unifying factors are deliberately created, or 'invented' in Eric Hobsbawm's terms.[6] In this case, Greece, which has been shown to have such a strong if ambiguous pull upon the imaginations of those living at the beginning of the nineteenth century, was particularly suited for a new nationalist 'enterprise'.

Traditionally critics have viewed the west's contribution to the war, and particularly that of the Philhellenes, as hopelessly idealistic and eccentrically divorced from reality. Byron is believed to have sacrificed his life for Greek independence, and thereby associated his name forever with heroic and committed military action abroad.[7] Shelley's *Hellas* is excoriated even more than Byron's work for its naivety and heady idealism.[8] In part the writers' idealising nationalism should not seem surprising, if we accept the degree of inventing or fictionalising which goes on when national feelings arise. Perhaps every nationalist struggle needs those who articulate what can and must be imagined. Yet it is also clear that Byron's *Childe Harold* and Shelley's *Hellas* rather question than confirm the predominant philhellenic rhetoric, which sought to establish an apparently natural connection between the Greeks and the west. Indeed the literariness of their work articulates the complications of identity and allegiance which are often lost in the exigency of war. After teasing out the conflicting interests and concepts of the nature of Greek identity which were masked by the overwhelming philhellenism of the war, I will examine the writings of Byron and Shelley which they produced when their imagining of Greece confronted a complicated reality.

NATIONAL FEELINGS

Three years into the war, the Rev. Thomas Smart Hughes articulated the British response to the Greek desire for independence:

> It is a cause, we repeat, possessing claims altogether unparalleled: and this without even once adverting to the heavy but unpaid debt of gratitude that we owe to Greece as one of the fountains of our literature, and parent of those models of eloquence and taste which have formed the brightest studies of our youth, and present to our maturer age comforting sources of instruction and delight.[9]

Until the outbreak of the war, the British had appropriated Greece as their own and used it to express their sense of themselves, their values and their national origins. Now their imaginative possession of the country called for a 'debt of gratitude' just as a child might return to support a parent. The 'debt' was focused in part around the importance of ancient Greece for the nation's childhood, both metaphorically for the childhood origins of the nation and literally in its education. Leigh Hunt wrote of the direct connection between the spirit of Greece and the subsequent character of his country:

> I have, in common with thousands of my fellow countrymen, derived the greatest gratification and the sweetest delight in the perusal of those immortal writings, which dignify the human character, which elevate us above ourselves, and which place the acquirements of past ages almost above the competition of modern times. I am bold to acknowledge that I feel for the distresses of that land, from the mental resources of whose inhabitants, in the age of Homer, of Thucydides, of Pericles, and of Demosthenes, England herself has derived her admiration and her adoption of freedom of government, of liberality of sentiments, and of patriotic enthusiasm.[10]

Momentarily Leigh Hunt's enthusiasm for the British Greeks could falter: 'If we know anything at all of the Greeks, we can hardly help being reminded of them at every turn of our lives.' But ideas of difference are quickly banished when the qualities of Greekness are remembered to lie at the heart of British education and culture. 'We can hardly open a book – we cannot look at a schoolboy – we cannot use a term of science but we read of the Greeks, or have thoughts that may be traced to them, or speak their very language.'[11]

Further debts to Greece were also incurred when it was recalled that she represented the last bastion of Christianity before the vast field of Asiatic Islam. Preserving Christian Greece from infidel hordes was as important as defending the Christian heart of Britain. Poems appeared in the popular magazines pressing the Christian case:

> O holy that cause! – and the light of its sign
>   Shall blaze upon temple and tower;

> Nor longer the Crescent in mockery shine
>   Mid the holiest relics of power.
>
> And far the rude hordes of the Moslem shall flee,
>   Their place in the desert to find,
> From that beautiful home which God made for the free,
>   And filled with the glories of mind.[12]

The pagan Greece of Hunt's Thucydides, Pericles and Demosthenes
might be thought to conflict with the Christian Greece. But in the
phrases 'the beautiful home which God made for the free', and the
'glories of mind', one can detect the developing Christian appropriation of ancient Greek culture, so that there was no longer a discrepancy.[13] Even Shelley, grasping for any means possible to whip
up support for the war, resorted to pointing out the Christian
allegiance between the Greeks and the British:

> The war of the Cross against the Crescent, for which our fathers
> bled, now sanctified still more by its being the overthrow of a
> cruel Empire, and the establishment of freedom and happiness
> in one of the finest provinces of the earth, must fill every heart,
> from the hoary veteran to the schoolboy, with enthusiasm and
> anxiety.

The effort to unify support, 'from the hoary veteran to the schoolboy', meant that factional differences were to be forgotten, and
personal political obsessions, such as Shelley's atheism, were laid
aside. Attempting to stress that 'we are all Greeks' required a unity
of purpose among the 'we' if the close relationship implied by 'are'
was to remain unproblematic.

But of course behind the apparent unity, there were problems,
differences, complications. Greece could be appropriated by different people to represent different arguments, and it is possible to
detect voices from both conservative and liberal groups among the
philhellenes, supporting the Greek cause but for widely different
motives. The liberals were attracted to the principles of freedom
and self-determination which the Greek cause seemed to them to
imply. They seized upon Greece as a symbol of resistance to the
Establishment, masking a real concern for Britain and its state of
liberty in their interest in Greece.[14] The London Greek Committee,
set up to raise funds in support of the Greek War of Independence,

comprised many names, like Sir Francis Burdett, John Cam Hobhouse and 'Radical Jack' Lambton, who were keen supporters of British parliamentary reform.[15] Major John Cartwright, the radical politician then in his eighties, wrote a pamphlet, 'Hints to the Greeks', as a contribution to the Greek cause.[16] The Greek war also appealed to utilitarians like Jeremy Bentham, who were concerned with trade and economic freedom. In 1823 Bentham published *A Constitutional Code for any Nation*. Word must have quickly reached the Greeks, because the following year the Greek provisional government wrote to him asking for advice in drawing up the new Greek constitution.[17] Bentham was enthusiastic, and also offered to educate three Greek boys in England, who could then return to Greece and spread his philosophy.[18] But his suggested code was never enacted, because it failed to take into account the idiosyncrasies of Greek history and culture.[19] What Bentham was interested in was not so much the particular details of the Greek national consciousness but rather the dissemination of his libertarian ideas, believing as he did that all countries were the same, equally susceptible to social and economic improvement. The battle for Greek national independence was simply the site in which he could experiment with his views.

On the other hand, those who had no desire to change anything at home and who admired the British establishment and would never support demands for greater freedom in a domestic context also joined the philhellenes. Since Greece was becoming associated with the central sources of British culture, it was thought to reflect upon the state of Britain, upon its upbringing, education and character. The enslavement of the Greeks was therefore somehow a slur upon Britain and its values. A letter in the *Southampton County Chronicle* expresses this view: 'Feeling as we do, for the Greeks, a people endeared to us by the most innocent and most lasting associations, those of our schoolboy recollections, we cannot but feel some anxiety for every negotiation in which they may form a subject.'[20] Even Lord Castlereagh was moved to ask whether the descendants of 'those in admiration of whom we have been educated, be doomed . . . to drag out, for all time to come, the miserable existence to which circumstances have reduced them'.[21] Once war broke out, arguments about Greeks deserving freedom and enjoying the innate sympathy of the west could develop a different perspective for some conservatives. The right-wing *Courier* admitted the difference war made to its former beliefs:

There is not a man breathing, we presume, whose mind has been
expanded by the love of antiquity, and whose opinions partake of
the spirit of the age in which we live, who would not devoutly
exclaim 'May the Greeks be free!' But the statesman and the
politician would pause ere they acted upon this impulse.[22]

In this passage, the contrast is made between the Everyman who
dreams of Greek freedom and the politician who has to make
decisions and act upon them. Privately people could sympathise,
but publicly no action seemed possible. Suddenly parallels could
be drawn between Greek demands for freedom and the campaigns
of those across Europe who were rebelling against the reinstitution
of the *anciens régimes* after the fall of Napoleon: 'The independence
of Greece could only spring from the dislocation of the existing
political relations of Europe.'

Yet, in general, the Greek demand to be independent was perceived to be fundamentally different from the other nationalist
movements of the post-Napoleonic-war years, such as the Carbonari movement in Italy and the resistance in Spain. Edward Blaquiere, one of the leaders of the London Greek Committee, stressed
the difference between the Greek nationalist group, the Philiki
Hetairae, and other nationalist movements:

Most rebellions are organised by secret societies, but no other
resemblance exists between the Hetairists and the Carbonari. The
revolts in Western Europe failed because their supporters had not
spirit enough to defend them, an imputation to which Greece can
never be liable.[23]

The belief that Greece should be free was not based solely on
political reasons, on beliefs about independence and liberty, as
were the other nationalist movements, but crucially it was also
associated with classical culture, with education and with art, and
so it could be seen to transcend politics. The whole question of
Greek independence was universalised and simplified. 'There are
few either in the Old or the New World', wrote Count Peter Gamba,
Byron's friend, 'whithersoever the light of civilisation extends, who
have not proclaimed themselves friendly to the regeneration of
Greece.'[24]

Besides the achievement of maintaining a unified rhetoric despite
the plethora of motives, there was the task of maintaining the ideal

morale of philhellenism in despite of war. Men took the notion of the 'debt of gratitude' seriously in their prosecution of the war. The London Greek Committee was formed in 1823 to raise money for the cause. Meanwhile individual enthusiasts from all over Europe journeyed to Greece to fight, forming their own army – the Battalion of Philhellenes – in the absence of a recognisable Greek army, in May 1822. Sir Richard Church, finally appointed commander of the Greek land forces in 1827, summed up the almost religious fervour which he felt for the Greek cause in a letter to his brother in 1822:

> . . . to go to Greece I must make heavy sacrifices – must give up my position in the English service, and my commission as lieutenant-governor. I am willing to give up the reality and prospect of these advantages. I feel that the glorious enterprise in a just cause has more attractions for me than these pleasurable enjoyments.[25]

Yet while men like Church expressed such views, accounts were filtering back about the chaos and disillusion that marked the real war effort. There were reports that European and Greek fighting forces were proving incompatible on the field, because they operated different military tactics. The Greeks saw no shame in retreat if fortune was turning against them, nor did they feel any compunction in violent massacre of their enemies if they were given the chance. They boasted about the barbaric slaughter of beleaguered Turks at Monemvasia and Tripolisa in 1821. The British, on the other hand, prided themselves on fortitude in defeat and in certain war codes of etiquette which they had devised and expected others to follow. In the early years of the war, volunteer Philhellenes, defending the town of Navarino against Turkish attack, shut the gates of the town to prevent the undisciplined Greeks, as they saw them, leaving in panic.[26] The Battalion of Philhellenes was disbanded a few months later, after the disastrous battle of Peta caused by the chaotic disagreements between the Greeks and the British. Some Philhellenes had already abandoned the campaign, disappointed that it failed to live up to their expectations of heroic adventure and that it was apparently conducted more like tribal guerilla warfare, with looting and primitive butchery. Count Peter Gamba records meeting two Germans in Italy on their return from Greece, full of tales of the reality of the Greek struggle.[27]

But the Germans' tales did not deter Count Gamba and Lord Byron themselves from setting sail for Greece, and many others like them. Despite the discrepancies from popular myth, the same pre-war philhellenic arguments continued and volunteers set out for Greece even after the Battalion was no more. The enthusiasm was maintained by a strenuous effort to distinguish between the Turks and the Greeks in the fighting. Delacroix's painting of the Turkish massacre at Scio in 1822 depicted an emphatic contrast between the brutal Turkish conquerors, dark and menacing on their bucking horses, and the victimised Greeks, mostly female, white, pure and sympathetic.[28] While Turkish atrocities like Scio were reported, accounts of Greek looting and barbaric killing at Monemvasia and Tripolisa, were discounted. Rev. Hughes added his weight to the argument:

> But the most atrocious part of all to be played, is the endeavour of some persons to assimilate the Greek character in point of systematic cruelty, as they call it, with that of the Turks themselves, and for this purpose they continually report the old story of the barbarities practised at the capture of Tripolisa. . . . I have the best reasons for asserting that the cruelties of the Greeks at Tripolisa have been greatly exaggerated.[29]

While there was a great desire to separate the Greeks – 'us' – from the Turks – the menacing 'them' – there was also tremendous fear of the Turkish ability to 'assimilate' the Greeks and thereby to contaminate the clearcut distinctions. The fear added greater urgency to the war effort, to rescue the Greeks before they became too Turkish. Hughes's description of the state of affairs in Greece provoked anxious responses, calling for hasty recovery of the Greeks before they became thoroughly oriental:

> It is argued that the cruelties, which have been charged on the Turks, have been practised in a similar way by the Greeks themselves. If such is the fact, this is the strongest possible reason for assisting the Greeks to realise their national independence, because by making them free you will inspire them with all the generous sentiments of free-born men.[30]

But sometimes it proved impossible to maintain that the Greek and Turks were different. 'The accounts from Constantinople present a horrid scene of massacre of every creature, Greek or Frank, from the highest to the lowest', the *Gentleman's Magazine* admitted. In these circumstances, observers argued that the modern Greeks were genetically different from the perfect ancient Greeks, and should not be allowed to distort the memory of that exemplary civilisation. Leigh Hunt added his weight to the argument in his grudging praise for the people he could not even bring himself to call Greek:

> The other nations of Europe have been struggling more or less with their several tyrannies for ages; but now we see an effort made against their oppressors even by that mixed and degraded race, the descendants of the effeminate population of the Lower Roman Empire, who were beaten and trod upon by successive tribes of Goths and Huns, and finally reduced into abject slavery by the victorious enthusiasts of the Mahometan faith. Adversity however has strengthened their bodies and purified their minds; and now they have risen up from under their burdens and contumelies, and have spoken out among the nations, if not in the pure dialect of their ancestors, at least in a spirit not unworthy of Athenians and Spartans.[31]

In *Travels in Greece and Albania* (1830), Hughes disparaged the people he found living in Greece as 'that unfortunate race, occupants of that soil, if not the legitimate descendants of those heroes, whose names still shed a blaze of glory over the land which contains their ashes'.[32] The solution was to restore the ancient culture, which was now perceived to reside in the west, and to convert the modern inhabitants through western efforts to what were perceived to be ancient Greek values and way of life.

It is a measure of how far the ideal Greece was popularly separated from the real situation in the Levant that a novel by Thomas Hope, *Anastasius*, which recounted the adventures of a contemporary Greek brigand in gruesome detail, had little impact upon people's beliefs. The author stressed the 'realism' of the tale, his 'scrupulous regard to truth' in his depiction of barbarous Greek customs. Yet the book met with popularity and approval. 'Anastasius is a greater villain than Gil Blas ... an Oriental profligate', wrote Francis Jeffrey in the *Edinburgh Review*, but 'there are few books in the English language which contain passages of greater power, feeling and eloquence.'[33] The reaction from the *Quarterly* was similar, attacking Anastasius as 'a scoundrel of the deepest dye', but full of admiration for the work: 'it is an extraordinary performance, displaying not only an intimate acquaintance with everything peculiar to the east, but a knowledge of mankind in general'.[34] It appears to have been only Shelley who recognised a potential conflict posed by the book. He acknowledged the quality of the work, writing to Mary that 'It is a very powerful – and very entertaining novel – and a faithful picture they say of modern Greek manners.'[35] Yet how can one praise the Greeks after reading *Anastasius*, he wondered. His preface to *Hellas* attempted to wriggle out of the problem: 'In fact the Greeks, since the admirable novel of *Anastasius* could have been a faithful picture of their manners, have undergone most important changes.' The brutal depiction of Greece is placed by Shelley in the past subjunctive – 'could have been' – so that it seems as distant and unlikely as possible, while the philhellenic dream is represented by the simple past verb – 'have undergone' – so that it becomes undisputable truth. Shelley could not divorce the contemporary Greeks from the popular ideal conception of them nor could he negotiate the division between the reality depicted and his ideal to allow for links and blurring of definitions. His solution was to actualise the ideal, and to render uncertain and distant the real.

Under the pervasiveness of western writing about Greece, it is hard to determine exactly the state of Greece before and during the war. *Anastasius* may have been no more realistic than the idealising, classical accounts of the country, since it was designed to appeal to the western fascination with the exotic.[36] What is clear is that Greece was very different from how it was perceived by western countries. For a start, it was far less oppressed than western enthusiasts were eager to portray it, with Christians being granted a considerable degree of religious freedom.[37] Moreover, until the call for freedom, the Greeks had no concept of nationality as we understand it, despite western interest in the state of the nation. The Greeks identified either with the former Byzantine empire or with immediate family or tribal groups. The former Byzantine empire was united not by countries and geographical frontiers but by common religious ties. Allegiance was owed not to public, secular leaders as was taken for granted in the West but to a spiritual centre, the Patriarch at Constantinople. Centres of Greek culture continued throughout the Greek diaspora, and particularly along the Black Sea, in Constantinople and Trabizond, maintaining ancient Greek scholarship in religious centres and monasteries, and thus constructing the Greek inheritance as a product of the ortho-dox church. Beyond religious links, there were loyalties on a local level. Bandit groups, known as klephts, acknowledged no allegi-ance to either a nominal Greek or Turk leadership, but worked, and robbed, for themselves. Armateli were formed to fight the lawless klephts, but frequently turned klepht themselves.[38] There was no idea of Greece as a country, and even the name Hellas was hardly used. The Greeks lived in regions such as the Morea or Epirus; they called themselves not Greeks but the Romaioi, an allusion to the old Roman Empire based at Byzantium or Constantinople, and the classical land of Hellas was virtually forgotten. Kolokotrones re-called in his autobiography, 'The society of men was small. It was not until our revolution that all the Hellenes became acquainted. There were men who knew no village one hour away from their own.'[39] Trelawny recounted a typical scene during the war:

> The Turkish horse go blindly through the ravines like a drove of buffaloes, and the Greeks, hidden among the rocky heights, rush down on them like wolves, and fusilade them under cover of the rocks. Their sole object is plunder. This is not war but carnage.[40]

Trelawny was not above some exaggeration himself, but when his account is compared with other reports, such as those of the con-temporary historians Thomas Gordon and George Finlay,[41] of the fighting methods of the Greeks, and the descriptions of the leading warriors – Kolokotrones, Odysseus – there is conjured up a telling picture of small factional guerilla warfare based on a society of isolated groups more enthusiastic about Turkish loot than Hellenic freedom.[42]

Against this background of what the west would term primitive tribal organisation, the Greeks who had travelled and been edu-cated in Europe sought to inculcate western ideas of liberty, nation-hood, revolution. Many were drawn to France and imbibed the new ideas about nationalism and independence which had been articulated by the ideologues behind the French Revolution. Rhigas, the leader of a revolutionary movement about twenty years before the Greek uprising of 1821, derived many ideas from French Jacobins and even adapted the 'Marseillaise' to suit the Greek con-text.[43] Adamantios Korais, author of *Mémoire sur l'État Actuel de la Civilisation dans la Grèce*, lived from 1781 in self-imposed exile in

Paris where he witnessed the events of the French Revolution at first hand.[44] Prince Mavrocordato stayed in Pisa for some time and was in close contact with the Shelley circle in Italy before travelling to Greece to organise the Battalion of Philhellenes. Prince Hypsilanti, the phanariot or high-ranking Greek civil servant, began an uprising from the haven of Jassy, Moldavia. Leaders, then, came from outside, with outside ideas, with outside aid, in order to stage a war of independence against Turkish oppression. Indeed Capodistrias, the Russian foreign minister, was positively welcomed because he had never been to Greece, and so was happily neutral. The men brought what they considered enlightenment, Western learning, and, crucially, literacy.[45] Adamantios Korais was convinced that the key to Greek liberation was through knowledge and learning, and so in 1805 he launched a new publishing project sponsored by the Zosimas brothers, wealthy Greek merchants, aimed at publishing editions of Classical Greek texts for Greek readers. These editions were intended to reawaken Greek interest in their ancient past, and at the same time disparaged the medieval, religious heritage. As a result of Korais' efforts, this period in Greek history has since been dubbed the Greek Renaissance or the Greek Enlightenment, significantly using Western European terms.[46]

The method of allowing Western ideals, such as literacy and learning, to become second nature in Greece means that it is difficult to determine what was imposed from outside and what arose from within, or, as Eric Hobsbawm terms it, what 'was constructed from above' and what 'was viewed from below'.[47] The very concept of independence, of revolution and nationalism, was derived from the French Revolution in the west and was not endemic to native Greek culture; and yet revolutionary secret societies, inspired by increasing reading and learning, were formed voluntarily within Greece or the Balkan area.[48] One such group was the 'Philiki Hetairia', formed in 1814 to liberate Greece from Ottoman rule and existing mainly in marginal diaspora communities.[49] The rhetoric of the Greek leaders was western. Hypsilanti stressed the national identity of Greece as it was perceived in the west and the need for Greeks to unite and to resist external oppression. But he expected this external perception of Greece to become the internal consciousness of the new nation. 'Let us recollect, brave and generous Greeks,' he wrote, 'the liberty of the classic land of Greece; the battles of Marathon and Thermopylae; let us combat upon the tombs of our ancestors, who, to leave us free, fought and died.'[50]

Hypsilanti harked back to the ancient example, recalling these famous battles and the supposed ancient characteristics of courage and independence. He addressed his people as Greeks, the ancient Ἕλληνες, and asserted that they were bound to the west, as both its inspiration and its product:

> The civilised people of Europe are busy in laying the foundations of their own happiness and, full of gratitude for the benefits they received from our ancestors, desire the liberty of Greece. Showing ourselves worthy of our virtuous ancestors, and of the age, we hope to deserve their support and their aid, and many of them, partisans of liberty, will come to fight by our side.[51]

The west would support Greece only if it adopted the characteristics which the west had created as associated with Greece: 'showing ourselves worthy of our ancestors . . . we hope to deserve their support'. Thus from necessity, the Greek leaders created a new western Greece of the philhellenic mould, and discountenanced those who would not adapt, calling them 'Asiatic', non-Greek, different people:

> The country will recompense her true children who obey her voice, by the price of glory and honour. But she will reprove as illegitimate, and as Asiatic bastards, those who shew themselves deaf and disobedient to her will, abandoning their name, like that of traitors, to the malediction of posterity.[52]

This threatening tone from Hypsilanti renders ironic such sentiments as Leigh Hunt's published in *The Examiner*: 'The Greeks fight with one heart and soul, because they have all their wrongs and sufferings in common.'[53] The Greeks were not united. Indeed only those who accepted the new identity urged by the leaders and the new ideas of the enlightenment were acknowledged and included. They adopted the beliefs, became indistinguishable from the west, became the new Greece. Others, in contrast, were separated out, excluded just as the Turks were during the war. There was some resistance, although it remained unwritten, passive. Writers since, such as Ion Dragoumis and Anghelos Sikelianos, have expressed doubts about western ideas and suggested an alternative vision.[54] But the feelings of resistance went largely unnoticed in the general desire to invent a universal national tradition and identity.

BYRON'S WAR

Given the extent to which the imagination shaped the pattern of the war and the creation of the new country, it is not surprising that the poets felt they had a vital role to play. Byron is commonly regarded as the philhellenic poet who contributed most to the ideology of the war. While privately he was uncertain about the Greek capacity for self-liberation, publicly he became the focus for the philhellenic efforts.[55] Although he actually travelled to Greece in a non-military capacity to distribute funds collected by the London Greek Committee, his presence there was portrayed as that of a saving warrior. He of course helped to promote this idea by donning a Homeric helmet before setting sail from Italy, and by having his arrival in Greece painted as if he were a powerful general, a latter-day Napoleon.[56] When he died at Missolonghi from the fever raging there, his death was described as a heroic self-sacrifice, a battlefield death, and helped to galvanise more support for the war, both among the British and the Greeks. 'Thus has perished, in the flower of his age, in the noblest of causes, one of the greatest Poets England ever produced', ran the glowing obituary in the *Gentlemen's Magazine*.[57] And in Greece, the poet Andreas Kalvos suggested that Byron's death would lead to a Greek resurrection as the sunset leads to the star of hope.[58] The Greek newspaper, Ελληνικα Χρονικα, edged the edition of 9 April 1824 with black in mourning for Lordhos Vyronos.[59] In a war which was being waged as a result of the imagination and ideals, an idealised symbolic death was more powerful than all the thousands dying on real battlefields. A Greek literary critic wrote later:

> The Greeks are eternally grateful to this philhellene poet, not for his military success, nor for his financial aid . . . but for his sincere love for Greece and its people. By means of his verse, he praised the ancient glory of Greece, mourned the miseries of her slavery, and finally gave his life in the struggle for her national liberation.[60]

The emerging national poet of Greece, Demetrios Solomos, who also wrote the poem, 'Hymn to Liberty', which was to become the national anthem, composed an elegy for Byron after he died.[61]

Byron had played a large part in fostering the philhellenic myth by his poetry. The opening verses of *The Giaour* lament the gloomy and ruined state of modern Greece under Turkish rule, and imply a symbolic connection between the conquered state of the country and the shadowy existence of Leila, only glimpsed in fragmentary phrases in the poem and subject to the wills of her husband and her lover. Further lament for Greece occurs in the song, in *Don Juan* III, 'The Isles of Greece', which mourns the modern Greek tendency to seek private pleasure rather than public war and heroic resistance:

> In vain – in vain: strike other chords;
> Fill high the cup with Samian wine!
> Leave battles to the Turkish hordes,
> And shed the blood of Scio's wine!
> (737–40)

Polarisations are complicated here by the implied comparison between the ancient Greeks and the 'Turkish hordes', both of whom relish battles, while the feminised modern Greeks prefer wine and delight. The impact of the song becomes even less clear when its narrative frame, the feasting and idyllic setting of Haidee's island, is also considered. Are such heroic, philhellenic sentiments out of place in the modern, more peaceful and more enjoyable world in which Haidee lives? Or does Haidee's joy, which is shattered moments later by the violent return of her father, illustrate all the more clearly the need for a return to perceived ancient heroism for which the singer calls? The canto as a whole, therefore, makes more complicated the relationship between nostalgia, heroism and political activity than is suggested when the poem, 'The Isles of Greece', is read in isolation.

But the poem which had most impact upon philhellenic thinking was *Childe Harold's Pilgrimage*, first published in 1812. Many a philhellene, crossing Europe to join the fight in Greece, carried Byron's poem in their pocket. The poem provided a mental map of contemporary Europe, charting where fact met fiction and linking places and events to appropriate moods. The second canto mixed elegiac nostalgia for the classical Greek past with despondency over the modern Greek present:

> Spirit of freedom! when on Phyle's brow
> Thou sat'st with Thrasybulus and his train,
> Couldst thou forebode the dismal hour which now
> Dims the green beauties of thine Attic plain?
> (702–5)

Byron evoked great names from the classical past – Thermopylae, Eurotas – like talismans to stir up emotion. In keeping with the rhetorical idealisation of classical Greece, the land, although now ruined, is almost sacred: 'Wher'er we tread 'tis haunted, holy ground'. Yet despite the tangible spirit to be found in Greece, it is apparently only Byron, the hero from the west, who can sense it. The Greeks seem impervious:

> Ah Greece! they love thee least who owe thee most;
> Their birth, their blood, and that sublime record
> Of hero sires, who shame thy now degenerate horde!
>
> (789–91)

Despite the protests in the poem that it is the Greeks themselves who must free their country, Byron adopts the philhellenic rhetoric that it is somehow the duty of the west to liberate their own Greece. The similarity between the gloomy western hero Childe Harold and the gloomy state of ruined classical Greece suggests some ancestral connection between the two. At the beginning of the second canto, for example, Byron moves swiftly from mourning his lover John Eddleston – 'There thou! – whose love and life together fled / Have left me here to love and live in vain' – to mourning the decayed Greece – 'Here let me sit upon this massy stone / 'The marble column's yet unshaken base'.[62] The hidden past of Byron's life and the glorious past of Greek culture become subsumed in Byron's all-encompassing melancholy.

Yet while Byron obviously inculcates the philhellenic myths of the British debt to Greece and the importance of the classical past, he also subtly questions and attempts to dispel them. Alternative figurings of Greece appear, besides the received philhellenic constructions. The famous passage lamenting the 'Fair Greece! Sad relic' of western creation is preceded by an account of the life of the Albanians in north-west Greece, with their alternative, nomadic and unwestern lifestyle, and their almost paradisal surroundings:

> From the dark barriers of that rugged clime,
> Ev'n to the centre of Illyria's vales,
> Childe Harold pass'd o'er many a mountain sublime,
> Through lands scarce noticed in historic tales;
> Yet in famed Attica such lovely dales

Are rarely seen; nor can fair Tempe boast
A charm they know not; loved Parnassus fails,
Though classic ground and consecrated most,
To match some spots that lurk within this lowering coast.

(406–14)

Albania, in Byron's description, succeeds in surpassing with its pastoral beauty the original home of pastoral, classical Greece. Byron's 'Illyria' inevitably recalls Shakespeare's Illyria at the beginning of *Twelfth Night*. Viola's early lines, 'And what should I do in Illyria? / My brother, he is in Elysium', draw an alliterative connection between Illyria and Elysium. Could Byron's Illyria also be a kind of Elysium? The suggestion is that he has discovered a Shakespearian paradise unknown in 'classic ground'.

The scholarly prose notes to *Childe Harold* also contain alternative versions and images of Greece. Byron includes a note about the Romaic language, and an appendix containing what amounts to a Romaic phrasebook for the traveller together with a comparison between the Lord's Prayer in classical Greek and the Lord's Prayer in Romaic. His translations of a Greek war song and a modern Greek love song also point out the contrast sharply. The hegemony of Athens as the predominant image is also questioned:

'Athens', says a celebrated topographer, 'is still the most polished city of Greece'. Perhaps it may be of Greece, but not of the Greeks; for Joannina in Epirus is universally allowed, amongst themselves, to be superior in the wealth, refinement, learning and dialect of its inhabitants. The Athenians are remarkable for their cunning.[63]

But most significantly, in contrast to the poem's presentation of the west's apparent authority over the history of Greece, the notes admit the west's lack of knowledge about Greece:

The fact is, we are deplorably in want of information on the subject of the Greeks, and in particular their literature, nor is there any probability of our being better acquainted, till our intercourse becomes more intimate, or their independence confirmed. The relations of passing travellers are as little to be depended on as the invectives of angry factors; but till something more can be attained, we must be content with the little to be acquired from similar sources.[64]

The prose notes describe an alternative, alien Greece, which refuses to conform to the western model and which remains mysterious and unable to be categorised. As a result, Byron tones down his political aspirations for the country in the footnotes. Instead of allusions to Thermopylae and Marathon and heroic warfare, there is a measured assessment of the political situation: 'The Greeks will never be independent; they will never be sovereigns as heretofore, and God forbid they ever should! but they may be subjects without being slaves. Our colonies are not independent, but they are free and industrious and such may Greece be hereafter.'[65] Perhaps even these sentiments could be construed as perpetuating the philhellenic rhetoric. The analogy with Britain's colonial relationship suggested here is simply a more honest description of the philhellenic dream – creating a western Greece. But, on the other hand, Byron's measured tone seems to suggest an understanding, on his part, of the autonomous existence of Greece, of its difference from the west and thus its inability to conform to the western agenda of freedom and independent national identity.

HELLAS

In contrast to Byron, Shelley has frequently been criticised for his naivety or his excessive idealism in his attitude to the war. Suffering from 'schoolboyish delusions', he is thought to have dreamt about an impossibly idealised Greece while Byron, the realist, went out to confront the Turkish enemies on the ground.[66] His famous statement in the preface to *Hellas* has served to foster this perception: 'We are all Greeks. Our laws, our literature, our religion, our arts have their roots in Greece.' The apparent assumption in this statement that Greekness is an easily assumed quality, which epitomises western civilised values and which can be shared by anyone, jars with the knowledge of those immersed in the brutal realities of the nineteenth-century Balkan war. But Shelley's other writings, his correspondence and particularly *Hellas*, suggest that his response to the war was very different. Like Byron, through whom after all the sense of contemporary Greece was partly mediated, Shelley both fosters and questions the philhellenic myth.

Indeed *Hellas* focuses attention upon the consequences of unremitting philhellenic enthusiasm, and complicates the simple divisions demanded by idealistic rhetoric.

When the news of the Greek uprising reached the Shelley household in Italy, there were some signs of excitement. Mary wrote an ecstatic letter to Claire, 'Greece has declared its freedom. . . . The Morea, Epirus, Servia are in revolt. Greece will most certainly be free';[67] while Shelley sent off emotive propaganda letters to the *Examiner* and the *Morning Chronicle*, with a translation of Hypsilanti's proclamation. But in private, like Byron, Shelley held reservations about the affair, revealing in his correspondence that he understood the situation beyond the rhetoric and that he found the chaos within Greece hard to endure. He admitted that Prince Mavrocordato, one of the leaders of the fight for freedom, was proving not so attractive in the flesh: 'The Greek Prince comes sometimes, and I reproach my own savage disposition that so agreeable accomplished and aimiable [*sic*] a person is not more agreeable to me'.[68] Noticeably here Shelley inverts the expected division between west and east, so that the irreconcilable distance between himself and the Greek is caused by his own 'savage disposition' and the Greek's 'accomplished and aimiable' character. Beyond the personal reasons for doubt and the awareness of the cultural difference of the Greeks, Shelley appears to have expressed uncertainties about the Greek capacity to reform and to resuscitate their freedom. He wrote to Mary from Ravenna:

> We have good rumours of the Greeks here and of a Russian war. I hardly wish the Russians to take any part in it – My maxim is with Aeschylus 'τὸ δυσσεβὲς – μετὰ μὲν πλείονα τίκτει, σφετέρᾳ δ'εἰκότα γέννᾳ. There is a Greek exercise for you. – How should slaves produce anything but tyranny – even as the seed produces the plant.[69]

This reference to slaves could apply purely to the Russians, but the descriptions by other writers of the oppression and state of servitude suffered by the Greeks lead one to conclude that Shelley was concerned about the consequences of the Greeks' own slavish situation. Indeed his recognition in private of the actual conditions and nature of the Greeks put an end to his dreams of visiting Greece. After hearing the news of the uprising, he wrote to his cousin Tom Medwin:

Massacres of the Turks have begun in various parts. – This is a sufficient objection to our Grecian project even if other circumstances would permit my being one of the party. – There is nothing I so earnestly desired as to visit Greece; but the fates do not seem propitious to my desires.[70]

Shelley was aware of the distance between his imaginative possession of Greece and the alien country. Only Mary retained the simple dream of unity. 'What a delight', she wrote to Claire, 'it will be to visit Greece free.'[71]

Despite Shelley's private doubts about the success of the war and the character of its participants, however, he felt compelled to support the Greek cause in public. More than that, he was stirred into writing one of the greatest propaganda pieces of the war, *Hellas*. The ostensible purpose of *Hellas* is indicated by Shelley's various letters to his publisher urging speedy publication. 'As the subject is in a certain degree of a transitory nature', he wrote to Ollier, 'I send it to you, instead of printing it here, in the full confidence that you will at my request not delay to send it to the press.'[72] He wanted *Hellas* to be printed quickly before its topicality and value as propaganda to encourage British interest in the new revolt was lost. The simple methods of propaganda are openly acknowledged in the preface, which argues that the more complicated details of truth have no place in this type of writing:

Common fame is the only authority which I can alledge [sic] for the details which form the basis of the poem, and I must trespass upon the forgiveness of my readers for the display of newspaper erudition to which I have been reduced. Undoubtedly, until the conclusion of the war, it will be impossible to obtain an account of it sufficiently authentic for historical materials.[73]

Just as the diverse motives behind the west's interest in Greece or the heterogeneity among the Greeks were compressed into the unifying rhetoric of philhellenism, so Shelley reduced the diversity of 'historical materials' into the simple verse of propaganda.

The lyric verses of *Hellas* contain many of the same arguments as the many anonymous philhellenic verses which appeared in the contemporary journals. The representation of Greece as semi-sacred, as the origin of western culture and values, as possessing a benign, abstract spirit of freedom, was essential to the arguments of

philhellenism. Felicia Hemans had argued as much in her poem
Modern Greece, which drew on the popular reception of *Childe
Harold*:

> Grandeur may vanish, conquest be forgot. –
> To leave on earth renown that cannot die,
> Of high-souled genius is th' unrivalled lot.
> Honour to thee, O Athens! thou hast shown
> What mortals may attain, and seized the palm alone.[74]

Shelley describes Greece as almost unworldly in its perfection. He
inverts Byron's insistance on manliness and portrays the perfect
Greece as feminine:

> But Greece was as a hermit's child,
>   Whose fairest thoughts and limbs were built
> To woman's growth, by dreams so mild,
>   She knew not pain nor guilt.
>
> (996–9)

In another of Shelley's nationalist poems, 'Ode to Liberty', inspired
by the uprising in Spain, Greece is portrayed as perfect beyond
belief and historical reality:

> Athens arose: a city such as vision
>   Builds from the purple crags and silver towers
> Of battlemented cloud, as in derision
>   Of kingliest masonry.
>
> (61–4)

Again subverting Byron's celebration of physical ruins and broken
masonry, Shelley's Athens of insubstantial cloud becomes more
important and longlasting, because not historically contingent,
than the 'kingliest masonry' of rival civilisations.

It is partly the need to stir the audience to a cause, whether it is
Greece or Spain, that provokes this exaggerated language and
simple view. The simplicity of the understanding of the processes
of revolution is reflected in the easy verse structure of the lyrics:

> Another Athens shall arise,
> And to remoter time

> Bequeath, like sunset to the skies,
> The splendour of its prime.
>
>   (1084–7)

The details of revolution, of historical process and legacy, are glossed over in the hazy metaphor of sunset. How is Athens *like* sunset? How exactly can an Athens-like civilisation spread its political ideals to other peoples and avoid problems of resistance, distortions, conservatism? These questions are quelled by the effortlessness of alternating rhyme – arise/skies and time/prime. The comforting closure of these lines soothes concerns about the problems of revolutionary activity.

The desire in the choruses to gloss over the problems of the implication of the ideal Greek image means that there is less sense of the contrast in Shelley's poem between Greece of the historical past and Greece of the present than there is in Byron and other contemporary writers. A typical poem urged its audience to

> Look round on the tombs of your fathers, whose fame
> In the bright page of history told,
> Should teach you to give to your country a name,
>   Or die like the martyrs of old![75]

The anonymous author of this verse does not concern himself with the difference between the metaphor of Greece, with its connotations of perfection and liberty, and the actual country in the Balkans. Byron actually plays upon the difference, placing his poems specifically and capitalising on the fact that he knew the country well. The contrast he sets up between the place in his time and the place of the past becomes the inspiration for freedom, symbolising the power of Greece:

> The mountains look on Marathon –
>   And Marathon looks on the sea;
> And musing there an hour alone,
>   I dream'd that Greece might still be free.[76]

But while occasionally referring to Thermopylae or Marathon, Shelley preferred the simplicity of abstracting his depiction of Greece totally from fact and place. The Greece that was associated with liberty was portrayed as timeless, not fixed by any temporal definitions.

> Temples and towers,
> Citadels and marts and they
> Who live and die there, have been ours
> And may be thine, and must decay.
> But Greece and her foundations are
> Built below the tide of war,
> Based on the chrystalline sea
> Of thought and its eternity.
>
> (692–9)

The Greece of philhellenic ideology – 'below the tide of war' – was not to be confused with historical or real events or phenomena. Shelley rejected the evocation of fifth-century classical Greece popular with his contemporaries. The past, he thought, was impossible to revive and could not be connected to their ideal of Greece. A fragment, intended for *Hellas* but eventually omitted, is revealing:

> Could Arethuse to her forsaken urn
> From Alpheus and the bitter Doris run,
> Or could the morning shafts of purest light
> Again into the quivers of the Sun
> Be gathered – could one thought from its wild flight
> Return into the temple of the brain
> Without a change, without a strain, –
> Could aught that is, ever again
> Be what it once has ceased to be,
>   Greece might again be free![77]

If Greece were the historical source of freedom, and the fruits of anything could return to their source, according to the fragment, Greece could be revived. But the fruit cannot return to the seed, and the historical Greece is not the source of freedom. History was not to be confused with the propagandist image, and nor was place. Shelley posits in *Hellas* a future 'Greece' in the west, America.

> If Greece must be
> A wreck, yet shall its fragments reassemble
> And build themselves again impregnably
>   In a diviner clime
> To Amphionic music on some cape sublime

Which frowns above the idle foam of Time.
(1002–7)

With these sentiments, Greece becomes a metaphor for the
principle of liberty and independence everywhere, applicable to
situations in America, Spain, even – covertly – Britain.[78] 'This is the
age of the war of the oppressed against the oppressors', Shelley
wrote in the preface to *Hellas*. 'A new race has arisen throughout
Europe, nursed in the abhorrence of opinions which are its chains,
and she will continue to produce fresh generations to accomplish
that destiny which tyrants foresee and dread.'[79]

   In the choruses, then, there is a case for finding an extreme form
of philhellenism in *Hellas*, a philhellenism which simplifies historical complications to a single idealised image, and which finds
history so distasteful that it avoids it altogether.[80] However, there
is clearly far more to *Hellas* than such propaganda. While the lyric
choruses deal with visions and aspirations, the work as a whole
centres on the dramatic realisation of his fate by Mahmud, in a way
which confronts the emotions and conflicts of war and unsettles the
philhellenic choruses.[81] The drama is based upon the Aeschylean
tragedy *The Persians*, which enacted the defeat of the Persians by
the Greeks in the battle of Salamis in 480 BC. Like Aeschylus's play,
Shelley's *Hellas* witnesses the events from the Turkish, or Persian,
point of view, and his hero is the king of the Turks. Unlike Aeschylus's play, the drama ends with the temporary victory of the Turks,
and unlike *The Persians*, the chorus consists not of Persians but
of Greek captive women who express the lyric hopes for Greek
liberty.

   The inversion of values and viewpoint which the tragic form
necessitates upsets the clearcut divisions of philhellenic rhetoric.
The reader's sympathy is naturally drawn towards the hero,
Mahmud, and yet he is Turkish, the 'wrong' side. Mahmud's conscience and feelings are laid bare to the reader so that all his fears
and weaknesses are known. Indeed there are several allusions to
Shakespeare's *Macbeth*. Count Cenci invokes Macbeth only to
prove his even greater evil. Totally shameless, he does not even
need night to 'scarf up the tender eye of pitiful day' since he does a
deed 'which shall confound both day and night'.[82] But Mahmud
invokes Macbeth's conscience, the last vestiges of his humanity. He
is haunted by dreams and visions presaging his doom like Macbeth. 'The times do cast shadows . . . and these are of them', he says

to his messenger, recalling the lines about the witches in Macbeth;[83] and later as he grows visibly weary during the drama, 'Tomorrow and tomorrow are as lamps / 'Set in our path to light us to the edge'.[84] Mahmud's allusions to Macbeth's tortured mental suffering increase the reader's sympathy for him. Like Macbeth – unlike, noticeably, Aeschylus's Xerxes – Mahmud is conscious and repentant of the evil he is creating, and equally powerless to prevent it now that it has begun:

> Silence those mutineers – that drunken crew,
> That crowd about the pilot in the storm.
> Aye! strike the foremost shorter by a head. –
> They weary me and I have need of rest.
>
> (191–4)

But Mahmud cannot find rest, because his mind is in turmoil. Given a vision of the future by Ahasuerus who appears like Darius's ghost, he witnesses the times changing in spite of his agency, and the pity is in his realisation of his lack of power:

> What meanest thou? thy words stream like a tempest
> Of dazzling mist within my brain – they shake
> The earth on which I stand, and hang like night
> On Heaven above me. What can they avail?
> They cast on all things surest, brightest, best,
> Doubt, insecurity, astonishment.
>
> (786–91)

The revolutionary movement of time disturbs Mahmud's conception of order so that he is filled with 'doubt' and 'insecurity'. For, like many other Romantic heroes of this time, Mahmud is bewildered by the speed of the impersonal roll of history and the mass will of the people. Like Hyperion and the deposed gods of Keats's poem, like Shelley's Cyclops in his translation, Mahmud is being overtaken by events and the revolutionary mob, and cannot 'stem the torrent of descending time' (350). There is a strong contrast between the individual, tragic figure of Mahmud trying to come to terms with change, and the impersonal voices of the chorus.[85] Mahmud's individualism centres around his consciousness, his dreams and fears so that he begins to transcend his world with his new understanding, his enlightenment from Ahasuerus:

everything 'is but a vision' (780). Byron's Sardanapalus is a similarly
isolated, monarchical figure. He is distanced from his people,
unaware of their views just as Mahmud is distanced from his
people's jubilation at their victory in *Hellas*. But Sardanapalus's
isolation stems from his positive belief in an alternative way of
life, in the pursuit of love not war: 'I had rather lose an empire than
thy presence.'[86] Mahmud's isolation is more elusive. It stems from
his consciousness, his consciousness that all division among humanity is insubstantial and yet that he is somehow on the losing
side of such a division. Mahmud's mind becomes the focus of
reality for him, because all else is insubstantial and temporal. And
in contrast to this, the chorus articulates a scientific vision of the
inevitability of change and progress, the necessary victory of the
Greeks:

> Worlds on worlds are rolling ever
> From creation to decay.
>
> (197–8)

Mahmud's attractive individualism and the chorus's alienating
and impersonal character further upset the clearcut divisions of
good and bad necessary for propaganda. Whereas the proponents
of philhellenism were shown continually to need to separate west
from east, Greek from Turk, and to categorise and define, the
dynamics of the tragic drama blur and deny those definitions. The
assured expressions of promised victory for the Greeks attain almost a cruel tone when set in direct juxtaposition with the agony of
Mahmud. The confusion over definition in the drama, or as
Mahmud puts it, the 'doubt, insecurity, astonishment', replicates
the difficulty experienced by the philhellene in representing Greece
unambiguously and unproblematically.

Hellas reveals a lack of ease with the simplicity and categorisation
promoted by the propaganda of war. War falsely imposes definitions of right and wrong which cannot be so simple while the
brutality of war itself serves to render definitions more impossible.
Shelley believed that the violence of war made all its participants
alike. In *Prometheus Unbound*, Prometheus and Jupiter are virtually
identical. In *Hellas*, the fortunes of war fluctuate between the
Greeks and the Turks. Unlike *The Persians*, which is one long tale of
disaster and lament for the Persians, the first messenger reports one
Turkish victory and one Greek victory. Reports of widespread

rebellion throughout the Ottoman Empire are countered by the blood-curdling rout of the Greeks at the end of the play:

> Shout in the jubilee of death! the Greeks
> Are as a brood of lions in the net
> Round which the kingly hunters of the earth
> Stand smiling.
>
> (931–4)

The image of the net recalls another of Aeschylus's great plays, the *Agamemnon*, in which Clytemnestra captures her husband in a net and kills him, only to perpetuate the cycle of killing and revenge, as the two factions in the family unite in the horror of violent murder. Like the tit-for-tat murders in the House of Atreus, the fluctuations of victory and defeat undergone by both Turk and Greek serve to transcend the distinctions between them, so that they become indistinguishable from each other through the course of war. This lack of distinction is highlighted at the climax of the drama when the Turkish victory is announced. Mahmud is unmoved, still despairing and mentally defeated. The Greek chorus, on the other hand, begin a chorus of optimism: 'The world's great age begins anew, / The golden years return' (1060–1). Which is the victor? Which is the Greek?

EPILOGUE

An editorial in the *Pall Mall Gazette* of 25 August 1865 began, 'If nobody were to talk about Greece, there would be no philhellenes', but it seems equally that if there were no philhellenes, there would be no Greece for anyone to talk about. The west set in motion the idea of an independent, unified Greece according to western revolutionary and nationalist ideals and contributed to the institution of the state of Greece in 1830. Indeed at the Treaty drawn up in 1832, representatives from Britain, France, Russia and Bavaria were present, but nobody from Greece. The western allies brought over the second son of the King of Bavaria to serve as the new monarch. They set up a western legal system and quickly founded a university in 1837. They established the new capital at Athens to conform with their classical notion of the country, rather than at Nauplia, which formed the capital in the first three experimental years of independence, or at Janina, the largest town in the early nineteenth century, or indeed in Constantinople, centre of the Byzantine heritage. They encouraged the reintroduction of 'katharevousa', the pure ancient Greek, instead of the corrupted Romaic or 'demotic'. And while the borders of independent Greece were altered and extended throughout the century, and are still disputed today, they expected the borders to correspond with the ancient geographical definitions of Greece, rather than with the Byzantine. In effect, they had created a real nation to correspond with their imagination.

The tensions which lay behind the establishment of Greece are still evident in the country today. A bastion of the modern British holidaymaker in the heart of Eastern Europe, a member of the European Union surrounded by the impoverished members of the defunct Warsaw Pact, Greece betrays its origins as the creation of the west in despite of its geographical position. Athens enjoys an uneasy status as a capital, a dusty and soulless modern city almost overwhelming the bizarre ancient temple at its heart. There are no rings of history between the ancient and modern cities, but only the determined use of the Parthenon icon as in some way a symbol of the city's confused identity and orientation. Yet in the capital's museums, hints of a second capital, the capital of the soul. Every artefact from Istanbul is resolutely, and wistfully, labelled 'From Constantinople'.[87] The people are torn between east and west by what Patrick Leigh Fermor has termed the 'Helleno-Romaic' dilemma, a division between the logical, public-orientated aspect of the mind symbolised by western Hellenism, and the passionate, private aspect symbolised by the religious demands of the eastern Byzantine and Ottoman Empire:

> 'Hellene' is the glory of ancient Greece; 'Romaic' the splendours and the sorrows of Byzantium, above all the sorrows. 'Hellenism' is symbolised by the columns of the Parthenon; Byzantium . . . by the great dome of St Sophia . . . a St Sophia turned into a mosque filled with turbans and flanked by minarets, with all her mosaic saints hidden under whitewash and the giant koranic texts of the occupying Turks; the Greeks meanwhile, exiles in their own land, celebrate their rites in humbler fanes.[88]

Nikos Kazantzakis, the most renowned recent Greek writer, has called this phenomenon in the make-up of Greece the 'double-born soul of Greece', and describes the confusion for the Greek, able to express only one half of his character and finding that the tradition for the articulation of the other eastern part has been lost:

> For a Greek, the journey through Greece is a fascinating, exhausting ordeal. The voices that fascinate most are not those which awaken the loftiest and most uncompromising ideals in his mind; and yet he is ashamed to make the gesture of wakening those less important, though still beloved departed.[89]

The method by which Greece came into being in the 1820s, with its struggle to conform to one set of ideals or another, has been set fast into the fabric of the country, so that its true character is for ever in doubt and is shaped by the conflicting demands of dominating external ideologies.

Since the creation of Greece is the peculiar product of Romantic Hellenism, the country has frozen in time the particular expectations and images of the early nineteenth century. The invented nation illustrates, in its constitution and self-perception, the aspiration of the west to re-imagine the past in its own image and to forge links abroad in order to gain a sense of identity. As Greece was established in 1830, so notions of Greece, 'the idea of Greece which keeps us together' as Fermor's train-guard asserts, were instituted, perfected, for the new nineteenth century. The political constitution of Greece ensured the permanence of philhellenic ideas, and officially denied the earlier historical conditions and allegiances.

A similar institutionalisation has affected the reception of Shelley. In the corner of University College in Oxford, there is a large shrine, opened in 1893 under the auspices of Shelley's daughter-in law, to commemorate the college's most famous student.[90] In the coolness of the silent sanctuary, the marble white body of Shelley lies stretched upon the plinth. He is naked like a pastoral Adonis and elegantly sprawled in the iconic pose of the dying Jesus, while around him gather cherubs and angels. Above is an excerpt from *Adonais*: 'The One remains, the many change and pass'. Iron bars prevent the ordinary public from approaching the statue, from sullying its innocence with their world of fallen experience. The marble statue of Shelley crystallised Victorian ideas of Greek beauty as well as nineteenth-century ideas of the poet, ideas which emphasised his lyrical unworldliness and repressed his political opinions and the disruptive impact of his writing.

While critics since the Victorian period have reassessed Shelley's poetry and rescued his politics and revolutionary writing from marmoreal petrification, his Greece has remained behind bars, a site supposedly of hushed silent worship, as divinely idealised as Byron's philhellenic Greece: 'Where'er we tread tis haunted, sacred ground.' It is only now, when Kazantzakis's Greek journeyman can 'waken' the forgotten 'voices' that articulated other views of Greece or when we can appreciate how Shelley's poetry expresses and explores the tensions of imagining another culture, that we are able to rethink former, apparently permanent, ideas of Greece and to sharpen and remould our understanding of Shelley's hellenism.

Notes

Unless otherwise stated, London is the place of publication. Classical references are taken from the Loeb Classical Library texts, unless otherwise stated.

Explorations

1. Sir R. Livingstone (ed.), *The Legacy of Greece* (1921; reissued 1969), preface.
2. F. Schiller, *Ueber naive und sentimentalische Dichtung* (1795), *Naive and Sentimental Poetry and On the Sublime, Two Essays*, translated by J.A. Elias (New York, 1966), p. 85.
3. G. Highet, *The Classical Tradition: Greek and Roman Influences on Western Literature* (Oxford, 1949), p. 1.
4. B. Knox, *Backing Into the Future: The Classical Tradition and its Renewal* (1994), p. 15; J. Churton Collins, *Greek Influence on English Poetry* (London, Bath and New York, 1910), p. 53.
5. C.M. Bowra, *The Greek Experience* (1957), p. 1; F.E. Pierce, 'The Hellenic Current in English Nineteenth Century Poetry', *Journal of English and Germanic Philology*, 16 (1917), pp. 103–35; R.R. Bolgar (ed.), *Classical Influences on Western Thought 1650–1870* (Cambridge, 1979), p. 1.
6. M. Finley (ed.), *The Legacy of Greece: A New Appraisal* (Oxford, 1981), preface. In his anthology, *English Romantic Hellenism* (Manchester, 1982), Timothy Webb notes the variety of response to Greece but is not concerned with the question of influence. Even Richard Jenkyns' much admired *The Victorians and Ancient Greece* (Oxford, 1980) and Frank Turner's *The Greek Heritage in Victorian Britain* (New Haven, 1981) offer only sophisticated forms of the Casaubon cataloguing type.
7. P. Sherrard, *The Pursuit of Greece: An Anthology* (1964), pp. 2, 11–15.
8. L. MacNeice, *Autumn Journal* (1939), IX.
9. O. Talpin, *Greek Fire* (1989), p. 25.
10. B. Knox, *The Oldest Dead White European Males* (New York and London, 1993), p. 28.
11. J.A. Notopoulos, *The Platonism of Shelley: A Study of Platonism and the Poetic Mind* (Durham, North Carolina, 1949). For a similar idealising and escapist view of Romantic Greece, see T. Webb, *The Violet in the Crucible: Shelley and Translation* (Oxford, 1976).
12. See for Keats, E.B. Hungerford, *Shores of Darkness* (New York, 1941), p. 6; for Byron, F.E. Pierce, 'The Hellenic Current in English Nineteenth Century Poetry', p. 109. Mary Beard and John Henderson do not even mention Shelley, but argue that Byron's and Keats's vision

of Greece 'became the standard' in the nineteenth century: see M. Beard and J. Henderson, *Classics: A Very Short Introduction* (Oxford, 1995), pp. 14–16.

13. Keats, 'Ode to Psyche' (1820), ll. 50–3, 64–7.
14. M. Aske, *Keats and Hellenism* (Cambridge, 1985).
15. E.J. Trelawny, *Recollections of the Last Days of Byron and Shelley* (1858, new edn, 1906), pp. 136–7.
16. E.J. Trelawny, *Records of Shelley, Byron and the Author* (1878), p. 37.
17. Most books on Byron's hellenism take that heroism at face value. See H. Spender, *Byron and Greece* (1924); T.B. Spencer, *Byron and the Greek Tradition* (Byron Foundation Lecture, Nottingham, 1959); E. Longford, *Byron's Greece* (1975).
18. Shelley to Peacock, *Letters*, 23–4 January 1819.
19. Shelley, *Defence of Poetry*, Reiman and Powers, p. 487.
20. W.J. Bate, *The Burden of the Past and the English Poet* (1971).
21. See M. Worton and J. Still (eds), *Intertextuality* (1990).
22. L.P. Hartley, *The Go-Between* (1953), prologue.
23. E. Said, *Orientalism* (1978; republished, Penguin, 1991), p. 3.
24. M. Bernal, *Black Athena: The Afroasiatic Roots of Western Culture*, 2 vols (1987–91), I, p. 236.
25. Said, *Orientalism*, p. 12.
26. See, for example, E. Hall, 'When is a Myth not a Myth?: Bernal's Ancient Model', *Arethusa*, 25.1 (Winter, 1992), pp. 181–201.
27. M. Bernal, *Black Athena*, I, p. 209.
28. H. Cixous, 'Sorties', in E. Marks and I. de Courtivron (eds), *New French Feminisms* (Brighton, 1980), p. 90.
29. L. Irigaray, *Speculum de l'Autre Femme*, translated as *Speculum of the Other Woman* by G.C. Gill (New York, 1985).
30. M. Green, *Dreams of Adventure, Deeds of Empire* (1980); P. Brantlinger, *Rule of Darkness: British Literature and Imperialism 1830–1914* (New York, 1988).
31. E. Said, *Culture and Imperialism*, (1993), pp. 95–116. See also N. Leask, *British Romantic Writers and the East: Anxieties of Empire* (Cambridge, 1992); J. Barrell, *The Infection of Thomas De Quincey: A Psychopathology of Imperialism* (New Haven and London, 1991).
32. P. Cartledge, *The Greeks: A Portrait of Self and Others* (Oxford, 1993).
33. E. Hall, *Inventing the Barbarian: Greek Self-Definition in Tragedy* (Oxford, 1989), p. 4.
34. H. Erskine-Hill, *The Augustan Idea in English Literature* (1983), pp. 234–66.
35. E. Gibbon, *Decline and Fall of the Roman Empire* (1776), chapter 2.
36. W. Leppman, *Pompeii in Fact and Fiction* (1968), pp. 48–91.
37. J. Stuart and N. Revett, *The Antiquities of Athens*, 4 vols (1762–1816).
38. R. Wood, *A Comparative View of the Antient and Present State of the Troad. To which is attached an Essay on the Original Genius of Homer* (1767). There was an earlier assessment of Homer in the eighteenth century – T. Blackwell, *An Enquiry into the Life and Writings of Homer* (1735). However, Blackwell was primarily concerned with Homer as a model of simplicity for contemporary writing, whereas Wood's

interest in Homer as a historical figure, of interest in his own right, pioneered a new way of regarding Homeric life.

39. D. Irwin (ed.), *Winckelmann: Writings on Art* (1972).
40. J.J. Barthélèmy, *Voyage de Jeune Anacharsis en Grèce, dans le milieu du quatrième siecle avant l'ére vulgaire*, 5 vols (Paris, 1788, trans. 1791).
41. C.M. Wieland, *The History of Agathon* (1766), translated by J. Richardson, 4 vols (1783), I, pp. xviii–xix.
42. A.W. Schlegel, *A Course of Lectures on Dramatic Art and Literature*, translated by J. Black, 2 vols (1815), Lecture II, p. 45.
43. See D. Constantine, *Early Greek Travellers and the Hellenic Ideal* (Cambridge, 1984) and H.N. Angelomatis-Tsougarakis, 'The Eve of the Greek Revival: British Travellers' Perceptions of Early Nineteenth Century Greece' (Unpublished DPhil Thesis, Oxford University, 1986).
44. J. Buzard, *The Beaten Track: European Travel, Tourism and the Ways to Culture* (Oxford, 1994).
45. F.A. Wolf, *Prolegomena ad Homerum; sive De Operum Homericorum prisca et genuina variisque mutationibus, et probabili ratione emendandi* (Halis Saxorum, 1795); J. Bryant, *A Dissertation concerning the War of Troy, and the Expedition of the Grecians, showing that no such expedition was ever undertaken, and that no such city of Phrygia existed* (1796); W. Francklin, *Remarks and Observations on the Plain of Troy* (1800); W. Gell, *The Topography of Troy, and its vicinity* (1804).
46. W. St Clair, *Lord Elgin and the Marbles* (1967), pp. 74–6.
47. Byron, Ravenna Journal, *BLJ*, Vol VIII, 11 January 1821.
48. F.M. Turner, 'Why the Greeks and not the Romans in Victorian Britain', in G.W. Clarke (ed.), *Rediscovering Hellenism: The Hellenic Inheritance and the English Imagination* (Cambridge, 1989), pp. 62–3.
49. E.S. Creasy, *Some Account of the Foundation of Eton College, and of the Past and Present Condition of the School* (1848), pp. 25–7; [Anon], *The Eton System of Education Vindicated: and its Capabilities of Improvement Considered* (1834).
50. N. Carlisle, *A Concise Description of the Endowed Grammar Schools in England and Wales*, 2 vols (1818).
51. D.S. Colman, *Sabrinae Corolla: The Classics at Shrewsbury School under Dr. Butler and Dr. Kennedy* (Shrewsbury, 1950); J.J. Findlay (ed.), *Arnold of Rugby: His School Life and Contributions to Education* (Cambridge, 1897).
52. Creasy notices the introduction of these particular authors at Eton too: *Some Account*, p. 58.
53. T. Arnold 'Rugby School', *Quarterly Journal of Education*, 7 (1834), pp. 240–1.
54. See Rev. Hunt's letter to Lord Elgin, in W. St Clair, *Lord Elgin and the Marbles*, p. 96.
55. W. St. Clair, *Lord Elgin and the Marbles*, pp. 172–9, 254–5.
56. G. Grote, *History of Greece*, 12 vols (1846–56), IV, pp. 234–42; W. Gladstone, *Studies on Homer and the Homeric Age*, 3 vols (1853), III, 'The Politics of the Homeric Age', pp. 1–144.

57. F.M. Turner, *The Greek Heritage in Victorian Britain* (New Haven, 1981), pp. 187–263.
58. C. Edwards (ed.), *Palimpsests: Reading Rome 1789–1945*, introduction [forthcoming].
59. R.M. Ogilvie, *Latin and Greek: A History of the Influence of the Classics on English Life from 1600–1918* (1964), p. 87. Ogilvie argues that, despite the 'transitional period', 'there is no sign of an Hellenic spirit permeating and transforming the conventional attitudes and morality inherited from the eighteenth century' (p. 82).
60. Evan Evans, *Some Specimens of the Poetry of the Antient Welsh Bards* (1764); Iolo Morganwg [Edward Williams], *Poems, Lyric and Pastoral*, 2 vols (1794); M. Edgeworth, *Castle Rackrent, an Hibernian Tale, taken from the facts and from the manners of the Irish squires, before the year 1782* (1800). For the rise of local nationalisms, see R. Porter and M. Teich (eds), *Romanticism in National Context* (Cambridge, 1988).
61. J. Horne Tooke, Επεα πτερεουτα, *or the Diversions of Purley* (1786); W. Cobbett, *Grammar of the English Language* (1819). See M. Butler, *Burke, Paine, Godwin and the Revolution Controversy* (Cambridge, 1984), p. 14.
62. J. Klancher, *The Making of English Reading Audiences 1790–1832* (Wisconsin, 1987), p. 3.
63. S. Behrendt, *Shelley and his Audiences* (Lincoln, Nebraska and London, 1989).
64. J.J. McGann, *The Romantic Ideology: A Critical Investigation* (Chicago, 1983).
65. L. Metzger, *One Foot in Eden: Modes of Pastoral in Romantic Poetry* (North Carolina, 1986).
66. L.J. Swingle, *The Obstinate Questionings of English Romanticism* (Louisiana, 1987). See also S.J. Wolfson, *The Questioning Presence: Wordsworth, Keats and the Interrogative Mode in Romantic Poetry* (Ithaca, 1986).
67. F. Stafford, *The Sublime Savage: A Study of James Macpherson and the Poems of Ossian* (Edinburgh, 1988), pp. 1–4.
68. H. Weinbrot, *Britannia's Issue: The Rise of British Literature from Dryden to Ossian* (Cambridge, 1993), pp. 526–56.
69. S. Smiles, *The Image of Antiquity: Ancient Britain and the Romantic Imagination* (New Haven and London, 1994), p. 47.
70. [J. Macpherson] Ossian, *Fingal, an Epic Poem* (1762).
71. Macpherson in fact translated the *Iliad* in 1773.
72. C.A. Sainte-Beuve, *Qu'est-ce qu'un classique?* (1850), translated as 'What is a Classic?' by J. Butler, in H. Adams (ed.), *Critical Theory since Plato*, rev. edn (New York, 1992), p. 568.
73. J. Guillory, *Cultural Capital: The Problem of Literary Canon Formation* (Chicago, 1993).
74. S. Shankman, *In Search of the Classic: Reconsidering the Greco-Roman Tradition, Homer to Valéry and Beyond* (Pennsylvania, 1994), p. ix. See also F. Kermode, *History and Value* (Oxford, 1988), pp. 114–15.
75. C.A. Stray, *Culture and Discipline: The Transformation of Classics in England 1830–1960* (Oxford) [forthcoming].
76. G.B. Taplin, *The Life of Elizabeth Barrett Browning* (1957), pp. 10, 25–32.

77. O. Smith, *The Politics of Language 1791–1819* (Oxford, 1984).
78. R. Cronin, *Shelley's Poetic Thoughts* (1981).
79. J.E. Hogle, *Shelley's Process: Radical Transference and the Development of his Major Work* (Oxford, 1988).

1 'Things Foreign'?: Classical Education and Knowledge

1. C. Lamb, 'On Christ's Hospital and the Character of the Christ's Hospital Boys', *Gentleman's Magazine* (June 1813), pp. 533.
2. Leigh Hunt, *Autobiography* (1850), pp. 104–5.
3. See in particular, O. Smith, *The Politics of Language* (Oxford, 1984); J. Bowen, 'Education, Ideology and the Ruling Class: Hellenism and English Public Schools in the Nineteenth Century', in G.W. Clarke (ed.), *Rediscovering Hellenism* (1989), pp. 161–86.
4. W. Cobbett, *The Life and Adventures of Peter Porcupine, with a full and fair account of all his Authorising Transactions* (Philadelphia, 1796), p. 13.
5. V. Knox, *Liberal Education, or a Practical Treatise on the Methods of Acquiring Useful and Polite Learning* (1781), p. 9.
6. Knox, *Liberal Education*, p. 101.
7. Knox, *Liberal Education*, pp. 10–11.
8. T. Paine, *The Age of Reason* (1794), p. 31. The preference for a concept of language based upon things – nouns – rather than upon verbs was linked to a politically liberal viewpoint: see Locke's theory of language in *Essay on Human Understanding* and Horne Tooke, Επεα Πτεροεντα (1786).
9. T. Paine, *The Age of Reason*, pp. 33–4.
10. 'Public Schools of England – Eton', *Edinburgh Review*, 51 (1830), p. 68.
11. N. Carlisle, *A Concise Description of the Endowed Grammar Schools* (1818). Carlisle's account is not completely reliable, since it was based upon the schools' own reports, which would be eager to claim the use of the Eton grammar, whether or not it was actually used. But the survey reveals the esteem with which the Eton system of education was viewed.
12. See M.L. Clarke, *Classical Education in Britain 1500–1900* (Cambridge, 1959), pp. 98–110.
13. See C.A. Stray, 'England, Culture and the Nineteenth Century', *Liverpool Classical Monthly*, 13.6 (June 1988), pp. 85–90.
14. A.H. Japp, *De Quincey Memorials*, 2 vols (1891), I, p. 38.
15. T. Keane, *Tom Paine: A Political Life* (1995), p. 26.
16. See W.J. Bate, *John Keats* (Cambridge, Mass., 1963), pp. 29–32.
17. W. Godwin, *Enquiry Concerning Political Justice* (1793), Bk I, chapter 4, p. 36.
18. Cobbett, *Peter Porcupine*, p. 11.
19. L. Hunt, *Autobiography* (1850), p. 130.
20. Byron, *Childe Harold* IV, stanza lxxv.
21. G. Lindop, *The Opium-Eater: A Life of Thomas De Quincey* (1981, reprinted 1993), p. 113. Hunt points out that children at Christ's Hospital had to choose between different schools of study – with the

result that he concentrated only on Latin grammar and never learnt his multiplication table or simple arithmetic (*Autobiography*, p. 103). For an example of the increasing feeling among middle-class trades-men of the irrelevance of standard education, see 'The Defects of a University Education, and its Unsuitableness to a Commercial People' (London, 1762): [lessons] 'being either totally or in part calcu-lated for the Disputes and Wranglings of the Divines, and of little use to the Lawyer or Physician, and still less to the Merchant or Gentle-man' (p. 5).

22. Peacock, 'Prospectus: Classical Education', *Works*, vol. VIII, p. 429.
23. W. Godwin to William Cole, 2 March 1802, in C. Kegan Paul, *William Godwin: His Friends and Contemporaries*, 2 vols (1970), II, p. 119.
24. For example, *The Pantheon* (1814) and *The History of Greece* (1822), written under pseudonym of Edward Baldwin and published by M.J. Godwin, his second wife.
25. J. Priestley, *Monthly Review*, XXVI (1762), p. 27. For further factual details on the Dissenting Academies, see J.W. Ashley-Smith, *The Birth of Modern Education: The Contribution of the Dissenting Academies 1660–1800* (1954).
26. Byron, *Childe Harold* IV, stanza lxxvi.
27. W. Godwin, *The Enquirer: Reflections on Education, Manners and Literature* (1797; reprinted, New York, 1965), p. 38.
28. W. Hazlitt, 'On Classical Education', *Collected Works*, I, p. 4.
29. W. Godwin, *Uncollected Writings 1785–1822: Articles in Periodicals and 6 Pamphlets*, ed. by J.W. Marken and B.R. Pollin, facsimile reproduc-tions (Florida, 1968), p. 438.
30. Rousseau, *Emile or On Education* (1762), translated by A. Bloom (Penguin, 1991), Bk III, p. 207.
31. Godwin, *Uncollected Writings*, pp. 438–9.
32. Hazlitt, 'On Classical Education', *Collected Works*, I, p. 416, notes; V. Knox, *Liberal Education*, p. 235.
33. Rev. D.H. Urquhart, *Commentaries on Classical Learning* (1803), p. 4.
34. For ideas on history, and its difference or similarity, see F. Meinecke, *Historicism: The Rise of a New Historical Outlook*, translated by J.E. Anderson (1972); and H. White, *Metahistory: The Historical Imagination in Nineteenth Century Europe* (Baltimore, 1973), p. 4. See also D.A. Rosenthal, *The Past is a Foreign Country* (Cambridge, 1985); S. Bann, *Romanticism and the Rise of History* (1995).
35. See the letter from Walter S. Halliday, dated 27 February 1857, quoted in Peacock, *Memoirs of Shelley*, p. 11.
36. T.J. Hogg, *The Life of Shelley*, 2 vols (1858), I, p. 127.
37. T.J. Hogg, *The Life of Shelley*, I, p. 97.
38. Shelley to Godwin, *Letters*, 29 July 1812.
39. Shelley to Godwin, *Letters*, 29 July 1812.
40. Shelley to his father, *Letters*, 6 February 1811.
41. Shelley to Godwin, *Letters*, 11 June 1812.
42. Shelley to Godwin, *Letters*, 11 June 1812.
43. Shelley to Godwin, *Letters*, 11 June 1812.
44. Shelley to Godwin, *Letters*, 29 July 1812.

45. A. Mellor, *Mary Shelley: Her Life, Her Work, Her Monsters* (1988), pp. 8–12, 226–7 n. 24.
46. Mary to Shelley, *MSL*, 28 October 1814.
47. Shelley to Mary, *Letters*, 25 October 1814.
48. 'I kiss your empty image', Shelley to Mary, *Letters*, 7 November 1814.
49. Shelley to Mary, *Letters*, 3 November 1814.
50. Shelley to Hookham, *Letters*, 18 August 1812.
51. Godwin, *Enquiry Concerning Political Justice*, p. 369. See also Hume's views on history in *Philosophical Essays concerning Human Understanding* (1748), pp. 132–3. For the scientific understanding of history, see H. White, *Metahistory*, pp. 12–13.
52. *Queen Mab*, canto I, 169–73.
53. Shelley ordered Locke's *Essay on Human Understanding* on 11 August 1810, shortly before going to Oxford. For an insight into his understanding of Locke's theory of causation, see his letter to Elizabeth Hitchener, 11 June 1811.
54. *Queen Mab*, canto II.108. For other references to chains, see I.188; VI.195.
55. For Shelley's debt to Holbach, see his letter to Godwin, 29 July 1812.
56. Holbach, *La Système de la Nature*, translated by H.D. Robinson (Boston, 1868, repr., New York, 1970), p. 20.
57. Holbach, *La Système de la Nature*, p. 31.
58. *Queen Mab*, canto VI, 171–3. For this purely necessitarian interpretation of the poem, see C. Baker, *Shelley's Major Poetry: The Fabric of a Vision* (New Jersey, 1948), p. 23.
59. *Edinburgh Review*, 51 (1830), p. 67.
60. Shelley to Hogg, *Letters*, 12 January 1811: 'Was not this then a cause, was it not a first cause – was not this first cause a deity – now nothing remains but to prove that this deity has a care, or rather that its only employment consists in regulating the present and future happiness of its creation. . . . Oh! that this Deity were the Soul of the Universe, the spirit of universal love.' Shelley finds Locke's physical world restrictive, despite the philosopher's frequent criticism of grammar in *Essay on Education*.
61. 'Godwin's Journal', in W. St. Clair, *The Godwins and the Shelleys: The Biography of a Family* (1989), p. 342.
62. The abrupt style is also strangely Greek. For an account of the particular association of the early Greek poetic style with parataxis, see B.E. Perry, 'The Early Greek Capacity for Viewing Things Separately', *Transactions of the American Philological Association*, 68 (1937), pp. 403–27.
63. A. Richardson, *Literature, Education and Romanticism: Reading as Social Practice, 1780–1832* (Cambridge, 1994), p. 57.
64. The chariot ride and oriental palace of William Jones's 'The Palace of Fortune' must lie behind Mab's chariot and palace. Shelley ordered Jones's *Works* on 24 December 1812. The name Mab probably derives either from *Romeo and Juliet*, I.iv.53–94 or from Milton's 'L'Allegro', l. 102.
65. Cixous, *The Laugh of the Medusa*, in E. Marks and I. de Courtivron (eds), *New French Feminisms* (Brighton, 1980), pp. 245–64.

216 *Notes*

66. *The Laugh of the Medusa*, p. 256.
67. Cixous, *The Newly Born Woman*, translated by B. Wing (Minneapolis, 1986), p. 88.
68. The idea that *Alastor* is actually a moral poem, warning about the dangers of solitude through the Narrator's tale of a deluded Poet, articulated most notably by Earl Wasserman, is now by and large rejected by critics. Certainly the uneasy connection between seduction and frustration renders any idea of morality or dogmatism problematic.
69. For the Caucasus river source as origin of the human race, see S. Curran, *Shelley's Annus Mirabilis: The Maturing of an Epic Vision* (California, 1975), p. 64; D.H. Reiman, *Percy Bysshe Shelley* (1976), pp. 37–8.
70. T. Taylor, 'Dissertation on the Eleusinian and Bacchic Mysteries', in K. Raine and G.M. Harper (eds), *Thomas Taylor the Platonist: Selected Writings* (1969). Wordsworth, *The Excursion*, III. 986. Peacock mocked the literary tradition which clamed to derive enlightenment from the contemplation of a river in his 'Ahrimanes', written probably in 1813. See Peacock, *Works*, ed. by H.F.B. Brett-Smith and C.E. Jones, 10 vols (1924–1934), vol. VII, pp. 265–70.
71. For woman as sex object, see C.M. Baer, ' "Lofty Hopes of Divine Liberty": The Myth of the Androgyne in *Alastor, Endymion and Manfred*', *Romanticism Past and Present*, 9.2 (1985), pp. 25–49.
72. Shelley, 'Treatise on Morals', *Prose*, p. 185.
73. This phenomenon gives rise to the title of the poem *Alastor* suggested by Peacock. The Poet is pursued by a fury or ἀλάστωρ but this could either be an external being, as portrayed by Aeschylus, or a product of the Poet's mind, as portrayed by Euripides in his *Orestes*. The comparison of the Poet with Orestes is illuminating. Both are undergoing processes of initiation, one to the world of secret, eroticised, knowledge, the other to the man's role in the *oikos*.
74. Shelley to Hogg, *Letters*, August 1815.
75. See in particular E. Strickland, Transfigured Night': The Visionary Inversions of *Alastor*', *KSJ*, 33 (1984), pp. 148–60; S. Fischman, 'Like the Sound of his Own Voice': Gender, Audition and Echo in *Alastor*', *KSJ*, 43 (1994), pp. 141–69.
76. M. O'Neill, *The Human Mind's Imaginings: Conflict and Achievement in Shelley's Poetry* (Oxford, 1989), p. 16.
77. L. Irigaray, *Ce Sexe qui n'est pas un*, in E. Marks and I. de Courtivron (eds), *New French Feminisms: An Anthology* (Brighton, 1980), p. 104.
78. The sense of the woman's existence beyond the capabilities of expression or 'fiction' therefore resists Hogle's interpretation of the woman as 'a mere fabrication': J.E. Hogle, *Shelley's Process: Radical Transference and the Development of his Major Works* (Oxford, 1988), p. 52.
79. 'Mont Blanc' ll.34–6; 'Essay on Life', *Prose*, p. 174.
80. Cixous, 'La', in *The Hélène Cixous Reader*, ed. by S. Sellers (1994), p. 59.
81. 'Essay on Life', *Prose*, p. 173.

2 'The Common-hall of the Ancients': Democracy, Dialogue and Drama

1. F.R. Chateaubriand, *Note sur la Grèce* (Paris, 1825), p. 9: 'There is no one who does not wish for the liberation of the Greeks.'
2. D. Read, *Peterloo: The Massacre and its Background* (1958); R.J. White, *From Waterloo to Peterloo* (1968); J. Stevenson, *Popular Disturbances in England 1700–1830* (1979), pp. 205–28; E. Evans, *The Forging of the Modern State: Early Industrial Britain 1783–1870* (1983), pp. 181–95.
3. A. Briggs, *The Age of Improvement* (1959), p. 214. The Six Acts included: prohibition of drilling and military exercises; empowerment of magistrates to search for arms; further limitation of the right to hold public meetings and restriction of the freedom of the press.
4. See Shelley's letter in support of Carlile to Leigh Hunt, intended for the *Examiner* but never published: *Letters*, 3 November 1819.
5. O. Smith, *The Politics of Language 1792–1819* (Oxford, 1984), p. 3.
6. P. Foot, *Red Shelley* (1980).
7. P.M.S. Dawson, *The Unacknowledged Legislator: Shelley and Politics* (Oxford, 1980); M. Scrivener, *Radical Shelley* (Princeton, 1982).
8. J.P. Klancher, *The Making of English Reading Audiences 1790–1832* (Madison, Wisconsin, 1987).
9. S. Behrendt, *Shelley and his Audiences* (Nebraska, 1989).
10. *Gentlemen's Magazine*, 92 (April 1822), Select Poetry, p. 358.
11. T. Paine, *The Rights of Man*, Parts I & II (1791–2), Pt II, chapter iii, p. 28.
12. T. Paine, *The Rights of Man*, Pt II, chapter iii, p. 33.
13. J. Gillies, *The History of Ancient Greece, Its Colonies and Conquests*, 2 vols (Dublin, 1786), I, dedication to the king, p. iii.
14. W. Mitford, *History of Greece*, 5 vols (1784–1818), Vol II (1790), pp. 111–12.
15. J. Gillies, *The History of Ancient Greece*, I, p. 109.
16. Mitford, *History of Greece*, Vol. I (1784), p. 257.
17. Rousseau, *The Social Contract* (1762), passim.
18. For a good account of the use of Sparta for political debate, see E. Rawson, *The Spartan Tradition in European Thought* (Oxford, 1969). See also O. Taplin, *Greek Fire* (1989), pp. 207–13.
19. W. Drummond, *A Review of the Governments of Athens and Sparta* (1794), pp. 186–7.
20. W. Drummond, *A Review of the Governments of Athens and Sparta*, p. 177.
21. Prometheus is described as φιλανθρωπος: see Aeschylus, *Prometheus Bound*, l.11. For Prometheus as rebel, see Chapter 5.
22. R. Holmes, *Shelley: The Pursuit* (1974), p. 342.
23. E. Shaffer, '*Kubla Khan*' and the Fall of Jerusalem: The Mythological Schools in Biblical Criticism and Secular Literature 1770–1880* (Cambridge, 1975), p. 105, 141.
24. R.P. Knight, *An Account of the Remains of the Worship of Priapus lately existing in Isernia; to which is added a Discourse on the Worship of Priapus*

and its Connexion with the Mystic Theology of the Ancients (1786); E. Darwin, *The Botanic Garden* (1791).

25. 'An Essay on the Devil and Devils', *Prose*, p. 266.
26. *Prose*, p. 268.
27. D. Hume, *A Treatise of Human Nature* (1739–40), Bk I, p. 219.
28. W. Drummond, *Academical Questions* (1805), preface, p. viii.
29. Drummond, *Academical Questions*, p. xv.
30. See L. Hunt, *Autobiography*, p. 68.
31. J. Spence, *Polymetis: or an Enquiry, concerning the Agreement between the works of the Roman Poets, and the Remains of the Ancient Artists* (1747), preface, p. iv.
32. T.L. Peacock, *Crotchet Castle* (1831), p. 134. Folliott is right. The main translation was an English version of A. Dacier, *The Works of Plato abridged, with an Account of his Life, Philosophy, Morals and Politics, together with a Translation of his choicest Dialogues* (1701). Thomas Taylor published a heavily neoplatonic translation of *Cratylus, Phaedo, Parmenides, Timaeus* in 1793. For more on eighteenth- century neglect, see P. Rogers, 'The Eighteenth Century', in A. Baldwin and S. Hutton, *Platonism and the English Imagination* (Cambridge, 1994), pp. 181–5.
33. Hume, *Dialogues Concerning Natural Religion* (1779), 'Pamphilus to Hermippus'.
34. Hume, *Dialogues Concerning Natural Religion*, 'Pamphilus to Hermippus'.
35. *Julian and Maddalo*, ll. 28–32.
36. *Julian and Maddalo*, ll. 36–48.
37. *Paradise Lost*, II, ll. 555–65.
38. Once disillusioned, Landor was to compare Napoleon with Xerxes, thus emphasising by implication his Peninsular War link with Xerxes' Athenian opponents: see *Imaginary Conversations*, 'Xerxes and Artabanus', p. 64. For Landor's military career, see R.H. Super, *Walter Savage Landor* (1957), pp. 85–90.
39. 'Pericles and Sophocles', *Imaginary Conversations*, p. 71.
40. 'Xerxes and Artabanus', *Imaginary Conversations*, p. 55.
41. K. Hanley, *Walter Savage Landor: Selected Poetry and Prose* (Manchester, 1981), p. xiv.
42. *The Examiner*, 4 November 1821.
43. See, for example, *Don Juan* V, ll.1269–70.
44. For the appropriateness of Peacock's names, see note in *Headlong Hall*, World's Classics (Oxford, 1929), p. 6.
45. *Headlong Hall*, p. 5.
46. Peacock to Hogg, 26 September 1817, *The Athenians: Being the Correspondence between Thomas Jefferson Hogg, and his friends Thomas Love Peacock, Leigh Hunt, Percy Bysshe Shelley and others*, ed. by W.S. Scott (1943), p. 40.
47. B.R. Haydon, *Autobiography*, ed. by T. Taylor (1926), p. 271.
48. 'A Refutation of Deism', *Prose*, pp. 118–19.
49. See Landor's self-parody, *A Satire on Satirists* (1836), p. 36: 'It is said indeed that he is such an old- fashioned pedant and conceited

incorrigible prig, that he will accept no engagement and he will write to please himself.'

50. Cobbett's *Political Register*, 1 October 1807. See also *The Examiner*, 5 October 1817.
51. See L. Nattrass, *William Cobbett: The Politics of Style* (Cambridge, 1995).
52. Byron to Augusta Leigh, *BLJ*, 15 October 1819.
53. *The Examiner*, 5 October 1817. Hunt's remarks about Cobbett's lack of education seem ironic now, given Lockhart's criticism of his own scholarly failings: see Chapter 3.
54. Shelley to Peacock, *Letters*, 20–1 June 1819.
55. Shelley to Peacock, *Letters*, 10 March 1820.
56. Shelley to Peacock, *Letters*, 20–1 June 1819.
57. Shelley to Peacock, *Letters*, 23–4 January 1819.
58. 'A Philosophical View of Reform', *Prose*, p. 245.
59. *Political Register*, 13 November 1819.
60. Shelley to Charles Ollier, *Letters*, 6 September 1819.
61. Shelley to Peacock, *Letters*, 9 September 1819.
62. 'A Proposal for Putting Reform to the Vote throughout the Kingdom', *Prose*, p. 162.
63. See in particular, S. Goldhill, *Reading Greek Tragedy* (Cambridge, 1986), 'The City of Words', pp. 57–78.
64. 'A Discourse on the Manners of the Ancient Greeks Relative to the Subject of Love', *Prose*, p. 217.
65. A. Pickard-Cambridge, *The Dramatic Festivals of Athens* (Oxford, 1968), p. 180.
66. D. Sutton, *The Greek Satyr Play* (Hain, 1980), p. 134.
67. It is possible, although there is no written evidence, that Shelley's understanding of the Greek satyr drama could have derived from Isaac Casaubon's treatise on satyr drama and satire, *De Satyrica Greacorum Poesi and Romanorum Satira* (Paris, 1605). Casaubon, significantly, was a Huguenot whose interest in Greek satyr was probably inspired by his non-conformity. His treatise contains a Latin translation of Euripides' *Cyclops* in the appendix.
68. To distinguish between the cyclops race and the name of the main anti-hero of Euripides' play, I have capitalised the hero's name, Cyclops, and left references to the race in lower case.
69. 'The Cyclops of Euripides', *SPW*, ll. 112–13.
70. For the political significance of diet in Shelley's writing, see T. Morton, *Shelley and the Revolution in Taste* (Cambridge, 1994), pp. 170–86.
71. 'The Cyclops', in *Bodleian Manuscripts Shelley e. 4, a facsimile edition with full transcription and textual notes*, ed. by P.M.S. Dawson (New York, 1987), fols 50r17–50v lb.
72. Timothy Webb notes the link between the Cyclops and Frankenstein's monster in *The Violet in the Crucible*, pp. 84–5, but does not emphasise the political associations.
73. 'The Cyclops', *Bodleian Manuscripts Shelley*, fols 73r2–6.
74. 'A Philosophical View of Reform', *Prose*, p. 235.
75. Mary Shelley, *The Poetical Works of Percy Bysshe Shelley*, 2nd edn (1839).

76. *Oedipus Tyrannus; or Swellfoot the Tyrant*, SPW, p. 390.

77. George Orwell's *Animal Farm* was probably partly inspired by Shelley's *Swellfoot* – Orwell read and enjoyed Shelley's poetry while still at Eton.

78. For the economy of Swellfoot's world, see T. Morton, *Shelley and the Revolution in Taste*, pp. 195–201.

79. See, for example, M. Heath, *Political Comedy in Aristophanes* (Gottingen, 1987) and S. Goldhill, 'Aristophanes and Parody', *The Poet's Voice: Essays on Poetics and Greek Literature* (Cambridge, 1991), pp. 167–222.

80. Bakhtin, *Rabelais and his World*, trans. by H. Iswolsky (Cambridge, Mass., 1968), pp. 11–12.

81. See, for example, T. Eagleton, *Walter Benjamin, or Towards a Revolutionary Criticism* (1981), pp. 148–9.

82. S. Goldhill, *The Poet's Voice*, p. 188.

83. See F. Macintosh, 'Under the Blue Pencil: Greek Tragedy and the British Censor', *Dialogos*, 2 (1995), pp. 54–70.

84. 'A Defence of Poetry', Reiman and Powers, 491. See T. Webb, 'Shelley and the Ambivalence of Laughter', in K. Everest (ed.), *Percy Bysshe Shelley: Bicentenary Essays* (English Association, Cambridge, 1992), pp. 43–62.

85. Pindar, *Olympian VI*, in F.J. Nisetich (trans.), *Pindar's Victory Songs* (Baltimore, 1980). For more on Thebes, see F. Zeitlin, 'Thebes: Theatre of Self and Society in Athenian Drama', in J.P. Euben (ed.), *Greek Tragedy and Political Theory* (1986), pp. 101–41; P. Cartledge, 'Theban "Pigs" Bite Back', *Omnibus*, 29 (1995), pp. 14–17.

86. E. Burke, *Reflections on the Revolution in France* (1790), p. 117: 'Along with its natural protectors and guardians, learning will be cast into the mire and trodden down under the hoofs of a swinish multitude'.

87. ' "We Pity the Plumage But Forget the Dying Bird": An Address to the People on the Death of the Princess Charlotte', *Prose*, p. 164.

88. *Swellfoot the Tyrant*, SPW, pp. 408–9.

89. For a similar retreat from previous democratic openness to publication for an elite class of reader, note Richard Payne Knight's republication of his earlier 'An Account of the Remains of the Worship of Priapus' (1786) as *An Inquiry into the Symbolic Language of Ancient Art and Mythology* (1818). For Payne Knight's comment on this retreat, see his *The Progress of Civil Society: A Didactic Poem* (1796), chapter IV, p. xvi.

3 'A Flowery Band': Pastoral, Polemic and Translation

1. A. Pope, 'A Discourse on Pastoral Poetry', *The Poems of Alexander Pope*, ed. by J. Butt (1963), p. 119.

2. Keats, *Endymion* (1818), I.12–18.

3. *Endymion*, I.7–10. Keats also clasps on to what are self-consciously created clichés of pastoral of ideal landscapes in 'Ode to a Nightingale' (1820).

4. T. Webb, *The Violet in the Crucible*, pp. 80, 62.
5. For another description of pastoral as escape, see R. Poggioli, *The Oaten Flute: Essays in Pastoral Poetry and the Pastoral Ideal* (Cambridge, Mass., 1975).
6. M. Butler, *Romantics, Rebels and Reactionaries*, 'The Cult of the South', pp. 113–37. See also R. Sales, *English Literature in History 1780–1830: Pastoral and Politics* (1983).
7. W. Empson, *Some Versions of Pastoral* (1950). See also L.A. Montrose, 'Of Gentlemen and Shepherds: The Politics of Elizabethan Pastoral Form', *ELH* 50 (1983), p. 415: 'Theories of pastoral have a way of turning into theories of literature.'
8. Hunt, *Foliage, or Poems Original and Translated* (1818), p. 18.
9. A. Ettin, *Literature and the Pastoral* (New Haven and London, 1984), p. 12.
10. R. Williams, *The Country and the City* (1973); J. Barrell, *The Dark Side of the Landscape: The Rural Poor in English Painting 1730–1840* (Cambridge, 1980); J. Haber, *Pastoral and the Poetics of Self-Contradiction* (Cambridge, 1994).
11. Haber, *Pastoral and the Poetics of Self- Contradiction*, p. 1.
12. S. Goldhill, *The Poet's Voice*, pp. 223–83. For the opposing view of early pastoral as perfect and unified, see T. Rosenmeyer, *The Green Cabinet: Theocritus and the European Pastoral Lyric* (California, 1969).
13. Mme de Staël, *De l'Allemagne* (1810; translated 1813).
14. *Quarterly Review*, 18 (January 1818), p. 327.
15. *Blackwood's Edinburgh Magazine*, 2 (October 1817), p. 38.
16. W.S. Scott (ed.), *The Athenians, being the Correspondence between Thomas Jefferson Hogg and his friends Thomas Love Peacock, Leigh Hunt, Percy Bysshe Shelley and others* (1943).
17. Hogg to Peacock, *The Athenians*, 8 September 1817.
18. Peacock to Hogg, *The Athenians*, 26 September 1817: 'water is best' (Pindar, *Olympian* I).
19. Hogg to Hunt, *The Athenians*, 22 January 1818. For Shelley's pagan rituals, see R. Holmes, *Shelley: The Pursuit*, p. 368. For Keats's wreath, see his poem 'On Receiving a Laurel Crown from Leigh Hunt'.
20. Peacock, *Rhododaphne, or the Thessalian Spell* (1818), preface, p. 3.
21. 'Review of Rhododaphne', *Prose*, p. 311. Although written in 1818, the review was not published until 1879, by H. Buxton Forman.
22. Hunt, *Foliage*, introduction, p. 16.
23. Hunt, 'The Nymphs', *Foliage*, p. vi.
24. *The Examiner*, 21 December 1817; 28 December 1817; 20 December 1818.
25. Hunt, *A Jar of Honey from Mount Hybla* (1848), p. 57.
26. Hogg to Shelley, *The Athenians*, 30 September 1817.
27. *Blackwood's Edinburgh Magazine*, 4 (January 1819), p. 475.
28. Keats to Hunt, *Letters of John Keats*, ed. by R. Gittings (Oxford, 1970), 10 May 1817.
29. A. Bennett, *Keats, Narrative and Audience: The Posthumous Life of Writing* (Cambridge, 1994), p. 3.
30. M. Dickstein, 'Keats and Politics', *SIR*, 25.2 (1986), pp. 175–81.

31. A. Bennett, *Keats, Narrative and Audience*, p. 1: 'Keatsian "solecism" is produced by the interlocking and conflicting energies which displace and redefine oppositions between beauty and truth, mortality and immortality, thought and feeling, dreaming and wakefulness, passivity and activity, life and death.' For a description of the confusion, see C. Ricks, *Keats and Embarrassment* (1974).
32. C. Reeve, *The Progress of Romance* (1785).
33. W.S. Landor, *Gebir; a Poem in Seven Books* (1798), VII, 197.
34. W.S. Landor, *Gebirus, poema* (1803).
35. Peacock, *Rhododaphne*, canto III, p. 49.
36. Peacock to Lord Broughton, 16 October 1843, British Library, Broughton Papers, Add MS 47225.
37. Hunt, 'The Nuptial Song of Julia and Manlius', *Foliage*, p. 103.
38. Hunt, 'The Nuptial Song of Julia and Manlius', *Foliage*, p. 110.
39. Shelley to Hunt, *Letters*, 14–18 November 1819.
40. Shelley, *Notes on Sculptures in Rome and Florence*, ed. by H. Buxton Forman (1879), p. 20.
41. Shelley to Hogg, *Letters*, 28 November 1817.
42. Shelley to Hogg, *Letters*, 20 April 1820.
43. Shelley to Peacock, *Letters*, 23–4 January 1819.
44. Shelley to Hogg, *Letters*, 21 December 1818.
45. Barrell, *The Dark Side of the Landscape*, pp. 1–2.
46. 'A Defence of Poetry' (1821), Reiman and Powers, p. 484.
47. C.A. Elton, *Specimens of the Classic Poets: In a Chronological Series from Homer to Tryphiodorus, translated into English Verse*, 3 vols (1814), p. xv.
48. 'Hymn to the Sun', Loeb, 1.8; G. Chapman, *The Hymns of Homer* (Chiswick, 1818), p. 130; Shelley, Bodleian Shelley MSS, Adds e. 12, fol. 221 (rev.), and *SPW*, ll. 11–12. Shelley read Chapman's translation in January 1818 while translating the hymns; see *The Journals of Mary Shelley*, ed. by P.R. Feldman and D. Scott-Kilvert, 2 vols (Oxford, 1987), I. p.190.
49. 'Hymn to the Earth', Loeb, l. 15; Shelley, *SPW*, ll. 5–9.
50. I. Rittson, *Homer's Hymn to Venus, translated from the Greek* (London, 1788), p. 2.
51. W. Godwin, *An Enquiry concerning Political Justice*, 3 vols (1793, 3rd edn 1796), Vol. II, Bk vii, p. 508.
52. 'Hymn to Venus', Loeb, 1.9; Chapman, p. 87; Shelley, *SPW*, l. 12.
53. 'Hymn to Venus', Loeb, l. 29; Shelley, *SPW*, ll. 26–7.
54. 'Hymn to Venus', Loeb, l.19; Shelley, Bodleian Shelley MSS, Adds e. 12, fol. 209 (rev.), and *SPW*, ll. 14–18. Timothy Webb adds a translation of the omitted lines in his edition of the text: see T. Webb, 'Shelley's Hymn to Venus', *Review of English Studies*, 21 (1970), pp. 315–24. A couple of the words from the omitted lines do appear in the margins of the original manuscript, but have been scored out and left not integrated into the main text.
55. 'Hymn to Venus', Loeb, l.28; Shelley, Bodleian Shelley MSS, Adds. e. 12, fol. 208 (rev.), and *SPW*, ll. 25–6. Webb adds a comma between 'deities' and 'divine' in his edition of the text, to render Shelley's

translation closer to the original Greek. But no comma appears in the original manuscript draft in the Bodleian (see plate) and the omission indicates Shelley's deliberate alteration of the balance of the sentence.

56. 'Hymn to Venus', Loeb, ll. 48–52; Shelley, *SPW*, ll. 47–53.
57. For the varying significance of 'φιλομμειδῆς, see D.D. Boedeker, *Aphrodite's Entry into Epic* (Leiden, 1974), pp. 33–7.
58. For 'serene' and 'safe', see the parallel endings of Shelley's 'Hymn to Castor and Pollux' and his translation of a poem of Moschus, *SPW*, p. 723.
59. 'Hymn to the Earth', *SPW*, ll. 7–9.
60. 'Hymn to the Earth', Loeb, ll. 6–7; Shelley, *SPW*, ll. 10–11.
61. J. Derrida, *Dissemination*, translated by B. Johnson (1981), pp. 71–2.
62. J.S. Clay, *The Politics of Olympus: Form and Meaning in the Major Homeric Hymns* (Princeton, 1989), p. 15.
63. Shelley, 'A Discourse on the Manners of the Ancient Greeks', *Prose*, p. 219.
64. *Works of Plato, translated from the Greek, nine dialogues by Floyer Sydenham and the remainder by Thomas Taylor*, 5 vols (1804), V, pp. 429–530.
65. 'A Discourse on the Manners', *Prose*, p. 222.
66. Plato, *The Symposium*, ed. by Sir K. Dover (Cambridge, 1980), p. 39, 191e9; Shelley, 'The Banquet', in J.A. Notopoulos, *The Platonism of Shelley*, p. 431.
67. Shelley, 'The Banquet', p. 425.
68. The Greek original metaphor: ὡςδ ὁπότ ὠκὺ νοημα δια στέρνοιο περήση / ἀνέρος ὅν τε θαμειαὶ ἐπιστρωφῶσι μέριμναι, / ἤ ὅτε δινηθ-ῶσιν ἀπ, ὀφθαλμων ἁμαρυγαί, / ὡς ἁμ' ἔπος τέ καὶ ἔργον ἐμήδετο κύδιμος Ἑρμῆς' (ll. 43–6); Chapman's translation: 'His word / And work had individual accord / All being as swiftly to perfection brought / As any worldly man's most ravished thought / Whose mind care cuts in an infinity / Of varied parts, or passions instantly / Or as the frequent twinklings of an eye' (p. 54).
69. E. Pound, *Homage to Sextus Propertius* (1934). For Pound's pastiche in his translation, see J.P. Sullivan, *Ezra Pound and Sextus Propertius: A Study in Creative Translation* (1964), esp. pp. 77–82.
70. For 'dialogic', see M. Bakhtin, *The Dialogic Imagination: Four Essays*, translated by C. Emerson and M. Holquist (Austin, Texas, 1981).
71. For 'bricolage', see R. Paulson, *Representations of Revolution* (New Haven and London, 1983), p. 18; and J. Mee, *Dangerous Enthusiasm* (Oxford, 1992), p. 8.
72. J.A.W. Heffernan, 'Adonais: Shelley's Consumption of Keats', *SIR* (1984), pp. 295–315. See also S.J. Wolfson, 'Keats Enters History: Autopsy, *Adonais* and the Fame of Keats', in N. Roe (ed.), *Keats and History* (Cambridge, 1995), pp. 17–45.
73. Jerrold E. Hogle, *Shelley's Process* (Oxford, 1988), pp. 296, 301.
74. E.Z. Lambert, *Placing Sorrow: A Study of the Pastoral Elegy Convention from Theocritus to Milton* (Chapel Hill, 1976), p. xv.
75. See, for example, Swinburne, *Atalanta in Corydon* (1865).
76. Keats, 'Ode to a Nightingale' (1820), l. 52.

77. Milton's *Lycidas*, the other text translating the experience of *Adonais*, is also self-referential, in the Moschus mould.
78. For Shelley's ideas on love and sameness, see Chapter 4.
79. For the deceptive polish and ornamentation of the elegiac tradition in *Adonais*, see R. Cronin, *Shelley's Poetic Thoughts* (1981), pp. 169–201.
80. See E. Wasserman, *Shelley: A Critical Reading*, pp. 473–502.
81. Shelley, 'The Ion', in J.A. Notopoulos, *The Platonism of Shelley: A Study of Platonism and the Poetic Mind* (North Carolina, 1949), p. 473.
82. J. Wallace, 'Shelley, Plato and the Political Imagination' in A. Baldwin and S. Hutton (eds), *Platonism and the English Imagination* (Cambridge, 1994), pp. 240–1.
83. Shelley, 'Sonnet, from the Italian of Dante', *SPW*, ll. 1–8.

4 'Hope Beyond Ourselves': Orientalising Greece

1. For the endemic polarity between Greek and barbarian in ancient Greek culture, see P. Cartledge, *The Greeks: A Portrait of Self and Others* (Oxford, 1993), pp. 35–62.
2. E. Said, *Orientalism* (1978), p. 56.
3. Said, *Orientalism*, p. 3.
4. Edith Hall argues that Euripides inverts the polarity between Greek and barbarian, not because of self-doubt, but for the 'striking rhetorical effects': see Hall, *Inventing the Barbarian*, p. 222. For a more ambiguous picture, see A. Poole, *Tragedy: Shakespeare and the Greek Example* (Oxford, 1987), p. 217: 'But the "terrible" is never entirely or surely "out there". It is in here already, within the gates, the alien in the very midst of what is most familiar.'
5. R. Schwab, *The Oriental Renaissance: Europe's Rediscovery of India and the East 1660–1880* (1950; translated, New York, 1984). For other non-political studies of influence, see E. Shaffer, *'Kubla Khan' and the Fall of Jerusalem: The Mythological School in Biblical Criticism and Secular Literature 1770–1880* (Cambridge, 1975); K.N. Joshi, *The West Looks at India* (Bareilly, India, 1969); J. Drew, *India and the Romantic Imagination* (Oxford, 1987); D.A. Rosenthal, *Orientalism: The Near East in French Painting 1800–1880* (New York, 1982).
6. E. Said, 'Orientalism Reconsidered', in F. Barker (ed.), *Literature, Politics, Theory* (1986), p. 225.
7. G.C. Spivak, *In Other Worlds: Essays in Cultural Politics* (New York, 1987). For other examples of imperialist or feminist criticism incorporating the new vocabulary, see H.K. Bhabha, 'The Other Question: Difference, Discrimination and the Discourse of Colonialism', in F. Barker (ed.), *Literature, Politics, Theory* (1986); J. de Groot, ' "Sex" and "Race": The Construction of Language and Image in the Nineteenth Century', in S. Mendus and J. Rendell (eds), *Sexuality and Subordination: Interdisciplinary Studies of Gender in the Nineteenth Century* (London and New York, 1989); S.L. Gilman, *Difference and Pathology: Stereotypes of Sexuality, Race and Madness* (New York, 1985).

8. M. Rossington, 'Shelley and the Orient', *Keats–Shelley Review*, 6 (1991), pp. 18–36; N. Leask, *British Romantic Writers and the East: Anxieties of Empire* (Cambridge, 1992), pp. 68–154.
9. The Greeks had always been perceived as children compared to the mature Romans but in the late eighteenth century this had become a matter for praise: see Bernal, *Black Athena*, p. 208.
10. Schiller, *Naive and the Sentimental Poetry*, translated by J.A. Elias, p. 87.
11. Shelley to Mr Gisborne, *Letters*, 16 November 1819.
12. For the difference between Greece and Rome, see F.M. Turner, 'Why the Greeks and not the Romans in Victorian Britain', in G.W. Clarke (ed.), *Rediscovering Hellenism: The Hellenic Inheritance and the English Imagination* (Cambridge, 1989), pp. 61–81.
13. H. Cixous, 'Sorties', *La Jeune Née*, in Marks and Courtivron (eds), *New French Feminisms*, p. 90.
14. *Monthly Magazine*, 32 (September 1811), p. 103.
15. W. Haygarth, *Greece, A Poem in Three Parts, with Notes, Classical Illustrations, and Sketches of the Scenery* (1814), preface.
16. W. Haygarth, *Greece*, p. 15.
17. M. Bernal, *Black Athena*, p. 209.
18. W. Haygarth, *Greece*, p. vi.
19. Winckelmann, 'On the Imitation of the Painting and Sculpture of the Greeks', *Winckelmann: Writings on Art*, ed. by D. Irwin (London and New York, 1972), p. 62.
20. Wordsworth, *The Excursion*, Bk IV, 718–20; Byron to Leigh Hunt, *BLJ*, 30 October 1815: 'The rivers are dry half the year – the plains are barren – and the shores still and tideless as the Mediterranean can make them – the Sky is anything but variegated – being for months and months – but "darkly – deeply – beautifully blue".'
21. Shelley to Peacock, *Letters*, 23–4 January 1819.
22. See J. Black, *The British and the Grand Tour* (1985), pp. 1–33.
23. J. Flaxman, *Lectures on Sculpture* (1829).
24. For an account of Goethe's interest in Greece, see H. Trevelyan, *Goethe and the Greeks* (Cambridge, 1941). For an account of Winckelmann's life, see W. Leppmann, *Winckelmann* (1971). For both, see E.M. Butler, *The Tyranny of Greece over Germany* (Cambridge, 1935). However, none of these books remarks particularly on the fact that neither Goethe nor Winckelmann ever visited Greece.
25. For an account of the changing significance of Italy for British writers, see K. Churchill, *Italy and English Literature 1764–1930* (1980).
26. J.C.L. Sismonde de Sismondi, *A Historical View of the Literature of the South of Europe*, translated by T. Roscoe, 4 vols (1823), I, p. 10.
27. Madame de Staël, *Corinna: or Italy*, translated by D. Lawler, 5 vols (1807), I, p. 30.
28. The lack of knowledge about Greece is often mentioned at the beginning of travel books. See, for example, W. Gell, *The Itinerary of the Morea* (1810) and W.M. Leake, *Travels in the Morea* (1830).
29. S. Owenson, *Woman: or Ida of Athens*, 4 vols (1809), III, pp. 118–34.
30. T. Moore, *Lalla Rookh: An Oriental Romance* (1817), pp. 11–12.

31. Shelley to Hogg, *Letters*, 28 November 1817.
32. The word 'paradise' derives originally from the Persian word for 'garden' – (old Persian) 'pairidaeza'.
33. *Epipsychidion*, ll. 422–3.
34. Byron to Hodgson, *BLJ*, 16 February 1812.
35. R.C. Dallas, *Recollections of the Life of Lord Byron 1810–1814* (1824), pp. 197–8.
36. See, for example, W. Jones, 'On the Gods of Greece, Rome and India', *Works*, 6 vols (1799), I, pp. 229–80.
37. R. Hole, *Remarks on the Arabian Nights' Entertainments* (1797).
38. W. Beckford, *Vathek, an Arabian Tale* (new edn, 1809), pp. 234–86. The custom of painting the eyes derived from the East – see M. Allen, *Selling Dreams: Inside the Beauty Business* (1981), pp. 158–60; W. Umbach (ed.), *Cosmetics and Toiletries: Development, Production and Use* (Chichester, 1991), pp. 5–6.
39. Byron, 'The Age of Bronze', *Poetical Works*, ll. 271–3.
40. J. Gillies, *The History of Greece*, (Dublin, 1786), p. 6.
41. W. Mitford, *The History of Greece*, 5 vols (1784–1818), II, p. 1.
42. The urgent need to distinguish Greek from Turk, provoked by their worrying similarity, will be discussed further in Chapter 6.
43. W. Gell, *The Itinerary of Greece* (1810), pp. ii–iii.
44. J.C. Hobhouse, *A Journey through Albania and Other Provinces of Turkey in Europe and Asia to Constantinople during the years 1809 and 1810* (1813), p. 147.
45. Shelley to Peacock, *Letters*, 26 March 1821.
46. W.M. Leake, *Travels in the Morea* (1830), preface.
47. *Monthly Magazine*, 37 (1814), p. 444.
48. J. Mill, *The History of British India*, 3 vols (1817), pp. xii–xx.
49. J. Dallaway, *Constantinople Ancient and Modern, with Excursions to the Shores and Islands of the Archipelago and to the Troad* (1797), p. 12.
50. E. Said, *Orientalism*, p. 36.
51. Majeed, *Ungoverned Imaginings: James Mill's History of British India and Orientalism* (Oxford, 1992).
52. For a good discussion of the problem of writing about place without entering into a relationship of dominance, see J. Bate, 'Wordsworth and the Naming of Places', *Essays in Criticism*, 39 (July 1989), pp. 196–216. For further thoughts on the difficulty of writing about another country, see R. Cronin, *Imagining India* (1989), p. 3.
53. T.K. Kolokotrones, *Kolokotrones: The Klepht and the Warrior: 60 Years of Peril and Daring, An Autobiography*, written by G. Tertzetis, translated by Mrs Edmonds (1892).
54. G. Konstantinidés, Istoría twn 'Aqhnwn (Athens, 1876) p. 1: 'The maxim 'know thyself' has rightly been hailed by our ancestors as the most important and fundamental principle of human wisdom.'
55. A. Korais, *Memoire sur l'État Actuel de la Civilisation dans la Grèce* (1803): 'Proud of their history and far from closing their eyes to the lights of Europe, the Greeks do not think of the Europeans as anything else than their debtors who should repay with triple interest the sum which they received from their ancestors.'

56. Said, *Orientalism*, p. 40.
57. L. Irigaray, *Speculum of the Other Woman*, translated by G.C. Gill (New York, 1985), p. 134. The ambiguity of the Greek national consciousness will be discussed further in Chapter 6, when consideration is given to the rhetoric of the Greek War of Independence.
58. 'Essay on Love', Reiman and Powers, p. 73.
59. 'Essay on Love', Reiman and Powers, p. 73.
60. N. Auerbach, *Woman and Demon: The Life of a Victorian Myth* (Cambridge, Mass., 1982). See also L. Lipking, *Abandoned Women and Poetic Tradition* (Chicago and London, 1988)
61. E. Longford, *Byron's Greece* (1975), p. 12; H. Spender, *Byron and Greece* (1924), p. 17.
62. See J. Calder, 'The Hero as Lover: Byron and Women', in A. Bold (ed.), *Byron: Wrath and Rhyme* (1983), pp. 103–24.
63. Shelley to Byron, *Letters*, 22 April 1818.
64. Shelley to Peacock, *Letters*, 17 December 1818.
65. *The Curse of Minerva* (1811).
66. For accounts of gender relations in Byron's *Oriental Tales*, see D.P. Watkins, *Social Relations in Byron's Eastern Tales* (London and Toronto, 1987); G.T. Hull, 'The Byronic Heroine and Byron's "Corsair" ', *Ariel*, 9 (1978), pp. 71–83.
67. Keats to George and Georgiana Keats, *The Letters of John Keats*, 31 December 1818; Keats to Fanny Brawne, 8 July 1819.
68. Keats to Fanny Brawne, *Letters of John Keats*, 15 July 1819.
69. Montagu to Abbé Conti, 1 April 1717, *Embassy to Constantinople: The Travels of Lady Mary Wortley Montagu*, ed. by C. Pick (1988), p. 104.
70. *Embassy to Constantinople*, p. 97.
71. *Embassy to Constantinople*, p. 98.
72. S. Owenson, *Woman, or Ida of Athens*, 4 vols (1809), I, p. 88.
73. M. Homans, *Women Writers and Poetic Identity: Dorothy Wordsworth, Emily Brontë, Emily Dickinson* (Princeton, 1980), p. 12.
74. B.C. Gelpi, 'The Politics of Androgyny', *Women's Studies*, 2 (1974), pp. 154–5.
75. For the appropriation of the feminine in the Romantic poetic sensibility, see A. Richardson, 'Romanticism and the Colonisation of the Female', in A. Mellor (ed.), *Romanticism and Feminism* (Indiana, 1988), pp. 13–25.
76. Hazlitt, 'Coriolanus', *The Characteristics of Shakespeare's Plays, Collected Works*, I. p. 214. See J. Kinnaird, *Hazlitt: Critic of Power* (New York, 1978), pp. 110–13.
77. Shelley, 'Defence of Poetry', Reiman and Powers, pp. 483, 503.
78. K.N. Cameron, 'The Planet–Tempest Passage in *Epipsychidion*', *PMLA*, 63 (1948), pp. 950–72.
79. *Epipsychidion*, l. 45.
80. *Epipsychidion*, preface, Reiman and Powers, p. 373.
81. M. O'Neill, *The Human Mind's Imaginings*, p. 158.
82. R. Pite, *'The Circle of our Vision': Dante's Presence in English Romantic Poetry* (Oxford, 1994), p. viii.
83. Rev. H.F. Cary, *The Vision; or Hell, Purgatory and Paradise of Dante Alighieri*, 3 vols (2nd edn corrected, 1819), p. xliii.

84. Mary Shelley recorded in her journal that Shelley read Dante's *Vita Nuova* on 31 January 1821. However, his frequent references to the work in his correspondence suggest a more protracted period of his reading.
85. Dante, *Vita Nuova*, translated by M. Musa (Indiana, 1973), canto II.
86. Shelley, 'The Banquet', in J.A. Notopoulos, *The Platonism of Shelley*, pp. 440–50.
87. Hogle, *Shelley's Process*, p. 279.
88. Bodleian Shelley MSS, Adds e. 12, fols 201–187 (rev). See also Shelley's reference to Diotima in 'Prince Athanase', *SPW*, ll. 224–9.
89. The degree to which it is an intentional failure of language is much debated. For the unavoidable failure argument, see F.D. McConnell, 'Shelleyan 'Allegory': *Epipsychidion*', *KSJ*, 20 (1971), pp. 100–12. For the view that the poem is deliberately ironic, see E. Schulze, 'The Dantean Quest of *Epipsychidion*', *SIR*, 21 (1982), pp. 191–216. The self-consciousness of the poem prevents the final resolution of this question.
90. N. Leask, *British Romantic Writers and the East*, p. 141.
91. O'Neill believes the final section is optimistic because 'it journeys constantly towards a transformed state' (p. 173); but the poet seems still weighed down by the failure and inescapable egotism of language. See also D.J. Hughes, 'Coherence and Collapse in Shelley, with particular reference to *Epipsychidion*', *ELH*, 28 (1961), pp. 260–83.
92. N. Brown, *Sexuality and Feminism in Shelley* (Cambridge, Mass., 1979), p. 23.
93. *The Witch of Atlas*, ll. 585–6.
94. *Epipsychidion*, Reiman and Powers, p. 373.
95. Shelley to Mr Gisborne, *Letters*, 18 June 1822.
96. E. Trelawny, *Recollections of the Last Days of Byron and Shelley*, p. 55.

5 'Grecian Grandeur': Authority, Tyranny and Fragmentation

1. H. Fuseli, 'The Artist in Despair over the Magnitude of Antique Fragments' (c. 1770–80), in P. Tomoroy, *The Life and Art of Henry Fuseli* (1972), p. 54. See plate.
2. 'A Discourse on the Manners of the Ancient Greeks', *Prose*, p. 217; 'Essay on the Revival of Literature', *Prose*, p. 180.
3. Burke, *Reflections on the Revolution in France, and on the Proceedings in Certain Societies in London relative to that event in a letter intended to have been sent to a Gentleman in Paris* (Dublin, 1790), pp. 143–4.
4. *Queen Mab*, Matthews/Everest, note to the line 'Necessity! Thou Mother of the World', p. 376.
5. 'A Philosophical View of Reform', *Prose*, p. 234.
6. See F. Haskell and N. Penny, *Taste and the Antique: The Love of Classical Sculpture 1500–1900* (New Haven and London, 1981), pp. 100–7. For a detailed and specialised account of the German reaction to Winckel-

mann, see G.A. Dolberg, *The Reception of Johann Joachim Winckelmann in Modern German Prose Fiction* (Stuttgart, 1976).

7. *MSJ*, 24, 27–9, 31 December 1818; 2–3 January, 14 March 1819.
8. See N.L. Pressly, *The Fuseli Circle in Rome: Early Romantic Art of the 1770s* (New Haven, 1979), p. vi.
9. H. Fuseli, 'Introduction to Academy Lectures', in D. Irwin, *Winckelmann: Writings on Art*, p. 10.
10. G.E. Lessing, *Laocoon, or the Limits of Poetry and Painting*, translated by W. Ross (1836).
11. J. Dallaway, *Of Statuary and Sculpture among the Ancients, with some account of specimens preserved in England* (1816), p. 34.
12. J.J. Winckelmann, 'On the Imitation of the Painting and Sculpture of the Greeks', in D. Irwin (ed.), *Winckelmann: Writings on Art*, p. 62; J. Dallaway, *Of Statuary and Sculpture among the Ancients*, p. 34.
13. A. W. Schlegel, *A Course of Lectures on Dramatic Art and Literature*, translated by J. Black, 2 vols (1815), Lecture II, pp. 46–7.
14. A. W. Schlegel, *A Course of Lectures on Dramatic Art and Literature*, Lecture IV, p. 91.
15. A. W. Schlegel, *A Course of Lectures on Dramatic Art and Literature*, Lecture IV, pp. 112–13.
16. B.J. Haydon, *The Diary of Benjamin Robert Haydon*, ed. by W.B. Pope, 5 vols (1960–63), 31 December 1818.
17. Keats, 'To B.R. Haydon, with a Sonnet Written on Seeing the Elgin Marbles', *Prose*, ll. 11–14.
18. B.R. Haydon, *Diary*, 30 June 1816.
19. B.R. Haydon to William Hamilton, *Correspondence and Table Talk, with a memoir by his son F.W. Haydon*, 2 vols (1876), I, 9 July 1818.
20. B.R. Haydon to Olenin, President of the Imperial Museum at St Petersburg, *Correspondence*, 10 August 1818.
21. Hazlitt, 'On the Elgin Marbles', *Essays on the Fine Arts*, in *Collected Works*, IX, p. 341.
22. Hazlitt, 'On the Elgin Marbles', *Collected Works*, IX, p. 327.
23. Hazlitt, 'Schlegel on the Drama', *Contributions to the Edinburgh Review*, in *Collected Works*, X, p. 81.
24. E. Burke, *A Philosophical Inquiry into the Origins of Our Ideas of the Sublime and the Beautiful* (1757), p. 41. See S. Monk, *The Sublime: A Study of Critical Theories in the Eighteenth Century* (Michigan, 1960); W.P. Albrecht, *The Sublime Pleasures of Tragedy: A Study of Critical Theory from Dennis to Keats* (Kansas, 1975); A. Leighton, *Shelley and the Sublime: An Interpretation of the Major Poems* (Cambridge, 1984), pp. 1–24.
25. F. Schiller, 'On the Sublime', in *'Naive and Sentimental Poetry' and 'On the Sublime'*, translated by J.A. Elias, p. 196.
26. E.D. Clarke, *Travels in Various Countries in Europe, Asia and Africa*, 6 vols (1810–1823), IV, p. 74. For an account of the sublimity of the past, see R. Macaulay, *Pleasures of Ruins* (1953), pp. 40–253.
27. T. Furniss, *Edmund Burke's Aesthetic Ideology: Language, Gender and Political Economy in Revolution* (Cambridge, 1993).

28. For the distinction between Romantic sublimity and Gothic, see R.D. Hume, 'Gothic versus Romantic: A Revaluation of the Gothic Novel', *PMLA*, 84 (March 1969), pp. 282–90. Josie Dixon explores the ambiguous significance of the fragmented antique in 'Hellenic Ideals in the Age of English Romanticism' (Unpublished MPhil dissertation, Oxford University, 1988), chapters III and IV.

29. See Kathleen Wheeler, *The Creative Mind in Coleridge's Poetry* (1981), pp. 27–8.

30. 'A Discourse on the Manners of the Ancients', *Prose*, p. 217.

31. C. Eaton, *Rome in the Nineteenth Century* (1852), p. 421.

32. Byron, *Childe Harold* IV, CXXIX. ll. 3–9.

33. Rev. T. Warton, 'The Pleasures of Melancholy' (1747), *Poetical Works*, ed. by R. Mant, 2 vols (1802), I, ll. 28–9.

34. M. Lewis, *The Monk* (1775). For the shocked response to the novel, see M. Butler, *Romantics, Rebels and Reactionaries*, p. 36. Shelley met 'Monk' Lewis in Geneva in 1816 – see R. Holmes, *Shelley: The Pursuit*, p. 344.

35. Keats, 'To B.R. Haydon, with a Sonnet Written on Seeing the Elgin Marbles', *Poems*, ll. 1–3.

36. B.R. Haydon, *Autobiography*, ed. by T. Taylor (1926), p. 68.

37. M. Volney, *The Ruins; or a Survey of the Revolutions of Empires* (1795), pp. 6–13.

38. Volney, *The Ruins*, p. xii.

39. Hazlitt, *The Spirit of the Age*, in *Collected Works*, IV, pp. 212–13.

40. T. McFarland, *Romanticism and the Forms of Ruin* (Princeton, 1981).

41. Shelley visited the Elgin Marbles in the British Museum on 13 February 1818: *MSJ*, p. 193.

42. The Laocoön statue was becoming a benchmark to test views about realism in art. See Lessing's contribution in *Laocoon*. It is unlikely that Shelley would have come across Lessing's work first hand, because the *Laocoon* was not translated in full until 1836, but his ideas filtered across through Fuseli. William Blake drew the statue of Laocoön from the plaster cast in the Royal Academy – watched over by Fuseli – to illustrate John Flaxman's essays on sculpture: see P. Ackroyd, *Blake* (1995), pp. 307, 349–51.

43. Byron to John Murray, *BLJ*, 12 October 1817.

44. See M. Aske, *Keats and Hellenism*, for a treatment of Keats's hellenism which is indebted to Bloom's theories.

45. *The Revolt of Islam*, *SPW*, p. 34.

46. *Prometheus Unbound*, Reiman and Powers, p. 135.

47. *Prometheus Unbound*, Reiman and Powers, p. 134.

48. L. Newlyn, *Paradise Lost and the Romantic Reader* (Oxford, 1993), pp. 144–51.

49. P. Tomoroy, *The Life and Art of Henry Fuseli*, pp. 39–40, 107–8, 113–14.

50. Byron, 'Prometheus' (1817); Mary Shelley, *Frankenstein, or the Modern Prometheus* (1818).

51. J.G. Robertson, *The Gods of Greece in German Poetry* (Oxford, 1924), pp. 10–11.

52. Goethe, 'Prometheus', *Goethe: Selected Poems*, translated by M. Hamburger (Boston, 1983), ll. 12–17.

53. Rev. R. Potter, *The Tragedies of Aeschylus* (Norwich, 1777).
54. The image of Prometheus as victim of political (and economic) oppression, with the potential for rebellion, was later famously used by Marx: see *Capital*, ed. by D. McLellan (Oxford, 1995), p. 362: 'The law, finally, that always equilibrates the relative surplus-population, or industrial reserve army, to the extent and energy of accumulation, this law rivets the labourer to capital more firmly than the wedges of Vulcan did Prometheus to the rock.'
55. E. Wasserman, *Shelley: A Critical Reading* (Baltimore, 1971), pp. 282–97. Wasserman argues that the 'borrowings' from Aeschylus are lifted out of context and left to destroy themselves, thus revealing 'the beautiful harmony that is potentially in Aeschylus's materials'. For a less harmonising account of the 'battle' that takes place in Act I, see J.E. Hogle, *Shelley's Process* (Oxford, 1988), p. 172.
56. Hazlitt, 'Schlegel on the Drama', *Collected Works*, X, p. 96.
57. Hogle (p. 170) and S. Curran, *Shelley's Annus Mirabilis* (San Marino, California, 1975) (pp. 33–5) argue that Shelley rewrote Schlegel because of his Judaic-Christian orthodox views. I argue that the source of Shelley's unease is less Schlegel's views and more the historical and political context of their reception.
58. *The Poetical Works of Percy Bysshe Shelley*, ed. by M.W. Shelley, 4 vols (1839), II, pp. 136–7.
59. W. Godwin [under the pseudonym of Edward Baldwin], *The Pantheon, or an Ancient History of the Gods of Greece and Rome* (1814), chapter 3.
60. Shelley, 'Hymn to Minerva', *SPW*, ll. 15–16.
61. Ovid, *Metamorphoses*, XI. 264: 'Thetis revealed herself; and after she had conceded, the hero embraced her.'
62. *Iliad*, I. 396–406.
63. L.M. Slatkin, *The Power of Thetis: Allusion and Interpretation in the Iliad* (California, 1991), pp. xv, 1–2
64. Charles Tomlinson identifies the connection between creative literary translation and the fluid world of Ovid's *Metamorphoses* in the poetry of T.S. Eliot and Ezra Pound in *Poetry and Metamorphosis* (Cambridge, 1983).
65. Ovid, *Metamorphoses*, translated by M.M. Innes (Harmondsworth, 1955), p. 230.
66. *Odyssey*, Book IV.
67. P. de Man, 'Shelley Disfigured', *The Rhetoric of Romanticism* (New York, 1984).
68. *The Triumph of Life*, ll. 248–51.
69. *OC*, 16–17, 668–80.
70. *The London Magazine* (1820).
71. T.A. Buckley (trans.), *The Tragedies of Aeschylus* (1849), p. xii.
72. T.A. Buckley (trans.), *The Tragedies of Aeschylus*, pp. xiii–xiv.
73. G.C. Swayne (trans.), *The Prometheus Chained* (Oxford, 1846), p. xii.
74. See, for example, G.C. Fox (trans.), *The Prometheus of Aeschylus* (London, 1835).
75. T.A. Buckley (trans.), *The Tragedies of Aeschylus*, p. xiv.

76. T. Medwin (trans.), *Prometheus Bound* (London, 1832).
77. Besides plagiarising Shelley, Medwin also lifts whole sentences from Schlegel's *Lectures* for inclusion in his preface, thus indicating the influence of Schlegel over Shelley.
78. *The Tragedies of Aeschylus*, p. xiv.
79. 'On Mr Shelly's [sic] Poem, "Prometheus Unbound" ', *John Bull*, 3 February 1822, p. 477. *John Bull* was an extreme Tory newspaper.

6 'We are all Greeks': The Greek War of Independence

1. *The Morning Chronicle*, 13 April 1821.
2. For the French Revolution as the product and producer of political ideology, see E.J. Hobsbawm, *The Age of Revolution 1789–1848* (1962; 2nd edn, 1977), pp. 73–100.
3. B. Anderson, *Imagined Communities* (1983), pp. 6–7; E. Gellner, *Nations and Nationalism* (Oxford, 1983), pp. 38–40.
4. J. Breuilly, *Nationalism and the State* (Manchester, 1982), p. 11; P. Sherrard, *The Greek East and the Latin West: A Study in the Christian Tradition* (Oxford, 1959), p. 179.
5. Homi Bhabha (ed.), *Nation and Narration* (London and New York, 1990), pp. 1–3.
6. E. Hobsbawm and T. Ranger (eds), *The Invention of Tradition* (Cambridge, 1983).
7. See N. Ferguson, 'So where's the demo?', *The Daily Telegraph*, 18 July 1995, p. 17.
8. See, for example, C.M. Woodhouse, *The Philhellenes* (Worcester and London, 1969), p. 47.
9. T.S. Hughes, 'An Appeal in Behalf of the Greeks' (1824), *The Pamphleteer*, Vol. 23, p. 219.
10. *The Examiner*, 14 October 1821.
11. *The Examiner*, 7 October 1821.
12. *The Gentleman's Magazine*, 92 (April 1822), Part II, Select Poetry, p. 636.
13. See also, for example, T.S. Hughes, *An Address to the People of England in the Cause of the Greeks, occasioned by the late inhuman massacre in the isle of Scio* (1822), in *The Pamphleteer*, Vol. 21, p. 8.
14. See C.M. Woodhouse, *The Philhellenes*, p. 81.
15. See R.E. Zegger, *John Cam Hobhouse: A Political Life 1819–1852* (New York, 1973).
16. J. Cartwright, *Military Hints to the Greeks* (1821) [written under the pseudonym, Nestor Lonchophorus].
17. Correspondence between the Greek provisional government and Jeremy Bentham, *The Works of Jeremy Bentham*, ed. J. Bowring, 11 vols (Edinburgh, 1843), IV, pp. 580–93.
18. A. Damaras, 'The Other British Philhellenes', in R. Clogg (ed.), *The Struggle for Greek Independence: Essays to mark the 150th anniversary of the Greek War of Independence* (1975), pp. 204–7.

Notes 233

19. E.G. Vallianatos, 'Jeremy Bentham's Constitutional Reform Proposals to the Greek Government', *Balkan Studies*, X (1969), pp. 325–34.
20. *The Southampton County Chronicle*, 19 September 1822, quoted in *The Pamphleteer*, Vol. 21.
21. R. Clogg, *A Concise History of Greece* (1992), p. 1.
22. *The Courier*, 16 October 1821.
23. E. Blaquiere, *The Greek Revolution: Its Origin and Progress*, quoted in the *Gentleman's Magazine*, 94 (1824), supplement Part I, p. 610.
24. P. Gamba, *A Narrative of Lord Byron's Last Journey to Greece, extracted from the Journal of Count Peter Gamba* (1825), p. 1.
25. Sir Richard Church to his brother, September 1822, in E.M. Church, *Sir Richard Church in Italy and Greece* (Edinburgh and London, 1895).
26. W. St. Clair, *That Greece Might Still Be Free: The Philhellenes in the War of Independence* (1972), p. 85.
27. *The Journal of Count Peter Gamba*, p. 7.
28. Delacroix, *The Massacre of Scio* (1824). See plate.
29. T.S. Hughes, *An Address to the People of England*, p. 182.
30. 'Mr Barker's Letter to Mr Hughes in the Cause of the Greeks', in *The Pamphleteer*, 21, p. 196. For similar views of the Turkish effects upon the Greek character, see Lord Erskine's letter to the Earl of Liverpool, also in *The Pamphleteer*; and T. Gordon, *The Greek Revolution* (1832), p. 32.
31. *The Examiner*, 15 April 1821.
32. T.S. Hughes, *Travels in Greece and Albania* (1830). The argument of the genetic difference between the ancient and modern Greeks received its most notorious airing by the Austrian historian, J.P. Fallmerayer, *Geschichteder Halbinsel Morea* (Tubingen, 1830).
33. *The Edinburgh Review*, 35 (March 1821), pp. 92–3.
34. *Quarterly Review*, 24 (January 1821), p. 512. See also *Blackwood's Magazine*, 10 (September 1821), p. 202. Byron wished he had been the author: M. Blessington, *A Journal of the Conversations of Lord Byron with the Countess of Blessington* (1834), p. 51.
35. Shelley to Mary, *Letters*, 11 August 1821.
36. See *Quarterly Review*, 24 (January 1821), p. 511: '[Thomas Hope has joined] that modern school of worthies, who, by the aid of a white forehead, a curling lip, raven hair and eyes, and the Turkish costume, have contrived to excite so powerful a sympathy in their favour.'
37. G. Finlay, *History of the Greek Revolution* (1861), p. 5.
38. R. Clogg, *A Concise History of Greece* (1992), pp. 15–17. 8
39. Kolokotrones, Διήγησι§ συμβάντων τη§ Ελληνικη§ φυλη§ άπο·τά 1770 έω§ τά 1836 (Athens, 1846), in G.D. Frangos, 'The Philiki Etairia', in Clogg (ed), *The Struggle for Greek Independence*, p. 90.
40. E. Trelawny, *Records of Shelley, Byron and the Author*, p. 180.
41. T. Gordon, *The Greek Revolution*, p. 312; T. Finlay, *History of the Greek Revolution*, pp. 172–81.
42. It is difficult to assess Greek conditions before the war accurately, because of the widespread illiteracy and the lack of written evidence. See Byron's note to *Childe Harold* II, on the paucity of contemporary

Greek literature, written in reply to an article in the *Edinburgh Review*, 16 (1810), pp. 55–61. For another comment on the lack of modern Greek literature, see the *London Literary Gazette*, 18 January 1823, no. 313, pp. 43–4.

43. E.J. Hobsbawm, *The Age of Revolution*, p. 174.
44. See R. Clogg, 'Korais and the Movement for Greek Independence', *History Today*, 53 (October, 1983), pp. 10–14.
45. On the importance of literacy for the rise of national consciousness, see B. Anderson, *Imagined Communities*, pp. 42–6.
46. See, for example, P. Sherrard, *The Greek East and the Latin West* (1959), pp. 179–86. Richard Clogg in contrast points out that because of Ottoman rule, Greece missed out on a Renaissance, Enlightenment and Industrial Revolution: *A Concise History of Greece*, p. 3.
47. E. Hobsbawm, *Nations and Nationalism since 1780: Programme, Myth, Reality* (Cambridge, 1990), p. 100.
48. For very different arguments on the Greek intrinsic sense of nation before the war, see T. B. Spencer, *Fair Greece Sad Relic* (1954), pp. 295–8; D. Dakin, 'The Formation of the Greek State', Clogg (ed.), *The Struggle for Greek Independence*, pp. 156–81.
49. See G.D. Frangos, 'The Philiki Etairia: A Premature National Coalition', in R. Clogg (ed.), *The Struggle for Greek Independence: Essays to mark the 150th anniversary of the Greek War of Independence* (1975), pp. 87–103.
50. *The Examiner*, 15 April 1821, and the *Morning Chronicle*, 13 April 1821. Another proclamation from Hypsilanti appeared in *The Moniteur*, a French newspaper.
51. *The Examiner*, 15 April 1821, and the *Morning Chronicle*, 13 April 1821.
52. Hypsilanti, *The Morning Chronicle*, 13 April 1821.
53. *The Examiner*, 22 April 1821. *The Examiner* significantly omits the part of Hypsilanti's speech which deals with 'Asiatic bastards' (15 April 1821).
54. For Dragoumis, see P. Sherrard, *The Greek East and the Latin West*, pp. 188–9; for Sikelianos, see P. Sherrard, *The Marble Threshing Floor: Studies in Modern Greek Poetry* (1956), pp. 132–3.
55. For Byron's doubts, see Byron to Thomas Moore, *BLJ*, 4 June 1821.
56. Byron's arrival at Missolonghi was painted by Theodorus Vryzakis, one of the leading nineteenth-century Greek painters, and hangs in the National Gallery, Athens.
57. *Gentleman's Magazine*, March 1824.
58. A Kalvos, 'The Britannic Muse' (Paris, 1826).
59. R. Fletcher, 'Byron in Nineteenth Century Literature', in Clogg (ed.), *The Struggle for Greek Independence*, p. 231.
60. E.G. Protopsaltos, 'Byron and Greece', in P. Graham Trueblood (ed.), *Byron's Political and Cultural Influence in Nineteenth Century Europe: A Symposium* (London, 1981), p. 105.
61. See R. Jenkins, *Dionysius Solomos* (Cambridge, 1940), pp. 87–97. The poem to Byron was called (in translation) 'Lyrical Poem on the Death of Lord Byron'.
62. *Childe Harold* II, ll. 73–4, 82–3. John Eddleston was the Trinity College choirboy with whom Byron was infatuated and whose death was one

of the motivations for Byron's departure on the Grand Tour. The deliberate confusion of distinction between the figures of Byron and Childe Harold replicates the confusion of distinction between the voice of the poet and the image of Greece.

63. *Childe Harold*, notes to canto II, papers referred to by notes to stanza 73.
64. *Childe Harold*, notes to canto II, notes written in the Franciscan convent, Athens, January 1811.
65. *Childe Harold*, notes to canto II, papers referred to by notes to stanza 73.
66. C.M. Woodhouse, *The Philhellenes*, p. 47; D. Howarth, *The Greek Adventure: Lord Byron and other Eccentrics in the War of Independence* (1976), p. 73.
67. Mary to Claire, *MSL*, 2 April 1821.
68. Shelley to Claire, *Letters*, 14 May 1821. Shelley's reaction to Mavrocordato was in marked contrast to Mary's. A few years later she wrote to John Howard Payne, *MSL*, 21 April 1826: 'I take more common interest in the affairs of Greece because I have known and even had an affection for Greeks.'
69. Shelley to Mary, *Letters*, 10 August 1821.
70. Shelley to Medwin, *Letters*, 4 April 1821.
71. Mary to Claire, *MSL*, 2 April 1821. See also her letters to Mrs Gisborne, 30 November 1821.
72. Shelley to Charles Ollier, *Letters*, 11 October 1821.
73. *Hellas*, Reiman and Powers, preface, p. 408.
74. Felicia Hemans, *Modern Greece* (1817), p. 43, stanza lxxxv.
75. *Gentleman's Magazine*, 92 (April 1822), Select Poetry, p. 358.
76. *Don Juan*, Bk III, ll. 701–4.
77. Shelley, 'Fragments intended for *Hellas*', *SPW*, p. 648.
78. The Greeks themselves saw the parallels between themselves and the Americans. See the 'Proclamation of the Messenian Senate at Kalamata to America', published in the *Courier*, 15 November 1821. For Shelley's application of the Greek metaphor to other countries and situations, see 'Ode to Liberty', *SPW*, pp. 603–10; 'Liberty', *SPW*, p. 622; 'Ode to Naples', *SPW*, pp. 616–20.
79. Shelley, preface to *Hellas*, Reiman and Powers, p. 410.
80. Most accounts of *Hellas* dwell purely on the ideas of the choruses. See P. Foot, *Red Shelley*, pp. 75–7; G. MacNiece, *Shelley and the Revolutionary Idea* (Cambridge, Mass., 1969), pp. 246–58; E. Wasserman, *Shelley: A Critical Reading*, pp. 374–413.
81. Carl Woodring explores some of the allusions to tragic drama in *Hellas*, but does not consider the implications of the work's tragic form in general: see C. Woodring, *The Politics of English Romantic Poetry* (1970), pp. 313–18.
82. *The Cenci*, II.i. 183; *Macbeth*, III.ii. 47.
83. *Hellas*, ll. 124, 127; *Macbeth*, I.iii. 79–80.
84. *Hellas*, ll. 644–5; *Macbeth*, V.v. 19–23.
85. For the alienated intellectual in the period, see M. Butler, *Romantics, Rebels and Reactionaries*, pp. 148–54.

86. Byron, *Sardanapalus, Poetical Works*, ll. 56–7.
87. This museum labelling is a product of the 'Great Idea' policy, first formulated in 1844, which aimed to extend Greek borders into the west coast of Turkey to incorporate all Greek-speaking communities into the state of Greece.
88. P.L. Fermor, *Roumeli* (1966; republished 1983), pp. 99–100.
89. N. Kazantzakis, *Travels in Greece*, translated by F.A. Reed (Oxford, 1965), p. 7.
90. The shrine was opened by Lady Jane Shelley, wife of Shelley's son, Percy Florence, in 1893. For details of the memorial, sculpted by Onslow Ford, see R.M. Smith, *The Shelley Legend* (New York, 1945, 2nd edn, 1967), pp. 142–3; S. Norman, *The Flight of the Skylark: The Development of Shelley's Reputation* (Oklahoma, 1954), pp. 258–60.

Select Bibliography

Unless otherwise stated, London is the place of publication.

Ackroyd, P., *Blake* (1995)

Aeschylus, *Prometheus Bound*, ed. M. Griffiths (Cambridge, 1983)

——, Loeb edition with English translation by H.W. Smyth, 2 vols (Cambridge, Mass., 1926)

Albrecht, W.P., *The Sublime Pleasures of Tragedy: A Study of Critical Theory from Dennis to Keats* (Kansas, 1975)

Allen, M., *Selling Dreams: Inside the Beauty Business* (1981)

Anderson, B., *Imagined Communities* (1983)

Angelomatis-Tsougarakis, H.N., 'The Eve of the Greek Revival: British Travellers' Perceptions of Early Nineteenth Century Greece' (DPhil. dissertation, Oxford University, 1986)

Aristophanes, Loeb edition with English translation by B.B. Rogers (Cambridge, Mass., 1924)

Arnold, T., 'Rugby School', *Quarterly Journal of Education*, 7 (1834), pp. 234–49

Ashley-Smith, J.W., *The Birth of Modern Education: The Contribution of the Dissenting Academies 1660–1800* (1954)

Aske, M., *Keats and Hellenism* (Cambridge, 1985)

Auerbach, N., *Woman and Demon: The Life of a Victorian Myth* (Cambridge, Mass., 1982)

Baer, C.M., ' "Lofty Hopes of Divine Liberty": The Myth of the Androgyne in *Alastor, Endymion* and *Manfred*', *Romanticism Past and Present*, 9.2 (1985), pp. 25–49

Baker, C., *Shelley's Major Poetry: The Fabric of a Vision* (New Jersey, 1948)

Bakhtin, M., *Rabelais and his World*, translated by H. Iswolsky (Cambridge, Mass., 1968)

——, *The Dialogic Imagination: Four Essays*, translated by C. Emerson and M. Holquist (Austin, Texas, 1981)

Baldwin, A. and S. Hutton (eds), *Platonism and the English Imagination* (Cambridge, 1994)

Bann, S., *Romanticism and the Rise of History* (1995)

Barrell, J., *The Dark Side of the Landscape: The Rural Poor in English Painting 1730–1840* (Cambridge, 1980)

——, *The Infection of Thomas De Quincey: A Psychopathology of Imperialism* (New Haven and London, 1991)

Barthélèmy, J.J., *Le Voyage du Jeune Anacharsis en Grece, dans le milieu du quatrième siècle avant l'ère vulgaire*, 5 vols (Paris, 1788, first translated 1791)

Bate, J., 'Wordsworth and the Naming of Places', *Essays in Criticism*, 39 (July 1989), pp. 196–216

Bate, W.J., *John Keats* (Cambridge, Mass., 1963)

—— , *The Burden of the Past and the English Poet* (1971)

Beard, M. and J. Henderson, *Classics: A Very Short Introduction* (Oxford, 1995)

Beckford, W., *Vathek, an Arabian Tale* (new edn, 1809)

Behrendt, S., *Shelley and his Audiences* (Lincoln, Nebraska and London, 1989)

Bennett, A., *Keats, Narrative and Audience: The Posthumous Life of Writing* (Cambridge, 1994)

Bentham, J., *The Works of Jeremy Bentham*, ed. J. Bowring, 11 vols (Edinburgh, 1843)

Bernal, M., *Black Athena: The Afroasiatic Roots of Western Culture*, 2 vols (1987–91)

Bhabha, H.K., 'The Other Question: Difference, Discrimination and the Discourse of Colonialism', in F. Barker (ed.), *Literature, Politics, Theory* (1986), pp. 148–72

—— (ed.), *Nation and Narration* (London and New York, 1990)

Black, J., *The British and the Grand Tour* (1985)

Blackwell, T., *An Enquiry into the Life and Writings of Homer* (1735)

Blackwood's Edinburgh Magazine, 1817–22

Blaquiere, E., 'The Greek Revolution: Its Origin and Progress', in the *Gentleman's Magazine*, 94 (1824)

Blessington, M., *A Journal of the Conversations of Lord Byron with the Countess of Blessington* (1834)

Bloom, H. *The Anxiety of Influence: A Theory of Poetry* (Oxford, 1973)

Boedeker, D.D., *Aphrodite's Entry into Epic* (Leiden, 1974)

Bolgar, R.R. (ed.), *Classical Influences on Western Thought 1650–1870* (Cambridge, 1979)

Bowen, J., 'Education, Ideology and the Ruling Class: Hellenism and English Public Schools in the Nineteenth Century', in G.W. Clarke (ed.), *Rediscovering Hellenism* (1989), pp. 161–86

Bowra, C.M., *The Greek Experience* (1957)

Brantlinger, P., *Rule of Darkness: British Literature and Imperialism 1830–1914* (New York, 1988)

Breuilly, J., *Nationalism and the State* (Manchester, 1982)

Briggs, A., *The Age of Improvement* (1959)

Brown, N., *Sexuality and Feminism in Shelley* (Cambridge, Mass., 1979)

Bryant, J., *A Dissertation concerning the War of Troy, and the Expedition of the Grecians, showing that no such expedition was ever undertaken, and that no such city of Phrygia existed* (1796)

Buckley, T.A. (translator), *The Tragedies of Aeschylus* (1849)

Burke, E., *A Philosophical Enquiry into the Origins of Our Ideas of the Sublime and the Beautiful* (1757)

—— , *Reflections on the Revolution in France, and on the Proceedings in Certain Societies in London relative to that event in a letter intended to have been sent to a Gentleman in Paris* (Dublin, 1790)

Butler, E.M., *The Tyranny of Greece over Germany* (Cambridge, 1935)

Butler, M., *Romantics, Rebels and Reactionaries* (Oxford, 1981)

—— (ed.), *Burke, Paine, Godwin and the Revolution Controversy* (Cambridge, 1984)

Buzard, J., *The Beaten Track: European Travel, Tourism and the Ways to Culture* (Oxford, 1994)

Byron, *Byron's Letters and Journals*, ed. by L.A. Marchand, 12 vols (1973–82)
——, *Poetical Works*, ed. by F. Page and corrected by J. Jump (2nd edn, Oxford, 1970)
Calder, J., 'The Hero as Lover: Byron and Women', in A. Bold (ed.), *Byron: Wrath and Rhyme* (1983)
Cameron, K.N., 'The Planet–Tempest Passage in *Epipsychidion*', *PMLA*, 63 (1948), pp. 950–72
Carlisle, N., *A Concise Description of the Endowed Grammar Schools in England and Wales*, 2 vols (1818)
Cartledge, P., *The Greeks: A Portrait of Self and Others* (Oxford, 1993)
——, 'Theban "Pigs" Bite Back', *Omnibus*, 29 (1995), pp. 14–17
Cartwright, J. [Nestor Lonchophorus], *Military Hints to the Greeks* (1821)
Cary, H., *The Vision; or Hell, Purgatory and Paradise of Dante Alighieri*, 3 vols (2nd edn, 1819)
Casaubon, I., *De Satyrica Graecorum Poesi et Romanorum Satira* (Paris, 1605)
Chapman, G. (translator), *The Hymns of Homer* (1616; Chiswick, 1818)
Chateaubriand, F.R., *Note sur la Grèce* (Paris, 1825)
Church, R., *Sir Richard Church in Italy and Greece*, ed. by E.M. Church (Edinburgh and London, 1895)
Churchill, K., *Italy and English Literature 1764–1930* (1980)
Churton Collins, J., *Greek Influence on English Poetry* (London, Bath and New York, 1910)
Cixous, H., 'Sorties', in E. Marks and I. de Courtivron (eds), *New French Feminisms* (Brighton, 1980), pp. 90–8
——, *The Laugh of the Medusa*, in E. Marks and I. de Courtivron (eds), *New French Feminisms* (Brighton, 1980), pp. 245–64
——, *The Newly Born Woman*, translated by B. Wing (Minneapolis, 1986)
——, 'La', in *The Hélène Cixous Reader*, ed. by S. Sellers (1994), pp. 59–67
Clarke, E.D., *Travels in Various Countries in Europe, Asia and Africa*, 6 vols (1810–23)
Clarke, M.L., *Classical Education in Britain 1500–1900* (Cambridge, 1959)
Clay, J.S., *The Politics of Olympus: Form and Meaning in the Major Homeric Hymns* (Princeton, 1989)
Clogg, R. (ed.), *The Struggle for Greek Independence: Essays to mark the 150th Anniversary of the Greek War of Independence* (1975)
——, 'Korais and the Movement for Greek Independence', *History Today*, 53 (October 1983), pp. 10–14
——, *A Concise History of Greece* (1992)
Cobbett, W., *The Life and Adventures of Peter Porcupine, with a full and fair account of all his Authorising Transactions* (Philadelphia, 1796)
——, *Grammar of the English Language* (1819)
——, *Cobbett's Political Register* (1802–35)
Colman, D.S., *Sabrinae Corolla: The Classics at Shrewsbury School under Dr. Butler and Dr. Kennedy* (Shrewsbury, 1950)
Constantine, D., *Early Greek Travellers and the Hellenic Ideal* (Cambridge, 1984)
——, *The Courier*, 1819–21
Creasy, E.S., *Some Account of the Foundation of Eton College, and of the Past and Present Condition of the School* (1848)

Cronin, R., *Shelley's Poetic Thoughts* (1981)

——, *Imagining India* (1989)

Curran, S., *Shelley's Annus Mirabilis: The Maturing of an Epic Vision* (California, 1975)

Dacier, A., *The Works of Plato abridged, with an Account of his Life, Philosophy, Morals and Politics, together with a Translation of his choicest Dialogues* (1701)

Dallas, R.C., *Recollections of the Life of Lord Byron 1810–1814* (1824)

Dallaway, J., *Constantinople Ancient and Modern, with Excursions to the Shores and Islands of the Archipelago and to the Troad* (1797)

——, *Of Statuary and Sculpture among the Ancients, with some account of specimens preserved in England* (1816)

Dante, A., *Vita Nuova*, translated by M. Musa (Indiana, 1973)

Darwin, E., *The Botanic Garden* (1791)

Dawson, P.M.S., *The Unacknowledged Legislator: Shelley and Politics* (Oxford, 1980)

The Defects of a University Education, and its Unsuitableness to a Commercial People (1762)

Derrida, J., *Dissemination*, translated by B. Johnson (1981)

Dickstein, M., 'Keats and Politics', *SIR*, 25.2 (1986), pp. 175–81

Dixon, J., 'Hellenic Ideals in the Age of English Romanticism' (MPhil dissertation, Oxford University, 1988)

Dolberg, G.A., *The Reception of Johann Joachim Winckelmann in Modern German Prose Fiction* (Stuttgart, 1976)

Drew, J., *India and the Romantic Imagination* (Oxford, 1987)

Drummond, W., *A Review of the Governments of Athens and Sparta* (1794)

——, *Academical Questions* (1805)

Eagleton, T., *Walter Benjamin, or Towards a Revolutionary Criticism* (1981)

Eaton, C., *Rome in the Nineteenth Century* (1852)

Edgeworth, M., *Castle Rackrent, an Hibernian Tale, taken from the facts and from the manners of the Irish squires, before the year 1782* (1800)

Edinburgh Review, 1816–22

Edwards, C. (ed.), *Palimpsests: Reading Rome 1789–1945* (forthcoming)

Elton, C.A., *Specimens of the Classic Poets: In a Chronological Series from Homer to Tryphiodorus, translated into English Verse*, 3 vols (1814)

Empson, W., *Some Versions of Pastoral* (1950)

Erskine-Hill, H., *The Augustan Idea in English Literature* (1983)

The Eton System of Education Vindicated: and its Capabilities of Improvement Considered (1834)

Ettin, A., *Literature and the Pastoral* (New Haven and London, 1984)

Euripides, Loeb text with English translation by A.S. Way, 4 vols (Cambridge, Mass., 1912)

——, Loeb text with English translation by D. Kovacs, 2 vols (Cambridge, Mass., 1994–5)

Evans, E., *The Forging of the Modern State: Early Industrial Britain 1783–1870* (1983)

Evans, Evan, *Some Specimens of the Poetry of the Antient Welsh Bards* (1764)

The Examiner, 1814–22

Fallmerayer, J.P., *Geschichte der Halbinsel Morea während des Mittelalters*, 2 vols (Stuttgart, 1830–36)

Fermor, P. Leigh, *Roumeli* (1966)
Findlay, J.J. (ed.), *Arnold of Rugby: His School Life and Contributions to Education* (Cambridge, 1897)
Finlay, G., *History of the Greek Revolution* (1861)
Finley, M. (ed.), *The Legacy of Greece: A New Appraisal* (Oxford, 1981)
Fischman, S., ' "Like the Sound of his Own Voice": Gender, Audition and Echo in *Alastor*', *KSJ*, 43 (1994), pp. 141–69
Flaxman, J., *Lectures on Sculpture* (1829)
Foot, P., *Red Shelley* (1980)
Fox, G.C. (translator), *The Prometheus of Aeschylus* (London, 1835)
Francklin, W., *Remarks and Observations on the Plain of Troy* (1800)
Furniss, T., *Edmund Burke's Aesthetic Ideology: Language, Gender and Political Economy in Revolution* (Cambridge, 1993)
Gamba, P., *A Narrative of Lord Byron's Last Journey to Greece, extracted from the Journal of Count Peter Gamba* (1825)
Gell, W., *The Topography of Troy, and its vicinity* (1804)
——, *The Itinerary of Greece* (1810)
——, *The Itinerary of the Morea* (1810)
Gellner, E., *Nations and Nationalism* (Oxford, 1983)
Gelpi, B.C., 'The Politics of Androgyny', *Women's Studies*, 2.2 (1974), pp. 151–9
Gentlemen's Magazine, 1816–24
Gibbon, E., *Decline and Fall of the Roman Empire* (1776)
Gillies, J., *The History of Ancient Greece, Its Colonies and Conquests*, 2 vols (Dublin, 1786)
Gilman, S.L., *Difference and Pathology: Stereotypes of Sexuality, Race and Madness* (New York, 1985)
Gladstone, W.E., *Studies on Homer and the Homeric Age*, 3 vols (1858)
Godwin, W., *Enquiry Concerning Political Justice* (1793, 3rd edn, 1796)
——, *The Enquirer: Reflections on Education, Manners and Literature* (1797)
—— [Edward Baldwin], *The Pantheon, or an Ancient History of the Gods of Greece and Rome* (1814)
—— [Edward Baldwin], *The History of Greece* (1822)
——, *Uncollected Writings 1785–1822: Articles in Periodicals and 6 Pamphlets*, ed. by J.W. Marken and B.R. Pollin, facsimile reproductions (Florida, 1968)
Goethe, *Goethe: Selected Poems*, translated by M. Hamburger (Boston, 1983)
Goldhill, S., *Reading Greek Tragedy* (Cambridge, 1986)
——, *The Poet's Voice: Essays on Poetics and Greek Literature* (Cambridge, 1991)
Gordon, T., *The Greek Revolution* (1832)
The Greek Bucolic Poets (Loeb edition), with English translation by J.M. Edmonds (Cambridge, Mass., 1912)
Green, M., *Dreams of Adventure, Deeds of Empire* (1980)
Groot, de J., ' "Sex" and "Race": The Construction of Language and Image in the Nineteenth Century' in S. Mendus and J. Rendell (eds), *Sexuality and Subordination: Interdisciplinary Studies of Gender in the Nineteenth Century* (London and New York, 1989), pp. 89–128
Grote, G., *History of Greece*, 12 vols (1846–56)

Guillory, J., *Cultural Capital: The Problem of Literary Canon Formation* (Chicago, 1993)

Haber, J., *Pastoral and the Poetics of Self-Contradiction* (Cambridge, 1994)

Hall, E., *Inventing the Barbarian: Greek Self-Definition in Tragedy* (Oxford, 1989)

—— , 'When is a Myth not a Myth?: Bernal's Ancient Model', *Arethusa*, 25.1 (Winter, 1992), pp. 181–201

Hanley, K. (ed.), *Walter Savage Landor: Selected Poetry and Prose* (Manchester, 1981)

Hartley, L.P., *The Go-Between* (1953)

Haskell, F., and N. Penny, *Taste and the Antique: The Love of Classical Sculpture 1500–1900* (New Haven and London, 1981)

Haydon, B.R., *Correspondence and Table Talk, with a memoir by his son F.W. Haydon*, 2 vols (1876)

—— , *Autobiography*, ed. by T. Taylor (1926)

—— , *The Diary of Benjamin Robert Haydon*, ed. by W.B. Pope, 5 vols (1960–63)

Haygarth, W., *Greece, A Poem in Three Parts, with Notes, Classical Illustrations, and Sketches of the Scenery* (1814)

Hazlitt, W., *Collected Works*, ed. by A.R. Waller and A. Glover, 12 vols (1901–6)

Heath, M., *Political Comedy in Aristophanes* (Gottingen, 1987)

Heffernan, J.A.W., 'Adonais: Shelley's Consumption of Keats', *SIR* (1984), pp. 295–315

Hemans, F., *Modern Greece* (1817)

Hesiod, Homeric Hymns and Homerica (Loeb edition), with English translation by H. G. Evelyn-White (Cambridge, Mass., 1936)

Highet, G., *The Classical Tradition: Greek and Roman Influences on Western Literature* (Oxford, 1949)

Hobhouse, J.C., *A Journey through Albania and Other Provinces of Turkey in Europe and Asia to Constantinople during the years 1809 and 1810* (1813)

Hobsbawm, E.J., *The Age of Revolution 1789–1848* (1962; 2nd edn, 1977)

—— and T. Ranger (eds), *The Invention of Tradition* (Cambridge, 1983)

—— , *Nations and Nationalism since 1780: Programme, Myth, Reality* (Cambridge, 1990)

Hogg, T.J., *The Life of Shelley*, 2 vols (1858)

—— , *The Athenians: Being the Correspondence between Thomas Jefferson Hogg, and his friends Thomas Love Peacock, Leigh Hunt, Percy Bysshe Shelley and others*, ed. by W.S. Scott (1943)

Hogle, J.E., *Shelley's Process: Radical Transference and the Development of his Major Work* (Oxford, 1988)

Holbach, *La Systéme de la Nature*, translated by H.D. Robinson (Boston, 1868)

Hole, R., *Remarks on the Arabian Nights' Entertainments* (1797)

Holmes, R., *Shelley: The Pursuit* (1974)

Homans, M., *Women Writers and Poetic Identity: Dorothy Wordsworth, Emily Brontë, Emily Dickinson* (Princeton, 1980)

Homer, *The Iliad* (Loeb edition), with English translation by A. T. Murray, 2 vols (Cambridge, Mass., 1925)

——, *The Odyssey* (Loeb edition), with English translation by A. T. Murray, rev. by T. E. Dimock, 2 vols (Cambridge, Mass., 1919, 2nd edn 1995)

Howarth, D., *The Greek Adventure: Lord Byron and other Eccentrics in the War of Independence* (1976)

Hughes, D.J., 'Coherence and Collapse in Shelley, with particular reference to *Epipsychidion*', *ELH*, 28 (1961), pp. 260–83

Hughes, T.S., *An Address to the People of England in the Cause of the Greeks, occasioned by the late inhuman massacre in the isle of Scio* (1822)

——, *An Appeal in Behalf of the Greeks* (1824)

——, *Travels in Greece and Albania* (1830)

Hull, G.T., 'The Byronic Heroine and Byron's "Corsair" ', *Ariel*, 9 (1978), pp. 71–83

Hume, D., *A Treatise of Human Nature* (1739–40)

——, *Philosophical Essays concerning Human Understanding* (1748)

——, *Dialogues Concerning Natural Religion* (1779)

Hume, R.D., 'Gothic versus Romantic: A Revaluation of the Gothic Novel', *PMLA*, 84 (March 1969), pp. 282–90

Hungerford, E.B., *Shores of Darkness* (New York, 1941)

Hunt, L., *The Story of Rimini* (1816)

——, *Foliage, or Poems Original and Translated* (1818)

——, *A Jar of Honey from Mount Hybla* (1848)

——, *Autobiography* (1850)

Irigaray, L., *Ce Sexe qui n'est pas un*, in E. Marks and I. de Courtivron (eds), *New French Feminisms: An Anthology* (Brighton, 1980), pp. 99–106

——, *Speculum de l'Autre Femme*, translated as *Speculum of the Other Woman*, by G.C. Gill (New York, 1985)

Irwin, D. (ed.), *Winckelmann: Writings on Art* (1972)

Jenkins, R., *Dionysius Solomos* (Cambridge, 1940)

Jenkyns, R., *The Victorians and Ancient Greece* (Oxford, 1980)

John Bull, 1822

Jones, W., *Works*, 6 vols (1799)

Joshi, K.N., *The West Looks at India* (Bareilly, India, 1969)

Kalvos, A., Καλβου και Χρηστοπουλου Λυρικα (Paris, 1826)

Kazantzakis, N., *Travels in Greece*, translated by F.A. Reed (Oxford, 1965)

Keane, T., *Tom Paine: A Political Life* (1995)

Keats, *Poems* (1820)

——, *Poetical Works*, ed. by H.W. Garrod (Oxford, 1956)

——, *Letters of John Keats*, ed. by R. Gittings (Oxford, 1970)

Kegan Paul, C., *William Godwin: His Friends and Contemporaries*, 2 vols (1970)

Kermode, F., *History and Value* (Oxford, 1988)

Kinnaird, J., *Hazlitt: Critic of Power* (New York, 1978)

Klancher, J., *The Making of English Reading Audiences 1790–1832* (Wisconsin, 1987)

Knight, R.P., *An Account of the Remains of the Worship of Priapus lately existing in Isernia; to which is added a Discourse on the Worship of Priapus and its Connexion with the Mystic Theology of the Ancients* (1786)

——, *The Progress of Civil Society: A Didactic Poem* (1796)

——, *An Inquiry into the Symbolic Language of Ancient Art and Mythology* (1818)

Knox, B., *The Oldest Dead White European Males: and other reflections on the classics* (New York and London, 1993)

——, *Backing Into the Future: The Classical Tradition and its Renewal* (1994)

Knox, V., *Liberal Education, or a Practical Treatise on the Methods of Acquiring Useful and Polite Learning* (1781)

Kolokotrones, T.K., Διήγησις συμβάντων της Έλληνικης φυλης άπο τα 1770 έως τα 1836, transcribed by G. Tertsetes (Athens, 1846)

——, *Kolokotrones: The Klepht and the Warrior: 60 Years of Peril and Daring, An Autobiography*, transcribed by G. Tertsetes, translated by Mrs Edmonds (1892)

Konstantinides, G., Ίστορία των 'Αθηνων (Athens, 1876)

Korais, A., *Memoire sur l'État Actuel de la Civilisation dans la Grèce* (1803)

Lamb, C., 'On Christ's Hospital and the Character of Christ's Hospital Boys', *Gentleman's Magazine* (June 1813)

Lambert, E.Z., *Placing Sorrow: A Study of the Pastoral Elegy Convention from Theocritus to Milton* (Chapel Hill, 1976)

Landor, W.S., *Gebir; a Poem in Seven Books* (1798)

——, *Gebirus, poema* (1803)

——, *A Satire on Satirists* (1836)

——, *Imaginary Conversations of the Greeks and the Romans* (1853)

Leake, W.M., *Travels in the Morea* (1830)

Leask, N., *British Romantic Writers and the East: Anxieties of Empire* (Cambridge, 1992)

Leighton, A., *Shelley and the Sublime: An Interpretation of the Major Poems* (Cambridge, 1984)

Leppman, W., *Pompeii in Fact and Fiction* (1968)

——, *Winckelmann* (1971)

Lessing, G.E., *Laocoon, or the Limits of Poetry and Painting*, translated by W. Ross (1836)

Lewis, M., *The Monk* (1775)

Lindop, G., *The Opium-Eater: A Life of Thomas De Quincey* (1981, reprinted 1993)

Lipking, L., *Abandoned Women and Poetic Tradition* (Chicago and London, 1988)

Livingstone, R. (ed.), *The Legacy of Greece* (1921; reissued 1969)

Locke, J., *Essay Concerning Human Understanding* (1690)

London Literary Gazette, 1823

The London Magazine, 1820–22

Longford, E., *Byron's Greece* (1975)

Lowenthal, D., *The Past is a Foreign Country* (Cambridge, 1985)

Macaulay, R., *Pleasures of Ruins* (1953)

McConnell, F.D., 'Shelleyan "Allegory": *Epipsychidion*', *KSJ*, 20 (1971), pp. 100–12

McFarland, T., *Romanticism and the Forms of Ruin* (Princeton, 1981)

McGann, J.J., *The Romantic Ideology: A Critical Investigation* (Chicago, 1983)

Mackintosh, F., 'Under the Blue Pencil: Greek Tragedy and the British Censor', *Dialogos*, 2 (1995), pp. 54–70

MacNeice, L., *Autumn Journal* (1939)

McNiece, G., *Shelley and the Revolutionary Idea* (Cambridge, Mass., 1969)

Majeed, J., *Ungoverned Imaginings: James Mill's History of British India and Orientalism* (Oxford, 1992)

Man, P. de, 'Shelley Disfigured', *The Rhetoric of Romanticism* (New York, 1984)

Marx, K., *Capital*, ed. by D. McLellan (Oxford, 1995)

Medwin, T., *Oswald and Edwin: An Oriental Sketch* (Geneva, 1820)

—— (translator), *Prometheus Bound* (London, 1832)

——, *The Life of Percy Bysshe Shelley* (Oxford, 1913)

Mee, J., *Dangerous Enthusiasm: William Blake and the Culture of Radicalism in the 1790s* (Oxford, 1992)

Meinecke, F., *Historicism: The Rise of a New Historical Outlook*, translated by J.E. Anderson (1972)

Mellor, A., *Mary Shelley: Her Life, Her Work, Her Monsters* (1988)

Metzger, L., *One Foot in Eden: Modes of Pastoral in Romantic Poetry* (North Carolina, 1986)

Mill, J., *The History of British India*, 3 vols (1817)

Milton, J., *The Complete Poetry of John Milton*, ed. by J. Shawcross (New York, 1963; rev. edn, 1971)

Mitford, W., *The History of Greece*, 5 vols (1784–1818)

Monk, S., *The Sublime: A Study of Critical Theories in the Eighteenth Century* (Michigan, 1960)

Montagu, Lady M. Wortley, *Embassy to Constantinople: The Travels of Lady Mary Wortley Montagu*, ed. by C. Pick (1988)

Monthly Magazine, 1796–1825

Montrose, L.A., 'Of Gentlemen and Shepherds: The Politics of Elizabethan Pastoral Form', *ELH* 50 (1983), pp. 415–459

Moore, T., *Lalla Rookh, an Oriental Romance* (1817)

Morganwg, Iolo [Edward Williams], *Poems, Lyric and Pastoral*, 2 vols (1794)

The Morning Chronicle, 1819–22

Morton, T., *Shelley and the Revolution in Taste* (Cambridge, 1994)

Nattrass, L., *William Cobbett: The Politics of Style* (Cambridge, 1995)

Newlyn, L., *Paradise Lost and the Romantic Reader* (Oxford, 1993)

Norman, S., *The Flight of the Skylark: The Development of Shelley's Reputation* (Oklahoma, 1954)

Notopoulos, J.A., *The Platonism of Shelley: A Study of Platonism and the Poetic Mind* (Durham, North Carolina, 1949)

Ogilvie, R.M., *Latin and Greek: A History of the Influence of the Classics on English Life from 1600–1918* (London, 1964)

O'Neill, M., *The Human Mind's Imaginings: Conflict and Achievement in Shelley's Poetry* (Oxford, 1989)

Orwell, G., *Animal Farm* (1945)

Ossian [James Macpherson], *Fingal, an Epic Poem* (1762)

Ovid, *Metamorphoses*, translated by M.M. Innes (Harmondsworth, 1955)

Owenson, S. (Lady Morgan), *Woman: or Ida of Athens*, 4 vols (1809)

——, *The Missionary* (1811)

Paine, T., *The Rights of Man* Parts I & II (1791–2)

——, *The Age of Reason* (1794)

The Pamphleteer, 1822–24

Paulson, R., *Representations of Revolution* (New Haven and London, 1983)

Peacock, *Rhododaphne, or the Thessalian Spell* (1818)

——, *Memoirs of Shelley*, ed. by H.F.B. Brett- Smith (1909)

——, *The Works of Thomas Love Peacock*, ed. by H.F.B. Brett-Smith and C.E. Jones, 10 vols (1924–34)

——, *Headlong Hall*, (Oxford, 1929)

Perry, B.E., 'The Early Greek Capacity for Viewing Things Separately', *Transactions of the American Philological Association*, 68 (1937), pp. 403–27

Pickard-Cambridge, A., *The Dramatic Festivals of Athens* (Oxford, 1968)

Pierce, F.E., 'The Hellenic Current in English Nineteenth Century Poetry', *Journal of English and Germanic Philology*, 16 (1917), pp. 103–35

Pindar, *Pindar's Victory Songs*, translated by F.J. Nisetich (Baltimore, 1980)

Pite, R., *'The Circle of our Vision': Dante's Presence in English Romantic Poetry* (Oxford, 1994)

Plato, *The Symposium*, ed. by Sir K. Dover (Cambridge, 1980)

——, *The Republic* (Loeb edition), with English translation by P. Shorey, 2 vols (Cambridge, Mass., 1935)

——, *The Ion* (Loeb edition), with English translation by W.R.M. Lamb (Cambridge, Mass., 1925)

Poggioli, R., *The Oaten Flute: Essays in Pastoral Poetry and the Pastoral Ideal* (Cambridge, Mass., 1975)

Poole, A., *Tragedy: Shakespeare and the Greek Example* (Oxford, 1987)

Pope, A., *The Poems of Alexander Pope*, ed. by J. Butt (1963)

Porter, R. and M. Teich (eds), *Romanticism in National Context* (Cambridge, 1988)

Potter, R. (translator), *The Tragedies of Aeschylus* (Norwich, 1777)

Pound, E., *Homage to Sextus Propertius* (1934)

Pressly, N.L., *The Fuseli Circle in Rome: Early Romantic Art of the 1770s* (New Haven, 1979)

Protopsaltos, E.G., 'Byron and Greece', in P. Graham Trueblood (ed.), *Byron's Political and Cultural Influence in Nineteenth Century Europe: A Symposium* (London, 1981)

'Public Schools of England – Eton', *Edinburgh Review*, 51 (1830)

Quarterly Review, 1816–22

Quincey, T. de, *Memorials*, ed. by A.H. Japp, 2 vols (1891)

Rawson, E., *The Spartan Tradition in European Thought* (Oxford, 1969)

Read, D., *Peterloo: The Massacre and its Background* (1958)

Reeve, C., *The Progress of Romance* (1785)

Reiman, D.H. (ed.), *The Romantics Reviewed: Contemporary Reviews of British Romantic Writers* (New York and London, 1972)

——, *Percy Bysshe Shelley* (1976)

Richardson, A., 'Romanticism and the Colonisation of the Female', in A. Mellor (ed.), *Romanticism and Feminism* (Indiana, 1988), pp. 13–25

——, *Literature, Education and Romanticism: Reading as Social Practice, 1780–1832* (Cambridge, 1994)

Ricks, C., *Keats and Embarrassment* (1974)

Rittson, I., *Homer's Hymn to Venus, translated from the Greek* (London, 1788)

Robertson, J.G., *The Gods of Greece in German Poetry* (Oxford, 1924)

Roe, N. (ed.), *Keats and History* (Cambridge, 1995)
Rosenmeyer, T., *The Green Cabinet: Theocritus and the European Pastoral Lyric* (California, 1969)
Rosenthal, D.A., *Orientalism: The Near East in French Painting 1800–1880* (New York, 1982)
Rossington, M., 'Shelley and the Orient', *Keats–Shelley Review*, 6 (1991), pp. 18–36
Rousseau, J.J., *The Social Contract* (1762)
——, *Emile or On Education* (1762), translated by A. Bloom (Penguin 1991)
Said, E., *Orientalism* (1978; republished, Penguin, 1991)
——, 'Orientalism Reconsidered', in F. Barker (ed.), *Literature, Politics, Theory* (1986), pp. 210–29
——, *Culture and Imperialism* (1993)
St Clair, W., *Lord Elgin and the Marbles* (1967)
——, *That Greece Might Still Be Free: The Philhellenes in the War of Independence* (1972)
——, *The Godwins and the Shelleys: The Biography of a Family* (1989)
Sainte-Beuve, C.A., *Qu'est-ce qu'un classique?* (1850), translated as 'What is a Classic?' by J. Butler, in H. Adams (ed.), *Critical Theory since Plato*, rev. edn (New York, 1992)
Sales, R., *English Literature in History 1780–1830: Pastoral and Politics* (1983)
Schiller, F., *'Naive and Sentimental Poetry' and 'On the Sublime', Two Essays*, translated by J.A. Elias (New York, 1966)
Schlegel, A.W., *A Course of Lectures on Dramatic Art and Literature*, translated by J. Black, 2 vols (1815)
Schulze, E., 'The Dantean Quest of *Epipsychidion*', *SIR*, 21 (1982), pp. 191–216
Schwab, R., *The Oriental Renaissance: Europe's Rediscovery of India and the East 1660–1880* (1950; translated, New York, 1984)
Scrivener, M., *Radical Shelley* (Princeton, 1982)
Shaffer, E., *'Kubla Khan' and the Fall of Jerusalem: The Mythological Schools in Biblical Criticism and Secular Literature 1770–1880* (Cambridge, 1975)
Shankman, S., *In Search of the Classic: Reconsidering the Greco-Roman Tradition, Homer to Valéry and Beyond* (Pennsylvania, 1994)
Shelley, M., *Frankenstein, the 1818 edition*, ed. by M. Butler (1993)
——, *The Last Man* (1826)
—— (ed.), *The Poetical Works of Percy Bysshe Shelley* (1839)
——, *The Letters of Mary Wollstonecraft Shelley*, ed. by B.B. Bennett, 2 vols (Baltimore, 1980–83)
——, *The Journals of Mary Shelley*, ed. by P.R. Feldman and D. Scott-Kilvert, 2 vols (Oxford, 1987)
Shelley, P.B., Bodleian Shelley Manuscripts, Adds. e. 12
——, *Notes on Sculptures in Rome and Florence*, ed. by H. Buxton Forman (1879)
——, *Shelley's Prose: or Trumpet of a Prophecy*, ed. by D.L. Clark (Albuquerque, 1954, new edn, 1988)
——, *The Letters of Percy Bysshe Shelley*, ed. by F.L. Jones, 2 vols (Oxford, 1964)
——, *Shelley: Poetical Works*, ed. by T. Hutchinson, corrected by G.M. Matthews (Oxford, 1970)

——, *Shelley's Poetry and Prose*, ed. by D.H. Reiman and S.B. Powers (New York, 1977)

——, *Bodleian Manuscripts Shelley e. 4, a facsimile edition with full transcription and textual notes*, ed. by P.M.S. Dawson (New York, 1987)

——, *The Poems of Shelley*, ed. by G. Matthews and K. Everest (1989), (1804–17)

Sherrard, P., *The Marble Threshing Floor: Studies in Modern Greek Poetry* (1956)

——, *The Greek East and the Latin West: A Study in the Christian Tradition* (Oxford, 1959)

——, *The Pursuit of Greece: An Anthology* (1964)

Sismonde de Sismondi, J.C.L., *A Historical View of the Literature of the South of Europe*, translated by T. Roscoe, 4 vols (1823)

Slatkin, L.M., *The Power of Thetis: Allusion and Interpretation in the Iliad* (California, 1991)

Smiles, S., *The Image of Antiquity: Ancient Britain and the Romantic Imagination* (New Haven and London, 1994)

Smith, H., *Amarynthus the Nympholet: A Pastoral Drama in Three Acts with Other Poems* (1821)

Smith, O., *The Politics of Language 1791–1819* (Oxford, 1984)

Smith, R.M., *The Shelley Legend* (New York, 1945, 2nd edn, 1967)

Sophocles (Loeb edition), with an English translation by H. Lloyd-Jones, 2 vols (Cambridge, Mass., 1994)

The Southampton County Chronicle, 1822

Spence, J., *Polymetis: or an Enquiry, concerning the Agreement between the works of the Roman Poets, and the Remains of the Ancient Artists* (1747)

Spencer, T.B., *Fair Greece Sad Relic* (1954)

——, *Byron and the Greek Tradition* (Byron Foundation Lecture, Nottingham, 1959)

Spender, H., *Byron and Greece* (1924)

Spivak, G.C., *In Other Worlds: Essays in Cultural Politics* (New York, 1987)

Staël, Mme de, *Corinna: or Italy*, translated by D. Lawler, 5 vols (1807)

——, *De l'Allemagne* (1810; translated 1813)

Stafford, F., *The Sublime Savage: A Study of James Macpherson and the Poems of Ossian* (Edinburgh, 1988)

Stevenson, J., *Popular Disturbances in Britain* (1979)

Stray, C.A., 'England, Culture and the Nineteenth Century', *Liverpool Classical Monthly*, 13.6 (June 1988)

——, *Culture and Discipline: The Transformation of Classics in England 1830–1960* (Oxford, 1997) (forthcoming)

Strickland, E., 'Transfigured Night': The Visionary Inversions of *Alastor*', *KSJ*, 33 (1984), pp. 148–60

Stuart, J., and N. Revett, *The Antiquities of Athens*, 4 vols (1762–1816)

Sullivan, J.P., *Ezra Pound and Sextus Propertius: A Study in Creative Translation* (1964)

Super, R.H., *Walter Savage Landor* (1957)

Sutton, D., *The Greek Satyr Play* (Hain, 1980)

Swayne, G.C. (translator), *The Prometheus Chained* (Oxford, 1846)

Swinburne, W.A., *Atalanta in Corydon* (1865)

Swingle, L.J., *The Obstinate Questionings of English Romanticism* (Louisiana, 1987)
Taplin, G.B., *The Life of Elizabeth Barrett Browning* (1957)
Taplin, O., *Greek Fire* (1989)
Taylor, T. (translator), *The Cratylus, Phaedo, Parmenides, Timaeus of Plato* (1793)
——, *Works of Plato, translated from the Greek, nine dialogues by Floyer Sydenham and the remainder by Thomas Taylor*, 5 vols (1804)
——, *Thomas Taylor the Platonist: Selected Writings*, ed by K. Raine and G.M. Harper (1969)
Tomlinson, C., *Poetry and Metamorphosis* (Cambridge, 1983)
Tompson, R.S., *Classics or Charity?: The Dilemma of the Eighteenth Century Grammar School* (Manchester, 1971)
Tomoroy, P., *The Life and Art of Henry Fuseli* (1972)
Tooke, J. Horne, Ἔπεα Πτεροεντα, *or the Diversions of Purley* (1786)
Toynbee, A.J., *The Western Question in Greece and Turkey* (1922)
Trelawny, E.J., *Recollections of the Last Days of Byron and Shelley* (1858)
——, *Records of Shelley, Byron and the Author* (1878)
Trevelyan, H., *Goethe and the Greeks* (Cambridge, 1941)
Turner, F.M., *The Greek Heritage in Victorian Britain* (New Haven, 1981)
——, 'Why the Greeks and not the Romans in Victorian Britain', in G.W. Clarke (ed.), *Rediscovering Hellenism: The Hellenic Inheritance and the English Imagination* (Cambridge, 1989), pp. 61–81
Umbach, W. (ed.), *Cosmetics and Toiletries: Development, Production and Use* (Chichester, 1991)
Urquhart, D.H., *Commentaries on Classical Learning* (1803)
Vallianatos, E.G., 'Jeremy Bentham's Consitutional Reform Proposals to the Greek Government', *Balkan Studies*, X (1969), pp. 325–34
Volney, M., *The Ruins; or a Survey of the Revolutions of Empires*, translated from French (1795)
Wallace, J.M.B., 'Shelley, Plato and the Political Imagination', in A. Baldwin and S. Hutton (eds), *Platonism and the English Imagination* (Cambridge, 1994), pp. 229–41
Warton, T., *Poetical Works*, ed. by R. Mant, 2 vols (1802)
Wasserman, E., *Shelley: A Critical Reading* (Baltimore, 1971)
Watkins, D.P., *Social Relations in Byron's Eastern Tales* (London and Toronto, 1987)
Webb, T., 'Shelley's Hymn to Venus', *Review of English Studies*, 21 (1970), pp. 315–24
——, *The Violet in the Crucible: Shelley and Translation* (Oxford, 1976)
—— (ed.), *English Romantic Hellenism 1700–1824* (Manchester, 1982)
——, 'Shelley and the Ambivalence of Laughter', in K. Everest (ed.), *Percy Bysshe Shelley: Bicentenary Essays* (Cambridge, 1992), pp. 43–62
Weinbrot, H., *Britannia's Issue: The Rise of British Literature from Dryden to Ossian* (Cambridge, 1993)
Wheeler, K., *The Creative Mind in Coleridge's Poetry* (1981)
White, H., *Metahistory: The Historical Imagination in Nineteenth Century Europe* (Baltimore, 1973)
White, R.J., *From Waterloo to Peterloo* (1968)

Wieland, C.M., *The History of Agathon* (1766), translated by J. Richardson, 4 vols (1783)

Williams, R., *The Country and the City* (1973)

Wilson, P.B., 'Classical Poetry and the Eighteenth Century Reader', in I. Rivers (ed.), *Books and their Readers in Eighteenth Century England* (Leicester, 1982), pp. 69–96

Winckelmann, 'On the Imitation of the Painting and Sculpture of the Greeks', translated by D. Irwin in *Winckelmann: Writings on Art*, ed. by D. Irwin (London and New York, 1972)

Wolf, F.A., *Prolegomena ad Homerum; sive De Operum Homericorum prisca et genuina forma variisque mutationibus, et probabili ratione emendandi* (Halis Saxorum, 1795)

Wolfson, S.J., *The Questioning Presence: Wordsworth, Keats and the Interrogative Mode in Romantic Poetry* (Ithaca, 1986)

——— , 'Keats Enters History: Autopsy, *Adonais* and the Fame of Keats', in N. Roe (ed.), *Keats and History* (Cambridge, 1995), pp. 17–45

Wood, R., *A Comparative View of the Antient and Present State of the Troad. To which is attached an Essay on the Original Genius of Homer* (1767)

Woodhouse, C.M., *The Philhellenes* (Worcester and London, 1969)

Woodring, C., *The Politics of English Romantic Poetry* (1970)

Wordsworth, W, *Poetical Works*, ed. by E. de Selincourt and H. Darbishire, 5 vols (Oxford, 1940–49)

——— , *William Wordsworth*, ed. by S. Gill (Oxford, 1984)

Worton, M., and J. Still (eds), *Intertextuality* (1990)

Zegger, R.E., *John Cam Hobhouse: A Political Life 1819–1852* (New York, 1973)

Zeitlin, F., 'Thebes: Theatre of Self and Society in Athenian Drama', in J.P. Euben (ed.), *Greek Tragedy and Political Theory* (1986), pp. 101–41

Index